PROCEDURAL HANDBOOK
FOR
INSTITUTES OF CONSECRATED LIFE
AND
SOCIETIES OF APOSTOLIC LIFE

Edited by

REV. MICHAEL JOYCE, C.M.
SISTER CATHERINE DARCY, R.S.M.
REV. ROBERT KASLYN, S.J.
SISTER MARGARET SULLIVAN, C.S.J.

CANON LAW SOCIETY OF AMERICA
The Catholic University of America
Washington, D.C. 20064

© Copyright 2001 by Canon Law Society of America
ISBN: 0-943616-89-1

All rights reserved. No part of this book may be reproduced in any manner without the permission of the copyright holder, except for brief quotations in critical reviews, and articles.

Canon Law Society of America
The Catholic University of America
Caldwell Hall, 431
Washington, D.C. 20064

2001

Contents

Introduction v
Abbreviations viii
Procedures for Governance in General 1
Institutes, Mergers and Suppression 31
Institute-Wide Policies 53
Admission of Candidates, Canons 641-645 63
Procedures for Formation: Canons 646-661 95
Membership: Fully Incorporated Members 111
Separation of Members from the Institute 135
Apostolate 167
Temporal Goods 195
Judicial Processes 209
Consecrated Life and the Sacrament of Order 219
Procedures for Secular Institutes 241
Societies of Apostolic Life 251

• • •

Index 261
Authors and Contributors 285

Introduction

In the canons pertaining to consecrated life and societies of apostolic life, *The Code of Canon Law* recognizes the need to balance fidelity to the traditions of a specific institute or society with an openness to today's world and to its needs. The code achieves this balance through norms which apply to all institutes and societies of apostolic life and through the principle of subsidiarity, expressed primarily by the phrase "according to proper law". In other words, the code explicitly recognizes both the need to establish norms common to all consecrated life and the need to provide for a certain freedom of action. This freedom allows institutes and societies—with the inspiration of the Holy Spirit and under the guidance of legitimate ecclesiastical authority—to adapt themselves to the particular circumstances of different cultures and countries as well as to new apostolic needs.

This combination of norms common to all consecrated and apostolic life and specific norms and policies of a particular institute or society can create difficulties for those persons charged with leadership. They must be aware not only of the requirements of the code but also those requirements expressed in their own law. We, the members of the Committee on Consecrated Life for the Canon Law Society of America, offer this *Procedural Handbook for Institutes of Consecrated Life and Societies of Apostolic Life* as a concise, ready reference to help institutes and societies work with the law. The committee hopes that leadership of institutes and societies, members, and vicars for religious find this resource helpful in their daily work.

This handbook itself reflects the rich variety of consecrated life and apostolic life through its authors and contributors. In its initial steps of developing the handbook, the Committee on Consecrated Life deliberately chose to involve a number of people to show the variety of the topics addressed and to engage in collaboration. The authors and contributors are not only members of institutes or societies but have devoted themselves to the study and practice of the law. Each chapter was written by one author frequently collaborating with contributors. As a consequence, each chapter reflects the experience and concerns of specific individuals. The handbook also addresses the variety of consecrated and apostolic life. Each chapter notes the differences between institutes of consecrated life, the newer form of secular institutes, and the distinct societies of apostolic life. The last two chapters of the handbook specifically present procedures unique to secular institutes and societies of apostolic life. These two forms are included in the handbook because secular institutes are a unique way of living the consecrated life and societies often proximate religious institutes.

This handbook deals with a variety of issues; a given author as well as the specific issue addressed determines the content and outline of the chapter. For example, chapter four on "Admission of Candidates" includes examples of documents necessary to the admission process. Chapter three, "Institute-Wide Policies," on the other hand, is more general, suggesting topics suitable for policy as well as specific items that should be included. The material and the author therefore determine the content of a chapter. At times, the handbook may appear more like a commentary than a book on procedures. The elements of commentary have been included to give some background for readers not versed in the law.

We realize that with a text of this type, individuals interested in a specific topic — for example, planning a general chapter or formulating a new policy on admissions — will not read the entire text. They will turn to the chapter which deals with their concerns. Consequently, each chapter therefore stands on its own with references as necessary to other chapters. Readers, however, are encouraged to read the first half of chapter one on "Procedures for Governance in General" which serves as a general introduction to terminology, types of law, and the types of texts used by institutes and societies to express their own norms, policies, and practices.

One further point needs to be made. Given the complex issues addressed by the law on consecrated life and societies of apostolic life and given the necessity of ensuring the protection of rights (both of the institute or society itself and of its members), those in leadership are encouraged to seek the advice of a competent canonist. If an institute does not have access to a canonist, referrals may be obtained from the diocesan chancery (through the Office of the Judicial Vicar or the Office of Canonical Affairs) or through the Office of the Executive Coordinator of the Canon Law Society.

The Committee on Consecrated Life takes this opportunity to thank the various authors and contributors in making the project a reality. It appreciates their patience in the production of the work. The committee also extends its gratitude to the Board of Governors of the Canon Law Society of America for the initial invitation to produce the handbook and for its ongoing interest, support, and challenges. A special note of gratefulness goes to Arthur J. Espelage, O.F.M. and Patrick Cogan, S.A., Executive Coordinators of the Canon Law Society of America, for their suggestions and expertise in publication. Without their efforts, this work would never have become a finished product.

     Committee on Consecrated Life

     Michael Joyce, C.M., Chair
     Catherine Darcy, R.S.M.
     Robert Kaslyn, S.J.
     Margaret Sullivan, C.S.J.

ABBREVIATIONS

A.A.	Vatican II, decree *Apostolicam actuositatem*, AAS 58 (1966) 837-864.
AAS	*Acta Apostolicae Sedis*, Rome, 1909-.
AG	Vatican II, decree *Ad gentes*, AAS 58 (1966) 947-990.
c.	canon
cc.	canons
CCEO	*Code of Canon Law of the Eastern Churches: Latin-English Edition.* Washington, D.C.: Canon Law Society of America, 1992
CD	Vatican II, decree *Christus Dominus*, AAS 58 (1966) 673-696.
CIC	*Code of Canon Law: Latin English Translation, New English Translation.* Washington, D.C.: Canon Law Society of America, 1999
CICLSAL	Congregation for Institutes of Consecrated Life and Societies of Apostolic Life
CLD	*Canon Law Digest*, ed. T. Bouscaren and J. O'Connor. Vols 1-6, Milwaukee-New York: Bruce, 1934-1969. Vols. 7-10, Chicago: Canon Law Digest, 1975-1986. Vol. 11., Washiington, D.C. Canon Law Society of America, 1991-.
LG	Vatican II, dogmatic constitutiion *Lumen gentium*, AAS 57 (1965) 702-712.
MR	Sacred Congregation for Bishops and Sacred Congregation for Religious and Secular Institutes, decree *Mutuae relationes*, May 14, AAS 70 (1978) 473-506.
PC	Vatican II, decree *Perfectae caritatis*, AAS 58 (1966) 702-712.
R.I.	Religious Instituute

CHAPTER ONE

Procedures for Governance in General

ROBERT J. KASLYN, S.J. [1]

Introduction

Governance in institutes of consecrated life and societies of apostolic life aims at fulfilling two purposes:

- To inspire the growth of the institute "according to the spirit of the founders and sound traditions" (c. 576) and
- To ensure that "All must observe faithfully the mind and designs of the founders regarding the nature, purpose, spirit, and character of an institute...." (c. 578; c. 732 applies this canon to societies of apostolic life "with due regard for the nature of each society").

Governance, therefore, implies both inspiration and oversight. Both aspects are necessary. Inspiration without oversight may result in disorganized activity and loss of ability to fulfill the aims of the institute [2]; oversight without inspiration may result in mere legalism and in abuses of authority. This chapter, "Procedures for Governance," presents general principles and procedures for *ordinary governance* and describes one example of *extraordinary governance*, the general chapter. These principles and procedures combined with the institute's proper spirit provide means for the institute to fulfill its mission, not only within itself, among its members, but also within the Church as a whole.

---

[1] Nancy Reynolds, S.P., Sally Tolles, D.H.S., Esther Redmann, O.S.U. and Dominica Brennan, O.P. contributed to the writing of this chapter.

[2] Unless the context indicates otherwise, the word *institute* will be used as a general term to include religious institutes, secular institutes, and societies of apostolic life.

This chapter will address the following issues as a foundation for governance in general:

- definition of governance in general, including subsidiarity;
- rights and obligations of members, including confidentiality;
- the relationship between major superiors and councils, in particular, the role of a council either to *consent* or *advise* a superior;
- types of law;
- record keeping, including archives;
- the relationship between a canonical and civil entity.

Following these principles and procedures for ordinary governance, this chapter will discuss the general chapter as one example of *extraordinary governance.*

FOUNDATIONAL PRINCIPLES OF GOVERNANCE

This section presents specific foundational principles and procedures for understanding the exercise of governance in institutes of consecrated life and societies of apostolic life. These principles and procedures aim at ensuring that those who exercise governance fulfill their responsibilities, both to the other members of the institute and to the Church. The existence of specific procedures, as well as common knowledge of them among the members of an institute, assist in encouraging good leadership as well as providing means to avoid abuses of authority.

Definition of Governance

Before beginning the discussion of specific topics, terminology must be clearly defined. One important principle which impinges frequently on the material in this chapter and throughout the handbook is that of subsidiarity. In many canons concerned with consecrated life, *The Code of Canon Law* frequently states, "unless otherwise determined in proper law." In other words, the code allows each institute, through its legitimately adopted constitutions and other directories and acts of chapters to determine specific modalities or procedures for dealing with issues that arise in the life of the institute. Subsidiarity therefore allows for greater adaptation to a particular ecclesial and cultural context and offers greater freedom for an institute to adapt to a specific situation. But difficulties arise in attempting to elucidate general principles; often, the phrase, "unless otherwise determined in proper law" must modify a statement of general principle. In other words, this handbook will refer not only to specific requirements in universal law but also to specific exceptions as allowed by universal law.[3]

Further, the code adopts a certain terminology which itself may be modified by proper law or legitimate custom; for example, use of *leadership* instead of *governance*; *president* in place of *superior*; *congregation* for *general chapter*. Given the plurality of terminology, this text will use terms provided by universal law albeit recognizing that the terms themselves may need translation to correspond to the terminology of a specific institute.

Rights and Obligations of Members

The *Code of Canon Law* explicitly lists rights and obligations of all the Christian faithful in canons 208-223. These canons apply to all the Christian faithful, including members of institutes. For the latter, the exercise of these rights and obligations occurs within the specific context of their condition: their membership in an institute or society and their profession of the evangelical counsels.[4] In canons 662-672, the code lists the obligations and rights of institutes and their members. In addition, other canons may also apply, depending upon the status of an individual and/or a particular institute or society, for example, the obligations and rights of the lay Christian faithful (cc. 224-231) or the obligations and rights of clerics (cc. 273-289)[5] Canon 670 summarizes the obligation of an institute to its members: "An institute must supply the members with all those things which are necessary to achieve the purpose of their vocations, according to the norm of the constitutions." Citing Domingo Andres, Elizabeth McDonough summarized this obligation as including:

- Sound, complete, approved proper law;
- Structural provision for general chapters, superiors, and councils;
- Systematic formation;
- Stable community life;

---

[3] For a discussion of universal, particular, and proper law, see section 'Types of Law' below.
[4] Some societies of apostolic life do not have religious vows nonetheless their members "strive for perfection of charity through the observance of the constitutions" (c. 731, §1).
[5] This is especially true for members of secular institutes whose consecration "does not alter the member's proper canonical condition among the people of God" (c. 771).

- Suitable options for apostolic action or internal work in keeping with the institutes mission; and
- Appropriate material goods for life, formation, work, and renewal.[6]

The following chapters will provide particular examples of these principles.

The listing of rights and obligations in canons 208-223 begins with the principle of equality among all the Christian faithful in canon 208; then canon 209 (the obligation to maintain communion with the Church) and 223 (the value of the common good) form a frame for specific rights and obligations listed in the intervening canons. The exercise of rights and obligations in the Church occurs within the specific context of a community of faith and the mission of that community to proclaim the divine message of salvation to all the world (c. 211). For consecrated life, this context is further particularized by the profession of the evangelical counsels – poverty, chastity, obedience. For societies of apostolic life without vows, observance of the constitutions particularizes this exercise. The needs of the community of faith can take precedence over individual rights (see c. 223); the free profession of evangelical vows also conditions an individual's rights, for example, the ownership of property is determined by the proper law of an institute or society. Nonetheless, members of institutes and societies do have rights which must be protected, as for example: the right to a good reputation (c. 220); the right to vindicate and defend the rights they possess (c. 221, §1); the right that penalties be inflicted according to law (c. 221, §3).

One of the most important areas concerns confidentiality. Canon 220 states: "No one is permitted...to harm the right of any person to protect his or her own privacy." As with the exercise of other rights, this right is conditioned by one's membership in an institute. But the natural right to privacy (and its concomitant right to protect one's reputation) is only conditioned and not completely eliminated for those in consecrated life. For example, in the context of "Admission of Candidates and Formation of Members," canon 642 specifically refers to canon 220. And in the context of "The Governance of Institutes," canon 630, §5 states: "Superiors, however, are forbidden to induce the members in any way to make a manifestation of conscience to them."[7] Through a request to enter an institute; through the request to profess the counsels, both temporary and perpetual; through the vows or other bonds of poverty, chastity, and obedience; and through the acceptance of a mission from the superior, an individual recognizes that the superiors might require confi-

---

[6] Elizabeth McDonough, "The Protection of Rights in Religious Institutes," in *The Jurist* 46 (1986) 169.

[7] Although an exception to this norm can be made in a particular institute, as is the case with the Society of Jesus.

dential information in order to make a prudential judgment concerning an individual's suitability or behavior. But the institute must have clear policies concerning access to confidential information, including location of and access to written materials, as well as time periods before they are destroyed.[8]

Major Superiors and Councils

Every major superior must have a council. There are no specifications as to the number of council members required except in the case of dismissal from an institute, in which case the council must have at least four members (c. 699). Canon 127 discusses the differences between *consent* and *counsel* (i.e., advice):

> §1. When it is established by law that in order to place acts a superior needs the consent or counsel of some college or group of persons, the college or group must be convoked according to the norm of can. 166 unless, when it concerns seeking counsel only, particular or proper law provides otherwise. For such acts to be valid, however, it is required that the consent of an absolute majority of those present is obtained or that the counsel is sought.

There are specific instances when the consent of the council is needed before a major superior may act and there are other cases when that superior simply needs to seek their advice.

Major superiors must have the *consent* of their council for:

- the validity of alienation or other business transactions which could potentially adversely affect the patrimony of the religious institute (c. 638, §3). The amount set for which a superior must seek both the consent of his/her council or the diocesan bishop (if a diocesan institute) or Holy See (if a pontifical institute) is $3,000,000.00 for the USA as of the date of publication.
- the erection, transfer, or suppression of a novitiate (c. 647, §1);
- an individual candidate to make the novitiate in a house other than the designated canonical novitiate (c. 647, §2);

---

[8] See the section below on the archives; see also the chapters which concern admission to the novitiate and admission to profession of the evangelical counsels. For further information on confidentiality see Patrick J. Cogan, S.A., *Selected Issues in Religious Law* (Washington, DC: Canon Law Society of America, 1997) 124-147.

- permission for a member to live outside a house of an institute for a longer period of time; this period may not exceed one year "except for the purpose of caring for ill health, of studies, or of exercising an apostolate in the name of the institute" (c. 665, §1);

- a perpetually professed member of an institute to transfer to another institute (c. 684, §1). In this case, the consent of two councils is required: the community in which the member is perpetually professed as well as the community to which the individual is seeking to transfer. Canon 730 applies this canon to secular institutes concerning transfer from one secular institute to another. Permission of the Apostolic See is required if the transfer is between a secular institute and a society of apostolic life or institute of consecrated life. Similarly, canon 744 requires this consent for transfer between two societies of apostolic life. If the transfer involves an institute of consecrated life, then the permission of the Holy See is required (§2).

- a member to transfer from one autonomous monastery to another monastery of the same institute or federation or confederation (c. 684, §3). In this case, the consent both of the major superiors and of the chapter of the receiving monastery.

- the granting for up to three years of an indult of exclaustration to a member with perpetual vows (c. 686, §1); to grant an indult of living outside the society to a definitively incorporated member of a society of apostolic life (c. 745). Two further qualifications in this canon should also be noted:

    if the member is a cleric, consent must first be obtained from the ordinary of the place where the cleric must reside;

    to extend the indult for more than three years or to grant an indult for more than three years requires consent of the Holy See (if an institute of pontifical right) or of the diocesan bishop (if of diocesan right);

- the petitioning of the diocesan bishop (for an institute of diocesan right) or of the Holy See (if of pontifical right) for imposed exclaustration on a member of the institute (c. 686, §3);

- the granting of an indult to leave the institute for a member in temporary profession (c. 688, §2);

- readmission without the requirement of repeating the novitiate of a member who left the institute after the novitiate or after profession (c. 690, §1). The superior of an autonomous monastery enjoys the same favor (c. 690, §2).

- the dismissal of a member (c. 699, §1). The council must have four members to perform a valid collegial act. The superior with the consent of the council may substitute for absent members or follow the specific procedure as provided in proper law. Canon 729 applies this norm to secular institutes and canon 746 to societies of apostolic life.
- the immediate expulsion from the religious house of a member in the case of serious exterior scandal or very grave imminent harm to the institute (c. 703). If there is danger in delay, then even the local superior with the consent of the council can expel the member.

Major superiors are to seek *consultation* from their councils for:

- admission to temporary profession (c. 656, 3°). This may be either a deliberative vote (i.e., binding on the superior) or consultative, depending upon the proper law of the institute. For secular institutes, canon 720 allows the constitutions to determine the roles of the major moderators with their council; for societies of apostolic life, canon 735 refers to the proper law of each society.
- exclusion of an individual from a further profession after the expiration of temporary profession (c. 689, §1);
- granting the expressed desire of a perpetually professed member who is seeking a dispensation from vows (c. 691, §1). The dispensation is granted by authority above the supreme moderator of the institute (the diocesan bishop for institutes of diocesan right; the Holy See if of pontifical right), but the personal opinion of the supreme moderator as well as that of the council is sent with the individual's request.
- issuing a declaration of dismissal for a religious who has either notoriously abandoned the faith or attempted marriage (c. 694, §2). Note that canon 729 applies this norm to secular institutes and canon 746 to societies of apostolic life).
- beginning a process of dismissal of a member from the institute (c. 697, 1°). Similar provisions are applied to secular institutes by canon 729 and to societies of apostolic life by canon 746.

Types of Law

Universal law refers to the law of the Latin Church found in the *Code of Canon Law*. There are two forms of special law: (1) Particular law is law which is applicable to a certain place or territory, e.g., a diocese or region; and (2) Proper law is a law which governs persons and which follows them wherever they go. Members of institutes are normally said to be governed by universal and proper law.

Canonically approved, well-written, proper law should preserve sound traditions, develop workable structures, elect good leaders, form new members, foster fidelity to the charism, provide possibilities for growth in love and holiness, as well as protect the rightful autonomy of the institute and preserve the rights of its members. Normally, proper law includes: (1) the fundamental norms or constitutions; (2) a complementary book to the constitutions giving them somewhat more specificity; (3) general directories or handbooks; and (4) regional or provincial statutes or policies. The level at which norms other than those required to be in the constitutions are elaborated will vary from institute to institute as appropriate. It is clearly the intent of the code that general norms be elaborated on the general level; and the norms more specific to places, cultures and missionary circumstances be elaborated at the level closest to those places, cultures, and missions.

The Constitutions

The constitutions require the approval of the general chapter as well as competent ecclesiastical authority. Constitutions of religious institutes tend to be more inspirational than juridic, stating important theological principles and only those juridic elements most basic to the institute (c. 587, §3). Constitutions are usually limited to those norms which are not likely to vary from one historical era to another. Those things likely to change with places, times, or circumstances, or which are clearly secondary or purely technical are not included in the constitutions (c. 587, §4). The following listing is the most basic material canonically required to be incorporated in constitutions:[9]

- ♦ a recognition of the needs which individual members of the institute may have in order to achieve the goal of their individual vocations i.e., spiritu-

---

[9]Depending on the type of incorporation into the society (without vows or by some bond), canon 732 applies canons 578-602 and 606 to societies of apostolic life. The canons on secular institutes (720-730) leave either to constitutions or proper law specific determinations of incorporation, governance, etc.

al and material resources such as retreats, days of recollection, finances, health care, education, professional updating, counseling (c. 670);
- a designation of the competent superior to give permission to members of the institute to publish writings dealing with questions of religion or morals (c. 832);
- An arrangement for the discipline of members and their separation from the institute (c. 587, §1);
- The constitutions of clerical institutes of pontifical right are to specify the manner of proceeding for the issuance of the dimissorial letters (c. 1019, §1). The constitutions of institutes having their own churches or oratories should specify the competent superior to grant permission to preach in the church or oratory (c. 765). Finally, the constitutions of clerical religious institutes should specify the manner in which major superiors make the profession of faith prescribed in canon 833 (c. 833, 8°).

Formation
- A development of norms regarding the incorporation and formation of member (c. 587, §1);
- a determination of one or several periods of apostolic activity for novices outside of the novitiate community (c. 648, §2).

Finances
- Some provisions for the manner of administration of temporal goods (cc. 635, §2 and 1251, §1);
- any exclusions or restrictions on the power of the institute, provinces, or houses to act in relationship to temporal goods (c. 634, §1).

Complementary Book

Because the constitutions state only the most basic general norms, further specification is usually required in a secondary, complementary book. The preparation or revision of this book normally pertains to the general chapter of the institute. The complementary book contains more detailed juridic elements and specifications of the constitutions which may require modification or adaptation from time to time. Any further specifications of competencies for the development of proper law should be included in the complementary book.

Directories or Handbooks

These norms are prepared on the general level to bring more specificity to the broad norms of the constitutions and complementary book. Their preparation may be the job of the general council or committees and advisory boards constituted on the general level. Approval of the directory or handbook may pertain to the superior general and general council or to the general chapter. Constitutions ought to specify the procedures for the preparation and approval of directories. If the constitutions are silent, the supreme moderator may approve a directory pending its ratification by the next general chapter.

The code seems to foresee four directories or handbooks concerning: general governance (c. 617), chapter procedures (c. 632), formation (c. 659, §2), and finances (c. 635, §2). Many of the following matters should be addressed in constitutions or the complimentary book. However, if that has not happened, they should be addressed in a directory or handbook. Canonically, the following matters have been left to the proper law of the institute and a level has not been specified:

Governance

- specification of the duties and powers of superiors (c. 617);
- delineation of the manner in which the supreme moderator is to exercise power over the provinces, houses, and members of the institute (c. 622);
- determination of the number of years of definitive profession required prior to election or appointment as a (non-major) superior (c. 623);
- provision for terms of office for superiors other than the supreme moderator (c. 624, §2);
- rationale for the removal or transfer of superiors from office (c. 624, §3);
- norms to be observed by superiors in the conferral of offices and by members during elections (c. 626);
- determination of the cases, besides those prescribed in universal law, in which superiors require the consent or counsel of their councils for the validity of their acts (c. 627, §2);
- designation of superiors to conduct, and the frequency of, visitations (c. 628, §1);
- arrangements for non-residential local superiors (c. 629);
- provisions for suitable confessors (c. 630, §2);

- specifications of the rights and obligations of the institutes and their members, such as:

    the manner of celebrating the liturgy of the hours (c. 663, §3);

    the manner of observing cloister (c. 667, §1);

    the designation of the superior competent to give permission to change dispositions of patrimonial goods (c. 668, §2);

- any exceptions to the provision that those things accruing to the religious by pension, subsidy or insurance are acquired for the institute (c. 668, §3);
- any provisions for the renunciation of goods after perpetual profession (c. 668, §4);
- provisions for goods acquired by members after an act of renunciation (c. 668, §5);
- a definition of the habit of the institute (c. 669, §1);
- requirements for a transfer from one autonomous monastery to another (c. 684, §3);
- a determination of time and manner of probation in the receiving institute in cases of transfers of professed members (c. 684, §4);
- an elaboration of serious causes for dismissal of the perpetually professed member beyond those specified in universal law (c. 696, §1);
- a statement of causes for dismissal of temporarily professed members (c. 696, §2).

Chapters and Other Gatherings

- determination of the order to be observed in the general chapter, especially for elections and other business (c. 631, §2);
- arrangements for individuals, as well as province and communities, to freely send ideas and suggestions to the general chapter (c. 631, §3);
- plans for other chapters or gatherings within the institute, their nature, authority, composition;
- manner of proceeding, and frequency of gatherings (c. 632);
- regulations governing the operations of those non-chapter bodies providing membership participation and consultation (c. 611, §1).

Formation
- norms regulating the admission of candidates to the novitiate (c. 641);
- impediments to admission to the novitiate beyond those specified in universal law (c. 643, §2);
- specification of testimony to be gathered regarding the requisite suitability of candidates and their freedom from impediments (c. 645, §3);
- establishment and definition of the program of formation for novices (c. 650, §1);
- provision for an extension of the period of the canonical novitiate for up to six months (c. 653, §2);
- definition of the period of temporary profession, within the norms specified in universal law (c. 655);
- delineation of the reasons for and length of time of any extension of temporary profession, in such a way that the entire time of temporary profession does not exceed nine years (c. 657, §2);
- norms establishing conditions for perpetual profession beyond those established by universal law (c. 658);
- definition of the program of continuing formation for all members of the institute (c. 659, §2);

Finance
- provisions for the goods of suppressed houses (c. 616, §1);
- norms governing the use and administration of goods so that the poverty appropriate to the institute will be fostered (c. 635, §2);
- provisions for the appointment of finance officers at each organizational level wihtin the institute (c. 636, §1);
- delineation of the manner in which finance officers and other administrators are to render an account of their administration to competent authority (c. 636, §2);
- designation of the boundaries of ordinary administration and of the requirements for valid acts of extraordinary administration (cc. 638, §1 and 1281, §2);

- provision for any administration of goods by a person who is not the immediate governing authority (cc. 638, §2 and 1279, §1);
- provision to reflect faithfully the content of canons 1291 through 1294 (c. 1295).

Provincial or Regional Statutes or Policies

In the case of larger widespread institutes, there may be norms or policies in the form of provincial or regional policy manuals or statutes. These are normally prepared and given preliminary approval at the level where they will be binding. The constitutions, complementary books, or directories should specify how pertinent local statutes or policies are to be developed and approved. Local statutes or policies specify, among other things, the content of the constitutions, complementary book, and directories, adapting their content to the local mission, culture, and needs of the institute.

Record Keeping in General and Archives in Particular

It is important that an institute, at its various levels, maintain documentation of policies and various actions undertaken by superiors and members. Proper record keeping provides consistency through changes in leadership and can assist in ensuring proper and consistent implementation of policies. John Allesandro's remarks concerning curial acts are pertinent here:

> Two of the values promoted by the maintenance of a written record are consistency and accountability. Without written policies and procedures, unity and coordination in today's complex world are not likely to be achieved. Writings represent decisions and commitments and offer the administrator a secure data base for consistent action and pastoral planning.[10]

Minutes should be kept of council meetings. They should

- give the date and place of the meeting;
- name persons present;
- record decisions taken;

---

[10] John A. Alessandro, "Title III: The Internal Ordering of Particular Churches," in *The Code of Canon Law: A Text and Commentary*, James A. Coriden, Thomas J. Green, Donald E. Heintschel, eds. (New York: Paulist Press, 1985), 386.

vote: consultative or deliberative;
if latter, whether secret;
numbers positive and negative, abstentions;
- be signed by the secretary;
- be approved by the council.

Acts: When a decision made in council must be communicated to another person, either to give information or to have action taken, a written act is made. Acts should be:

- assigned a protocol number, e.g. 23/01 (act 23 of 2001);
- dated, with the place given;
- signed by the superior and the secretary;
- imprinted with the official seal;
- copies are kept in the appropriate file.

Files: Record should be grouped for filing in such a way as to

- reflect the institute's organization;
- reflect how responsibility is exercised;
- serve as a basis for all files.

The following chart, for example, might be a guide for files at the local level of an institute.

FILES: OFFICE OF THE LOCAL SUPERIOR

Diocesan Level
    Local Ordinary
    Vicar for Religious
    Council for Religious
    Relevant Diocesan Boards
    Other

Level of Supreme Moderator
    Circulars
    Correspondence

Provincial/Regional Level
    Correspondence
    Superior
    Assistants/Councilors
    Secretary
    Treasurer
    Commissions/Standing Committees
    Publications

Local Level
    Personnel: folder for each religious
    Community
    Planning
    Ministries
    Visitation Reports
    Legal Affairs
    Corporation Business
    Other

Note:
- Minutes of community meetings should be retained in their own book.
- Annals of the community should be kept in their own book.
- Minutes of council meetings and corporation meetings should be kept separately and readily accessible to the superior and the secretary.

> ### SAMPLE OF AN ACT AT THE LOCAL LEVEL
>
> Protocol Number
>
> The local council of (the name of the community) of (city, state) approved an expenditure of twenty-seven thousand dollars ($27,000.00) for repairs to the roof of the east wing of the residence building.
>
> Vote: _____ Yes _____ No _____ Abstain
>
> Given at (place, city, state)
>
> Date:
>
> (Signature of Superior)
>
> (Signature of Secretary)
>
> (Seal)

Archives

Archives serve to gather, preserve, and make accessible valuable records relevant to the institute or local community. They serve administrative needs of governance and provide a basis for research. Just as importantly, they help maintain the identity of the institute, which is not only a historical entity, but a living organism continually developing. The data and materials of well-organized and maintained archives record its life.

The following is an indication of the kinds of things that should be found in archives. It is not an outline according to which archives should be set up. Each institute should develop its own record groups with the appropriate series of topics in each group. Each institute should also be aware of issues of confidentiality–under civil law and canon law–and of access, and develop policies and procedures accordingly.

For practical help, recourse can be had to the Society of American Archivists, 600 S. Federal, Suite 504, Chicago, IL 60605; to the Association of Catholic Diocesan Archivists, 5150 Northwest Highway, Chicago, IL 60630; to the Archivists of Congregations of Women Religious, 3333 Fifth Avenue, Pittsburgh, PA 15213-3165. Membership in such organizations provides opportunity for workshops at almost any level of need and access to helpful publications.

Official Documentation

- Government
- Constitutions, Rule
- Directory, Policies, Procedures
- History
- Institute
- Provinces
- Biographies
- Annals (duplicates)
- Formation/Education
- Foundations
- Ministries/Institutions
- Membership Listings
- Minutes of Chapters
- Minutes of Council Meetings
- Official Documents: Acts
- Finances
- Property and Buildings
- Correspondence: Roman Congregations, Local Ordinaries, Provincials, etc.

General Materials

- Books and Articles published by members
- Commemorative Booklets
- Community Newsletters
- Community Studies: ministry, government, finance, etc.
- Financial and Photographic Records of buildings, change in their use, etc.
- Journal Articles relevant to community or members
- Orders of Liturgical Ceremonies
- Photographs
- Prepared Publicity

Individual Religious Materials
Other Materials
> Artifacts–statues, paintings, sacred vessels, furniture, books–of artistic value or of
>
> significance in the history of the institute or house

SECRET ARCHIVES

Applying canons 489 and 490 to consecrated life, the manifest need exists to protect the confidentiality of all members, including former members. As canon 489 suggests for the diocesan curia, an institute should therefore make provision for

> [...]a secret archive or at least in the common archive there is to be a safe or cabinet, completely closed and locked, which cannot be removed; in it documents to be kept secret are to be protected most securely.

On analogy with canon 490, proper law should designate the major superior as the sole individual with the key to this archive. Proper law should already have provision in case of the sudden death of the major superior. The person upon whom leadership devolves in such a situation might be allowed access under specific conditions. Finally, proper law should clearly define the limited access to the secret archives. Such a policy properly enforced will encourage the freedom of individuals in discussing personal matters with the major superior and with medical personnel, including psychiatrists or psychologists.

The institute should have a clear policy on the location of specific types of documents. The secret archive should not include all documentation. The secret archives might include

- results of psychological testing, received either before admission or afterwards;
- results of medical testing, again, received either before admission or afterwards;
- for a clerical institute or one with clerics as members:
    records of dispensations from impediments and irregularities to orders or to the exercise of orders;
    documents concerning loss of the clerical state through invalidity, penalty or dispensation (see cc. 290-293);
- decree of dismissal from the institute (see c. 700)
- documentation of penal investigations concerning present or former

members; also documentation if penalties were imposed. Again on analogy with canon 489, §2, proper law should set a policy for the timely destruction of documents concerning criminal cases. Psychological records, although maintained in the secret archives, should be kept indefinitely in case need for them should arise such as in petitions for dispensation from obligations arising from ordination to the priesthood.

Given the complex legal situation in the United States concerning access to archives, the major superior should consult a civil lawyer in establishing or implementing a specific policy concerning the secret archives.

THE RELATIONSHIP BETWEEN A CANONICAL AND CIVIL ENTITY

Because canon law requires the use of civil legal structures to hold title to property and to protect church assets, the institute, and its province are incorporated under state statutes.

It should be noted that certain actions under specific conditions (for example, the alienation of property) are governed both by canon and civil law. Both canonical and civil legal advice should be sought. The following table by Cecilia Meighan, R.S.M., J.D. is a useful reference.

CANONICAL AND CIVIL REFERENCES

		RELIGIOUS INSTITUTE (RI)	CORPORATION (CIVIL)
I.	LEGAL STATUS	Collegial public juridic person (c. 115) recognized by competent ecclesiastical authority, whose members take vows as required by the constitutions of the institute (cc. 573-746)	Civil or religious not-for-profit corporation incorporated under appropriate state statute; person under civil law
II.	GOVERNING DOCUMENTS (Define duties and authority)	**Constitutions and Directory** *Constitutions* ♦ Nature, end, and spirit of R.I. ♦ Governance of R.I. ♦ Admission of candidates and formation of members ♦ Obligations and rights of R.I. and members ♦ Separation of members from R.I. ♦ Approved by CICLSAL or diocesan bishop *Directory, Policies, Procedures* ♦ Norms by which R.I. is governed ♦ Directory needs approval of chapter ♦ Policies and procedures need approval of council	**Articles (Charter) and Bylaws (Code of Regulations)** *Articles* ♦ General and specific purposed ♦ Indemnification of directors and officers ♦ 501(c)(3) requirements ♦ Dissolution clause *Bylaws* ♦ Specific responsibilities of Board of Directors ♦ Procedures for valid corporate acts ♦ Committee structure ♦ Designation of officers

	RELIGIOUS INSTITUTE (RI)	CORPORATION (CIVIL)
III. GENERAL PURPOSES	♦ Profess evangelical counsels ♦ Live a common life ♦ Share assets ♦ Undertake certain works of charity	♦ Follow the same set of directive–rule ♦ Further and promote charitable, religious, educational purposes [purposes must meet 501(c)(3) requirements of Internal Revenue Code ♦ Support the works of public charity of R.I. ♦ Receive and administer funds for religious and charitable purposes
IV. SPECIFIC PURPOSES	♦ Carry out the particular purpose(s) of R.I. according to constitutions, directory, and canon law	♦ Carry out business and administer property and assets of R.I. according to the Articles, Bylaws, and corporate law
V. GOVERNING BODY	Major Superior and Council; chapter when in session (elected by membership according to Constitutions)	Board of Directors (self perpetuating)
VI. FORMALITIES	♦ Council Meetings ♦ Separate agenda ♦ Separate minutes ♦ Annual reports ♦ Periodic meetings ♦ Financial reports ♦ Board of Directors Meetings	♦ Separate agenda ♦ Separate minutes ♦ Annual report ♦ Annual and regular meetings ♦ Proper notices ♦ Election of officers ♦ Annual budget/audit financial statements ♦ Corporate seal

	RELIGIOUS INSTITUTE (RI)	CORPORATION (CIVIL)
VII. RESPONSIBILITIES OF GOVERNING BODY	♦ Administrator of ecclesiastical goods (Book II, Title II, Art. 3 and Book V, Code) ♦ Perform acts of ordinary and extraordinary administration-alienation (transfer of property) ♦ Obtain permissions of competent authority ♦ Generalate level- receive request for approval from provinces; request necessary approvals from CICLSAL ♦ Province level- approve and make requests to generalate ♦ Attend to issues/matters as determined by Constitutions or Directory ♦ Preserve official records of a non-current nature in Congregation archives ♦ File reports as requested by appropriate canonical authority	♦ Receive gifts, bequests, grants in name of R.I. and in accordance with applicable canons ♦ Make contracts ♦ Sue and be sued ♦ Receive state or federal grants ♦ Approve merger of dissolution of corporation ♦ Hold property ♦ Purchase or lease real and personal property ♦ Sell, convey, dispose of real and personal property ♦ Receive, take title to, and use proceeds of stocks, bonds, etc. ♦ Keep corporate files, correct and complete books and records of accounts, transactions, and minutes of the proceedings of the Board of Directors and its committees ♦ Preserve official records of a non-current nature in administrative archives ♦ File reports with state/federal governments ♦ Hire, fire employees and administer personnel policies consonant with local, Reform and Control Act ♦ Fair Labor Standards Act ♦ Internal Revenue Code

	RELIGIOUS INSTITUTE (RI)	CORPORATION (CIVIL)
VIII. MINUTES	**Council Minutes** Should reflect actions taken on: *Canonical Issues* ♦ Admission of candidates ♦ Admission to novitiate ♦ Exclaustration ♦ Transfer ♦ Readmission ♦ Dismissal ♦ Dispensation ♦ Permissions for alienation *Personnel Issues* ♦ Education ♦ Sabbatical leave ♦ Placement *Sponsored Apostolates* ♦ Canonical approvals ♦ Membership ♦ Responsibilities ♦ Board of Directors *Reports* ♦ Committees ♦ Task forces ♦ Planning *Patrimony of the Institute* ♦ Purchasing ♦ Alienating	**Board of Directors Meeting** Should reflect quorum present ♦ Should follow requirements of state law re notice (date, time, place of meeting) or waiver of notice ♦ Should note minutes of previous meeting reviewed, approved, signed by secretary of president of Board ♦ Should note passage of corporate resolution required by banks, state or federal requirements, e.g. open bank accounts, change authorized signatures on accounts ♦ Should reflect passage of all corporate resolutions ♦ Other corporate matters Taxes Budget Property-sale, purchase, improvement Leases Loans Amendments of articles or bylaws Approval of merger or dissolution

	RELIGIOUS INSTITUTE (RI)	CORPORATION (CIVIL)
IX. CANONICAL REQUIREMENTS WITH CIVIL LAW IMPLICATIONS	♦ Patrimony ♦ Cessation of administration of property ♦ Wills	♦ Taxes ♦ Power of attorney ♦ Must meet requirements of state will statute

X. DOCUMENTS	♦ Personnel files
	   Cession instruments
	   Health records
	
	♦ Archives
	   Council meeting minutes
	   Personnel files of dispensed and deceased members
		♦ Property files
		   Deeds
		   Appraisals
		   Surveys
		   Mortgages
		   Leases
		
		♦ Financial file
		   Audits
		   Budgets
		   Reports
		
		♦ Contracts

PROCEDURES FOR GENERAL CHAPTERS

The Church guarantees to individual institutes "[a] just autonomy of life, especially of governance... by which they possess their own discipline in the Church and are able to preserve their own patrimony intact...." (c. 586, §1). The general chapter of an institute provides one very important means by which the institute not only exercises this rightful autonomy but also manifests the institute's "true sign of unity in charity" (c. 631, §1). The general chapter is distinct from other chapters of the institute, as for example, a provincial chapter (c. 632). The following outline, read along with proper law, may provide a means for developing guidelines for such bodies, for example, determining who can vote.

The principle of subsidiarity receives concrete expression in the universal law concerning chapters; often, the universal law stipulates *as determined by proper law or unless otherwise determined by proper law*. The following outline lists what is required by universal law, and it notes when options are left to proper law. Given this freedom, when questions arise concerning the convoking of a chapter, its members, voting, etc., a canonist should be consulted.

According to canon 631, §1, the chapter

- possesses supreme authority in the institute;
- represents the entire institute;
- its decisions bind all members.

Requirements

- protect patrimony of the institute; (Is this action keeping with the nature, end, spirit, character, and traditions of the institute?)
- promote suitable renewal;
- elect Supreme Moderator, a clear protection of the institute's rightful autonomy of governance.

    Qualification established in proper law, canon 623;

    Suitable period is required after perpetual or definitive profession, as determined by proper law or for major superiors by the constitutions;
- treat major business, particularly affecting the whole institute; proper law may also reserve certain items of business for the consideration of the general chapter (for example, erection or suppression of provinces, sale of property);
- publish norms binding on all, which reflects the collegial nature of the chapter.

How convoked

- Applying canon 166 to religious institutes, the supreme moderator convokes the general chapter; as determined in proper law, provides for election of delegates or arranges a *chapter of the whole* (for further specification, see below).
- Proper law should determine how preparation for the chapter should occur.

Officials of Chapter

- Unless otherwise determined by proper law, the supreme moderator is the presiding officer of the chapter.

- Tellers

    Canon 173 requires, prior to any election in a chapter, the designation of at least two tellers; these tellers must be members of the group.

    canon 173, §2: the tellers gather the ballots, determine in the presence of the presiding officer that the number of votes cast equals the number of electors (otherwise the election is invalid), reads the ballots and announce the votes each person received.

    Secretary appointed by the presiding officer; record accurately the acts of the election and preserve them.

Participation

- Canon 633 states that the general chapter should have as its purpose the concern and participation of all members for the good of the entire institute or community.
- Canon 631, §3 states that each member may submit proposals, suggestions or desires to the chapter. Chapter preparation should provide for feedback from membership. Proper law may determine the proper procedure

Membership

- Proper law may determine the procedure for electing members of the chapter.
- Must represent the institute as a whole (c. 631, §1)
- Canon 631, §2 specifies that the composition of the general chapter must be defined in proper law. Therefore, if the norm found there calls for a chapter composed of elected delegates, the institute is bound to observe that norm until

    a special indult is received granting permission for an exception or

    an amendment is passed by the general chapter and approved by competent ecclesiastical authority. Such as amendment would become operative for future chapters.

- Praxis of the Apostolic See regarding a *chapter of the whole*

    members of an institute have an acquired right to participate in making its decisions. Traditionally, each member has exercised this right by voting for delegates to the general chapter and by submitting proposals for the consideration of the chapter. If the composition and structure of the chapter were changed in such a way that only those persons who were physically present participated in decision-making, some and perhaps even many members of the institute might be effectively disenfranchised.

Institutes of less than 100 members have received permission for all members to elect the supreme moderator. Some larger institutes have received favorable responses if they have submitted a well-developed plan which provides for a truly whole-member chapter, that is one which will actually involve nearly all members. Key criteria include geographic proximity, impact on ministry and on financial resources, tradition of chapters in the particular institute, numbers of members who would be disenfranchised if they can neither come in person nor vote for a delegate and conduciveness of number for good decision making. In general the Apostolic See requires that chapter members be perpetually professed, indults have been granted as exceptions (see *Canon Law Digest* 10: 102-105).

Procedures for Election

- Convening of electors

    Canon 166, §1: all must be convened

    > notice of convocation valid if directed to domicile, quasi-domicile, or actual residence[11]

    > if one elector overlooked and not present

    >> election is valid

    >> canon 166, §2: the one overlooked can provide proof and the election rescinded by competent authority, provided recourse made within three days of the notice of election

    >> canon 166, §3: if more than one third electors overlooked, election is invalid by law itself

    > unless all those overlooked were present

    Canon 168: no mail or proxy voting unless

    > provided by proper law or statutes

---

[11] For the terms see cc. 100-107, especially c. 103.

Canon 167, §2: one present in the place of election but cannot be present due to illness at the election itself:

the written vote is collected by the tellers

- Eligibility to vote

    Requirements in voters

    canon 169: member of the group or college

    canon 171, 1°: capable of placing a human act

    if questions arise concerning a person's mental capacity (for example, suffering from Alzheimer's disease) canonical advice must be sought before election.

    Canon 171, 2°: active voice

    Members with active voice may vote; members with passive voice may be elected.

    The right to be elected – passive voice – has a corresponding obligation – allowing one's name to stand for election. Proper law may determine if a member can withdraw his or her name from the election but care must be taken to protect the right of the members to elect the best qualified for office.

    Exclaustrated members do not enjoy either active or passive voice (see c. 687)

    Canon 171, 3°: not excommunicated by judicial sentence or decree inflicting or declaring a penalty

    Canon 171, 4°: not notoriously defected from the communion of the Church

    Notorious indicates the defection is not simply known by some persons (and therefore public) but rather person has clearly and unambiguously defected from communion

    The phrase, *communion* of the Church, in the context of law of consecrated life, implies full communion with the Catholic Church as this may be judged in the external forum (see c. 205).

    Canon 171, §2: if any such ineligible person votes, then

    If the one elected received enough votes even subtracting the vote[s] cast by the ineligible, the election is valid.

If the one elected did not receive enough votes subtracting the ineligible votes[s], the election is invalid and another election must be held.

Canon 172, §1: requirements in the voting itself: free (no coercion by grave fear or fraud); *secret* (in the act of voting itself); *certain* (for a specific individual); *absolute* (without conditions; see c. 172, §2); *determinate* (clearly stated without ambiguity).

Canon 176 and The One Elected

- Canon 119: to be elected (unless otherwise provided in proper law)

    a majority of those who must be convoked are present;

    the person receives an absolute majority of those present;

    An absolute majority is fifty percent (50%) of those voting plus one.

    Abstentions are considered part of the total vote; so, for example, in a chapter consisting of 100 delegates, ten members abstain from the election for superior. To be elected, an individual needs 51 votes. Proper law, however, could determine that abstentions are not considered as part of the total; thus, in the example given, to be elected a person would need 46 votes.

    After two inconclusive ballots, the choice is limited to those two individuals who have received the most votes;

    If a tie exists among several members, then those persons senior in age stand for election in the following ballots.

    After three inconclusive ballots, the one senior in age is considered elected.

- Canon 177, §2: The one elected must be informed of the election (if not present) and has eight days to accept or decline the election.
- Canon 178: If the office does not require confirmation, the one elected acquires the office by acceptance of the election.

    Canon 153 allows for an election within six months prior to that office becoming vacant (for example, if the superior's term ends on June 1, the election may occur from January 1 to June 1). If, however, the election occurs before the expiration of the time period, the one elected acquires the office only when the office does in fact become vacant.

- Canon 179: If the election requires confirmation, then confirmation must be requested from the competent authority within eight days of the election.

Confirmation must be given in writing;

Confirmation is required for the validity of any acts; therefore, the one elected cannot act prior to confirmation.

Canon 174 allows for compromise (if provided in proper law) to transfer the right of election to a qualified individual or individuals, the electors must unanimously agree and express their consent in writing

Other matters decided by the General Chapter

- Canon 119, 2° provides for procedures other than elections (for example, adopting a new institute-wide policy). The general rule requires an absolute majority of those present (who are a majority of those who must be convoked) but does not limit the number of ballots. 2° also provides for the possibility of breaking a tie vote through the vote of the presiding officer.

CHAPTER TWO

NEW INSTITUTES, MERGERS, AND SUPRESSION

SHARON HOLLAND, I.H.M..[1]

Despite the existence of countless religious institutes, secular institutes, and societies of apostolic life in the Church throughout the world, the Spirit continues to give new founding gifts. These must be submitted to the competent authority of the Church in order to assure their authenticity. There are four major steps in the procedure from the original inspiration of a founder to the final possible step of pontifical recognition: inspiration, association, diocesan erection, and pontifical recognition.

The foundational canon is canon 579, which states: "Diocesan bishops, each in his own territory, can erect institutes of consecrated life by formal decree, provided that the Apostolic See has been consulted."

INSPIRATION

Before any juridic action, the inspiration which has been received by a founder must be evaluated by the hierarchy. Conciliar and post conciliar documents are rich in teaching which not only can help founders, but also can guide the bishops who have the responsibility of welcoming and distinguishing among charisms (*Lumen gentium* 12b).

---

[1] Marlene Weisenbeck, F.S.P.A. and Rita-Mae Bissonette, R.S.M. contributed to the writing of this chapter.

Criteria for discernment

Mutuae relationes, n. 51 helps explain contemporary procedural practices, offering criteria to bishops. What was written in 1978 regarding religious institutes can be applied also in evaluating certain other initiatives.

> In some regions there is noticeable a certain overabundance of initiatives to found new religious institutes. Those who are responsible for discerning the authenticity of each foundation should weigh—with humility, of course, but also objectively, constantly, and seeking to foresee clearly the future possibilities —every indication of a credible presence of the Holy Spirit, both to receive His gifts "with thanksgiving and consolation" (LG,12) and also to avoid that "institutes may be imprudently brought into being which are useless or lacking in sufficient resources" (*Perfectae caritatis* 19).

Bishops are asked to have a great openness, but also wise prudence and strong realism. Not every good initiative or work of good will is destined to be the beginning of a new institute of consecrated life or society of apostolic life. Those who are asked to evaluate a possible new form of consecrated life (c. 605) should study carefully articles 12 and 62 of the 1996 apostolic exhortation *Vita Consecrata*. These articles treat, respectively, new forms of consecrated life, and new forms of evangelical life.

At a time when many religious congregations, long established, find themselves struggling with diminishment issues, there is, in fact, also a certain phenomenon of new foundations and new forms of consecrated and of evangelical life. In an expression most uncharacteristic of canon law, the code recognized this future possibility in canon 605 (*Code of Canons of the Eastern Churches* [CCEO], c. 571).

Already recognized were two forms of *institutes* of consecrated life, religious and secular, and two individual forms of consecrated life, consecrated virgins and hermits (the Eastern code, and now *Vita Consecrata*, also add widows). Similar to the institutes but distinct and very diverse among themselves are the societies of apostolic life.

Canon 605 has left a possibility before us which we do not know exactly how to recognize. The Church's most recent experience with this came in 1947 when secular institutes were formally recognized as a *new* and complete form of consecrated life, lived *in the world*, expressed in secular occupations and organized without the common life typical of religious. These consecrated persons would be dedicated to a discreet leavening of the social fabric of a needy world.

Today we see, in many parts of the world, new growing religious institutes, but we also see new structures, which may or may not be new forms of consecrated life. New organizations today often are deliberately structured to represent a microcosm of the Church, with branches of celibate men and of celibate women, a branch of secular clerics and another of married couples. All share a common spirituality and mission; they want ecclesial recognition. Sometimes they ask explicitly to be recognized as a form of consecrated life. Bishops are faced with the discernment of which *Lumen gentium* and canon 605 speak.

Vita Consecrata offers some help in this discernment, without claiming to do so definitively. One of the commissions announced in the apostolic exhortation is precisely for the purpose of determining criteria of authenticity to help with the discernment necessary in these cases (n. 62-e). However, three numbers are of particular usefulness for dealing with such questions in the interim: n. 30 discussing the relationship between baptismal consecration and consecration through profession of the evangelical counsels; n. 12 on new expressions of consecrated life, and n. 62 on new forms of evangelical life.

Relationship to baptismal consecration

Article 30 responds to the Synod's desire for a clearer expression of the relationship between baptismal consecration and consecration through profession of the evangelical counsels, which, Vatican II teaches, is rooted in the former (*Perfectae caritatis* 5; *Lumen gentium* 44). Historically, religious profession has been presented as a sort of second baptism. Vatican Council II presented profession as a special and fruitful deepening of baptismal consecration; a means of drawing deeper into union with Christ and of being more authentically configured to him (cfr. *Redemptionis donum* 7).

But this new consecration also differs from baptismal consecration of which, states the text, "it is not a necessary consequence"(*Vita Consecrata* 30). All of the baptized are called to the chastity proper to their state of life, to obedience to God and the Church and to a reasonable detachment from possessions. All are called to holiness, to the perfection of charity (*Lumen gentium* 42). Baptism, however, does not ask for celibacy or perpetual virginity. It does not require renunciation of possessions or obedience to a superior in a form particular to the evangelical counsels. Here there necessarily enters the concept of distinct vocations. There is a fundamental equality of dignity through baptism, and there are distinct vocational gifts. The life of the evangelical counsels is a particular following of Jesus' way, as proposed by him to his disciples and personally lived by Jesus (*Vita Consecrata* 31). Chastity for the sake of the Kingdom is called the "door" of consecrated life (*Vita Consecrata* 32). This also provides a key for reading article 12 on new expressions of *consecrated* life and article 62 on new forms of *evangelical* life.

The distinctions made in these articles can be very helpful to those who deal directly with persons who feel called to make new foundations. The importance of this early stage of discerning charism is critical. Sometimes founders or foundresses themselves do not adequately recognize the diverse options for approval within the Church.

Emerging forms of consecrated life

In speaking of "new expressions of consecrated life," *Vita Consecrata* 12 recognizes both new foundations of traditional types and the renewal of existing institutes. Then it moves to "new experiments which are seeking an identity of their own in the Church" and which are awaiting official recognition from the Apostolic See, in the sense of canon 605, which reserves that recognition to the Holy See.

The underlying unity and the characteristic mark of all forms of consecrated life is the one call to follow Jesus—chaste, poor, and obedient—in the pursuit of perfect charity. This must mark new forms as well. What that means and does not mean is more fully drawn out in n. 62 on new forms of evangelical life.

Emerging forms of evangelical life

This article indicates some of the characteristics of new foundations emerging in the Church today, under the same action of the Holy Spirit. A first point of newness or originality is often that new communities are mixed: men and women; clergy and lay; married and celibate.

While there are diverse forms of commitment to evangelical life, these new communities tend to be characterized by "an intense aspiration to community life, poverty and prayer." Both clerics and lay persons have a share in the governance of such groups and the apostolate focuses on the new evangelization.

The text turns next to the importance of discernment regarding these charisms. If they are to be recognized as consecrated life, as a matter of principle, they must be founded upon the essential theological and canonical elements proper to the consecrated life. Here, in the footnote, reference is made to the initial doctrinal-theological canon of each code (*CIC* c. 573; *CCEO* c. 410).

Bishops are also offered some specific criteria for use at the diocesan level. In studying new groups, they must examine:

- the witness of life and the orthodoxy of founders;
- the spirituality of founders;
- their ecclesial awareness in carrying out their mission;
- methods of formation;
- the manner of incorporation;
- the suitability of members who desire to receive Holy Orders.

Article 62 moves next to clarify a point which now occurs with increasing frequency as new communities seek some form of ecclesial recognition: the question of married persons. Appreciation is expressed for the commitment of married persons and for the *consecration* received through the sacrament of matrimony in the sense of *Gaudium et spes*, n. 48. In some new organizations, conjugal chastity is confirmed by a vow. "However," the article continues, "by reason of the above-mentioned principle of discernment, these forms of commitment cannot be included in the specific category of the consecrated life."

Characteristics of Authentic Charisms

The above text from *Mutuae relationes* first indicates motives which are insufficient for a new foundation: simple usefulness or suitability in a field of action or the life of someone who has experienced devotional phenomena. The same n. 51 then lists characteristics of authentic charisms:

- its special origin from the Spirit, distinct, even though not separate, from special personal talents, which become apparent in the sphere of activity and organization;
- a profound ardor of love to be conformed to Christ in order to give witness to some aspect of His mystery; and
- a constructive love of the Church, which absolutely shrinks from causing any discord in Her.

In the same document, n. 12, there is a further indication of a genuine charism, that is, its newness or "genuine originality." The document acknowledges openly: "In its surroundings it may appear troublesome and may even cause difficulties, since it is not always and immediately easy to recognize it as coming from the Spirit." The necessary discernment will be aided by the list of qualities and attitudes which ought to characterize founders and their followers:

> fidelity to the Lord; docility to His Spirit; intelligent attention to circumstances and an outlook cautiously directed to the signs of the times; the will to be part of the Church; the awareness of subordination to the sacred hierarchy; boldness of initiatives; constancy in the giving of self; humility in bearing with adversities.

ASSOCIATION (CC. 298-329)

As a *charismatic* gift to the Church, a new institute begins without formality. However, as a charismatic gift *to the Church*, the time comes for seeking a first juridic recognition from the Church.

In the past, a new institute at this stage was referred to as a *Pious Union*. In the code, this reality is called an "association of the faithful." From canon 579, this stage is not obvious but the practice is not new. For a new institute, this is the time of growth, of clarification of its identity and of proof of its stability and authenticity. It is the time for developing its statutes or constitutions.

Role of Ecclesiastical Authority

The clearest reference to this stage is found in *Pastor Bonus*, n. 111, regarding the competence of the Congregation for Institutes of Consecrated Life and Societies of Apostolic Life. This in no way alters the responsibility of the diocesan bishop at this stage. Rather it indicates that such associations are a particular category, established with a view to a different future identity.

> Art. 111. Its competence also embraces the third orders and associations of the faithful which are erected with the intention that, after a period of preparation they may eventually become institutes of consecrated life or societies of apostolic life.

While the legislation regarding this stage is less specific, it is a critically important stage because it lays the foundation for the desired future. New groups seeking approval, and the bishops under whose guidance they are developing will find help in the above cited canons on associations. Some are of particular use in seeing the relationship to ecclesiastical authority.

Canon 299, §1: Associations will be purely private at first, a free initiative of individuals, established by private agreement among themselves. They may remain private unless established for purposes of teaching Christian doctrine or promoting public worship (c. 301, §1). If the name Catholic is to be used, however, there must be permission (c. 300). Obviously an association seeking recognition as an institute of consecrated life, will be working toward erection as a public association.

Canon 299, §2: The praise or recommendation of ecclesiastical authority will be of significant encouragement to a new association if and when the Bishop feels that this is merited. Such recommendation does not change the status of the association from being private, however, it gives a note of assurance to prospective members. The group remains under canons 321-326.

Canon 299, §3: To be considered a "recognized" association in the Church, its statutes must be "reviewed" by the competent authority i.e., the diocesan bishop (c. 312, §1,3°).

Canon 305: Associations are subject to the vigilance of ecclesiastical authority, the local ordinary of the diocese. The scope of this vigilance includes the integrity of faith and morals and ecclesiastical discipline. The bishop has the right of visitation according to law and statutes (cc. 396-398, especially 397). Associations are subject to the governing authority of the bishop according to the other canons on associations.

It is the diocesan bishop who may erect a public association in his own territory (cf. c. 312, §1,3°). This is done with a formal decree (cf. cc. 48, 50-51), in which it should be explicitly stated that this association is destined to become a religious institute (or a secular institute or a society of apostolic life).

The same bishop, with the same decree, has the authority to approve the statutes of the new association (c. 314). The statutes of an association must recognize a stronger role for the bishop than will be the case later for a diocesan institute. For, example, he retains a role in the designation of moderators as well as chaplains (c. 317). Nevertheless, the statutes (or constitutions) should be written to the greatest extent possible, according to the doctrine and canons which regulate the form of life intended by the founder.

Spiritual heritage of the institute

In canon 578 of the common norms for all institutes of consecrated life, there is an exhortation to remain faithful to the spiritual heritage of the institute. In the case of a new foundation, this heritage is just being formulated. This is the time of establishing what is the nature, end, spirit, and character of the institute being formed.

While these four terms from the canon are given diverse explanations at times, their general intent can guide those preparing statutes and those charged with the responsibility of approving them.

- What is the juridic nature of the new foundation? Is it to be religious? secular? monastic? apostolic? clerical? lay? Obviously these are not all mutually exclusive.
- What is the end or purpose which the founder wishes to accomplish? Why is a new foundation called for? To what needs does it respond?
- What is the spirituality of the new institute? What values of the Gospel urge the founder and his or her followers? What are the characteristics of the spirituality and how are they to be realized in the institute?
- What synthetic expression of the nature, end, and spirit gives the institute its particular identity?

According to the determination of this comprehensive identity, the statutes can be developed, including the most suitable form of consecration in a life of the evangelical counsels (or other form of commitment in a society of apostolic life), the most appropriate form of community life in common (or other provisions in the case of secular institutes), the apostolate, norms for formation, initial structures of governance; and in the case of clerical institutes, the provision for incardination at this early stage.

DIOCESAN INSTITUTE

Although a well established association will appear very much like a diocesan institute or society, it does not yet enjoy that rightful autonomy of life, in particular of government, which is spoken of in canon 586. It is not yet juridically an institute of consecrated life or a society of apostolic life.

It is at this third step in the overall process that canon 579 formally comes into play. It is at this point that one must consider the full meaning of the phrase "provided that the Apostolic See has been consulted." In the end, it will be the diocesan bishop who, by his decree, erects the new institute but first he requests a *nihil obstat* to proceed.

The list of required documents given to bishops wishing to present an institute includes the following points:

- The names of the founder and of the first superior general, with a brief *curriculum vitae* of each. Obviously the founder is the key person for understanding the new institute; from him or her comes the spiritual heritage to which future generations must remain faithful. Since it often happens that a bishop or priest begins an institute of women, it follows that the first superior general may well be a different, but also very important, figure in shaping the beginnings.

- An historical-juridical account of the institute from its beginnings, including a copy of the document by which the ecclesiastical authority first approved it. Reading this history, together with the material in point 1, the Church can consider the petition in the light of the characteristics and criteria called for by ecclesial documents. The decree of erection of the association of the faithful indicates a critical step in the juridic history. It often happens that 20 or more years pass from this decree to the petition for the *nihil obstat*. This too highlights the importance of laying sound foundations.

- The constitutions and the directory of the institute, revised in accordance with the *Code of Canon Law*. If, in fact, the statutes of the association of the faithful are well done, with necessary revisions according to experience, and with increasing clarity around the identity of the new foundation their preparation as constitutions for the new diocesan institute or society will not be difficult. If the members already are living with integrity the life intended by the founder, the changes needed will be, above all, in the area of government. Certain matters, once reserved to the bishop, will become the competence of the chapter and of the superiors. Further, the vows, or other sacred bonds, previously private, will become public or formally recognized by the Church.

    The proper law—constitutions and directory (by whatever title)—will be studied with care, according to what type of institute is envisioned. Observations will be sent to the diocesan bishop with the *nihil obstat* regarding recommended revisions to be made before his approval of the constitutions.

- Where applicable, there is to be included a picture of the religious dress of both a professed member and of a novice.
- Up-to-date statistics of membership (year of birth and of temporary and perpetual profession), of houses (including the place and diocese where they are located), and of the works of the institute.

  It is important to note that for the erection of a new institute of diocesan right, at least forty members are needed, the majority of whom have made perpetual private vows (or other form of permanent commitment) Before erecting an institute of consecrated life or a society of apostolic life, the Church asks proof of stability, of the capacity to persevere and grow in the service of the People of God. It is not prudent to recommend to the faithful, through the formality of diocesan erection, an entity which does not offer this hope of vitality.

  > Regarding statistics however, two exceptions are to be noted:
  > For secular institutes, there is no listing of houses as for religious institutes, since there is no obligation to common life or corporate works.
  >
  > For a new foundation dedicated to contemplation, approval is given to proceed with a smaller number.

- An account of the financial patrimony of the institute, including a declaration of debts. It is not necessary to send a detailed report, but one sufficient to indicate to what extent the institute enjoys financial autonomy and whether it has means for the support of its members and works.
- A statement regarding each of the following points:

  any facts of an extraordinary nature with reference to the institute, such as visions, etc.;

  particular devotions or exercises of piety, specific to the institute; and

  whether in the diocese of origin, there exists already any other institute with the same name and purpose.

- Testimonial letters from the diocesan bishops of those dioceses in which the institute is represented. These letters are to be sent directly to the Holy See, giving the opinion of the bishops about the following: usefulness, stability, discipline of the institute; formation of members; government; administration of goods; liturgical and sacramental dimensions; a sense of being with the Church, particularly in regard to the observance of ecclesiastical discipline as expressed in the common law of the Church and in the diocesan directives.

  The list concludes with the request that the equivalent of $200.00

(US) be forwarded with the documentation as a deposit for the expenses of the entire process.

Pontifical Recognition

The fourth stage, pontifical recognition, is an option but not an obligation. Nevertheless, if an institute has spread into diverse parts of the world, this recognition can reflect better its identity and facilitate its governance.

The documents and information to be sent to the Apostolic See are essentially the same as for the diocesan process, updated to the current situation. The number of members expected is about 100. It is the bishop of the principle house, at the request of the congregation who sends the petition, and it is the Holy See which grants the decree.

Mergers and Unions

Various possible reconfigurations of institutes are frequently referred to simply as *mergers*. Nevertheless, the realities are diverse and consequently so also the procedures to be followed in effecting mergers (*fusiones* in the text of the canon) or unions.

A typical example of a merger is that of a small institute being completely absorbed into another larger institute. After the merger, only the larger institute exists as a distinct entity.

In the case of a union of institutes, two, four, fifteen institutes unite to create one new institute composed of all of them but not identical to any one of them.

Rationale

Before examining the procedures as such, it is useful to recall why such mergers or unions might take place. In *Perfectae caritatis* we read the concern of the Council Fathers for institutes (and monasteries) which seemed to offer no hope of development. The words are strong:

> Religious foundations and monasteries, however, may sometimes be clearly devoid of any real chance of survival. When this is the conviction of the Holy

> See and the opinion of the local ordinaries, the acceptance of more novices should be forbidden. Such establishments should, if possible, be amalgamated with some other religious body or monastery of similar character and outlook, one with a more promising future. (*Perfectae caritatis* 21)

Number 22 then speaks of unions between institutes "if their constitutions and customs are practically the same and a kindred spirit animates them…especially when of themselves they are excessively small."

Ecclesiae sanctae II then published more specific norms. In n. 39 there is insistence on the importance of a suitable spiritual, psychological and juridical preparation. Number 40 notes the most important points to be taken into consideration: the good of the Church, the proper character of each institute, and the freedom of each member.

At the end of n. 41, there is an important canonical principle to be observed before proceeding to a merger or union: every religious is to be heard and all is to be done in charity.

Mergers

> Canon 582 reserves these procedures to the Apostolic See:
>
> > Mergers (*fusiones*) and unions of institutes of consecrated life are reserved to the Apostolic See only; confederations and federations are also reserved to it.

Despite this reservation, the greatest part of the preparation takes place before a formal petition is submitted to the Holy See. Considerable time and energy are needed for the spiritual and psychological as well as juridic preparation.

A small institute must study its situation well—the lack of vocations, the age of members, the institute's economic state, the difficulties in responding to apostolic commitments. All of the members need to participate in the discernment regarding a merger and having decided in favor of the idea, the superior general will most probably make contact with a number of institutes which have a similar purpose and spirituality.

The larger institute also needs to give careful consideration to the proposal and to its capacity to receive and integrate the members of the smaller institute. It may be the case that an eventual merger will affect one province in particular, in which case they should be involved in the discernment in a particular way.

Required documentation from institute requesting merger

The documents required eventually by the Holy See illustrate some of the kinds of information which will have been exchanged between the institutes beforehand.

The institute which is asking for the merger must present the following documentation.

- The petition of the superior general;
- A brief history of the institute;
- A list of the members: name, surname, date of birth, of temporary and of perpetual profession;
- A list of the houses, and the dioceses in which they are located and their ministry;
- The motives for requesting the merger (Why with this institute? How will this merger serve the well-being of the Church?);
- The method used for voting and the result of the voting: in favor and against (Such procedures may include various soundings of opinion, action in general chapter and an individual referendum involving all members.); and
- The intention of those who are opposed to the merger on the part of their institute.

Options for individual members

At this point a question often arises about what choices an individual who is opposed may have if his or her institute is deciding to merge with another institute. If those opposing a merger are few in number, their *No* will not prevent the process from going forward. However such persons have every right to charity and to a clear explanation of their canonical possibilities.

They may, of course, remain and move with their institute into the new, even though this would not be their preferred solution. Another option is to request an indult of transfer to another institute or they may ask an indult of departure. These are hard choices which require charity and patience. It must be clear, however, that if the merger is effected through a decree of the Holy See, all members pass into the new in their present status of vows unless they have taken some other action.

Required documentation from receiving institute

From the institute accepting the merger, less documentation is required. They must present a letter from the superior general, along with the consent of the general council. For this purpose, it is useful to submit an excerpt from the council minutes showing the formal act of readiness to accept the merger. The accepting institute should also present a brief history of the institute and the number of members.

Additional requirements

Both institutes must present an account of the process through which they have prepared their members for the merger. Likewise, both must have ascribed to a preliminary agreement for the disposition of temporalities according to the norms of canon and civil law. This agreement should be signed by both superiors general.

It is the usual case that the temporal goods of the institute asking to merge go to the institute accepting it. However, it is always necessary to observe the intent of benefactors and to observe civil law in addition to canon law. It is necessary to have prudent advice regarding the manner and timing of changing civil titles of ownership and making necessary changes in civil documents of incorporation for the institute and for apostolic works separately incorporated civilly.

The final piece of documentation comes from the bishops concerned. The *nihil obstat* is asked of bishops where the requesting institute is located, especially if it is of diocesan right or is a pontifical institute represented in only a few dioceses.

Unions

As noted, the notion of a union is that of two or more institutes each relinquishing their distinct juridic identity to mutually form one new institute, with a name and proper law they will agree upon, and bringing together their respective temporal goods, observing canon and civil law. Its internal structure will vary depending on the number of institutes, of members and the geographic spread of the new institute.

As noted above, the Church has encouraged the union of institutes having almost the same constitutions, practices and spirit. As is well known, there are many institutes which historically go back to one same founder and which are marked by the same spiritual heritage.

Spiritual and psychological preparation

It is often the case that before speaking of the union of institutes, there has been the formation of a federation in order to study together their common charism and to permit members to grow in mutual relationships. Federations frequently promote common projects not only of study but of apostolate; often formation resources have been shared. It is often from a federation-type structure that there emerges an informal organism which begins to coordinate efforts toward the spiritual and psychological preparation of members, prior to seeking juridic union.

Juridic preparation

The eventual procedures and documents are analogous to those for merger. However in this case, every institute is the institute which is asking for union and there is no receiving institute. Every institute must prepare and consult every religious. Each institute will study the matter in a general chapter, either ordinary or extraordinary.

While the code does not state the detail of these matters, it is the general practice that there must be a two-thirds vote in favor of union in the general chapter for an institute to continue to move forward toward a formal petition. After the chapters, there will be continuing preparations which, at a certain point, must include a new a consultation with every member in order to know his or her intention in the face of an eventual union. In this case, it is the practice of the Holy See to consider a petition only if at least 80% of the members express themselves in favor of being a part of the new institute to be created by the union.

As the process continues, a union requires preparations not called for in the case of mergers. Since the result will be an entirely new institute, it will have to have a new name. Likewise it will have to have its own proper law. Depending on the participating institutes there may be one text which can serve as a base for developing their new proper law. In some cases, a federation will already have moved to a common core text which can be the basis of development. Depending on the size and extension of the new institute, structures of governance will have to be decided upon. Provisional texts will often be reviewed in the individual general chapters of the participating institutes. Certain matters, such the composition of the first general chapter of the new institute and certain points of governance will have to be approved provisionally by the Holy See before the formal erection of the institute. Once it has been erected, some of the first acts of the new institute's general chapter will be the election of the general superior and council, and the approval of the constitutions to be submitted to the Holy See for formal approval.

As in the case of mergers, one of the documents presented with the petition for the union will be the preliminary financial agreements. Expert assistance is essential to make sure that not only canon law is properly observed but also the civil law of the places involved.

In cases of union, letters are asked from the bishops in whose dioceses the generalates are located. These are to be sent directly to the Holy See, expressing their opinion in the matter.

As in the case of mergers, every member, when the decree of establishment of the new institute goes into effect, becomes a member of the new institute, in the state he or she previously had in their original institute: perpetual vows, temporary vows, exclaustration, transfer. Anyone who has not taken positive steps to alter their status, moves into the new institute. Those who are definitely not in favor of the new have the same choices indicated for mergers. Obviously these options also remain after the institute has been erected.

SUPPRESSION

The suppression of an institute of consecrated life or a society of apostolic life, whether diocesan or pontifical, is reserved to Holy See:

> Canon 584—The suppression of an institute pertains only to the Apostolic See; a decision regarding the temporal goods of the institute is also reserved to the Apostolic See.

The same is true of the only house of a religious institute (c. 616, §2) and of the suppression of an autonomous monastery of nuns.

> Canon 616—§4. To suppress an autonomous monastery of nuns belongs to the Apostolic See, with due regard for the prescripts of the constitutions concerning its goods.

Initiation of suppression process

As has been seen, the Church prefers the merger or union of monasteries or institutes to their actual suppression. Should it be necessary however, the initiative may come from within the institute or monastery itself or from external ecclesiastical authority. The criteria have been seen in *Perfectae caritatis* 21-22. If there is a grave crisis of government or if there is scandal there may be motive for suppression, even initiated against the wishes of the members. However, an institute able to govern itself and to provide for its members has the right to continue.

Juridic steps

A first step toward suppression, whatever the source of the initiative, will be a formal visitation. For a diocesan institute, this will most probably be conducted by the diocesan bishop of the principal house, with the assistance of other appropriate persons. For a monastery, this may be by the bishop or a member of the First Order if there exists this relationship. In the case of a pontifical institute, a visitator would be named by the Holy See.

A visitation will include meetings with the Superior and Council, with the community and with each individual. This should provide an overall indication of the situation and the disposition of each individual. A detailed report would then be sent to the Apostolic See, requesting the suppression, and explaining the reasons for it, noting the dispositions of the chapter and the individual religious, explaining how accommodation can be made for the religious who remain (in other monasteries of the same Order, with other religious congregations, in diocesan facilities for aged religious), and recommendations—taking the constitutions of monasteries into consideration—for the resolution of financial questions and the temporal goods which exist or which may be realized from the sale of properties. As in other similar matters, sound legal and financial advice will indicate how just and charitable provision can be made for the remaining members, establishing trust funds if necessary.

If, as has been seen, careful and lengthy preparation is needed in the case of mergers and unions, the same is surely equally true of suppressions.

The suppression of groups which are still public associations of the faithful is regulated by canon 320.

COMMUNICATION WITH THE APOSTOLIC SEE

In a circular letter dated 2 January 1988, the then Congregation for Religious and Secular Institutes, presented norms for the implementation of canon 592, §1 regarding the reports to be periodically sent to the Apostolic See by supreme moderators. These reports are seen as an important help to the Congregation in carrying out its work of pastoral service to institutes of consecrated life and societies of apostolic life and in fostering their communion with the Holy See.

The report to be sent to the Congregation may be that which has been presented to the general chapter, but in a more concise form. The points to be included in the report from religious institutes and societies of apostolic life are, in summary, the following:

- a brief statistical report of members, houses, and parts of the institute;
- how the constitutions are valued and how authority in the institute is respected;
- how vocations are promoted and how formation is carried out;
- how fraternal life in community is lived;
- relationships with the Holy See, with diocesan bishops and with international, national, and regional conferences of major superiors;
- pastoral and apostolic activity in conformity with the charism;
- the general economic condition of the institute and any particular difficulties;
- more urgent difficulties; departure of members (cf. c. 704); and
- any other matters which show the real state of the institute.

The summary of the content of the reports from secular institutes is expressed in the following points:

- synthetic statistics of the members;
- promotion of vocations;
- apostolic commitment of individual members, formation, fraternal communion, and the relationship between director and members;
- ecclesial attitude in relationship to the Apostolic See, diocesan bishops, participation in world and national conferences;
- apostolic, social, activity, if the institute as such carries on such activity;
- the financial situation of the institute in general; any difficulties;
- more urgent difficulties; and
- other aspects regarding the actual situation.

CIRCULAR LETTER to the SUPREME MODERATORS of RELIGIOUS INSTITUTES and SOCIETIES of APOSTOLIC LIFE

Criteria for preparing reports which are to be sent periodically to the Holy See on the state of life in religious institutes and societies of apostolic life

Prot. n. SpR 640/85

The Holy See has a special interest in the state of religious institutes and societies of apostolic life and is concerned about their spiritual and apostolic growth, for this reason it follows their different situations with special care.

Therefore, in order that its work of pastoral service may be carried out more effectively and adequately and that the communion of Institutes with the Holy See may be fostered in accordance with canon 592 n. 1, it is very important that this same Holy See should be informed as to the situation and life of religious institutes according to circumstances of time and place.

In this way the Holy See can be a participant in the Lord (cf. Rom. 12, 15) in the joyful and sorrowful events of the institutes, and whenever possible in different situations—offer pastoral assistance in an appropriate fashion.

Toward this end the Congregation for Religious and Secular Institutes wishes to propose certain criteria for the reports that the supreme moderators of Institutes must make to the Holy See.

1. The report which the supreme moderator must make periodically to this Congregation can be that which he/she has already presented to the general chapter of the institute, but in summary form.

   If, however, the general chapter is not celebrated every six years, as is the practice in most Institutes, the report will still be sent at six yearly intervals according to the directions indicated below.

   The supreme moderators of religious institutes and of societies of apostolic life are asked to send the report for the first time after the celebration of the next ordinary general chapter of the institute or society.

2. This report should consist of the following:

   a) a brief and summarized statistical report of the members, the houses, and those parts immediately dependent that form the institute;

b) in what manner the constitutions are received and valued by the members, how the authority of the Institute is respected, what is the relationship between superiors and members;

c) what pastoral activity and encouragement of vocations takes place; what hopes are there for future growth of the institute; what is the early and ongoing formation, with special reference to the principal criteria and essential elements of such formation;

d) how fraternal life in community is lived;

e) what the relationship is with the Holy See, with the local bishop (especially regarding the apostolate and the liturgy), with the Unions of Superiors General, with the National Conference of Major Superiors, mentioning in what ways the superiors at the different levels participate in the meetings and works of these Union and Conferences;

f) the work of the Institute with regard to pastoral action, and the other works of the apostolate in conformity with the Institute's charism;

g) the economic condition of the institute, noting, at least in a general fashion, if there are particular difficulties;

h) the more urgent difficulties that must be provided for with special care, especially those dealing with the life and apostolic works of the institute, and the departure of members (cf. can. 704);

i) any other facts or aspects that might be called for that would clearly show the real state of the institute, for the purpose of promoting fruitful dialogue with this Dicastery.

The Congregation for Religious and Secular Institutes, while awaiting these periodic reports, asks God's blessing on all religious institutes, societies of apostolic life, and on all their individual members.

Rome, 2 January 1988 in the Marian Year.

Hieronymus, M. Card. Hamer, O. P. Praef.

Vincentius Fagiolo

Archiep. em. Theat. Vasten. secr.

To the Moderators General of Secular Institutes

The Apostolic See is heartily interested in the secular institutes of consecrated life, in their fruitful development, both spiritual and apostolic, and is solicitous about their manifold needs.

It is, therefore, very important that the communion of the institutes with the Apostolic See, according to what is recommended by c. 592, §1, be constantly strengthened through opportune information regarding their state and their life. In this way, the Apostolic See may participate in the Lord in the circumstances, both favorable and unfavorable (*Rom* 12:15 and as the case may be, offer its pastoral assistance.

For this purpose, the Congregation for Religious and for Secular Institutes proposes some criteria for the reports the supreme moderators of secular institutes are to hand in to the Apostolic See.

1. The report which the supreme moderator should submit to this Congregation can be the same as that presented to the general assembly of the institute, but in a more concise form; the acts of the assembly may be included. The supreme moderators are requested to send the first report after the celebration of the next general assembly.

2. The report shall contain the following data:

    a) synthetic statistics of the members;

    b) concerning the apostolate for vocations and the hopes for the future growth of the institute;

    c) about:

      1) the apostolic commitment of the individual members;

      2) initial and permanent formation;

      3) the fraternal communion according to the spirit of the institute, and the relation between the director and the members;

    d) regarding the ecclesial attitude in relation to the Apostolic See and the diocesan bishops; participation in world and national conferences;

    e) concerning any apostolic social or assistential activity, if the institute as such carries on such activity;

    f) about the financial situation of the institute, in general, with reference to any eventual difficulties;

g) regarding the more urgent difficulties which may have arisen especially in the life and apostolate of the institute;

h) other aspects which throw light on the actual situation of the institute;

The Congregation for Religious and for Secular Institutes, awaiting this requested information, invokes on all secular institutes and their members "peace and love with faith from God the Father and the Lord Jesus Christ" (*Eph* 6:23).

Rome, January 2, 1988, the Marian year.

Jerome Cardinal Hamer, O.P.

Archbishop Vincenzo Fagiolo

CHAPTER THREE

INSTITUTE-WIDE POLICIES

ROSEMARY SMITH, S.C.[1]

Well thought out, current congregational policies can be helpful to the superior faced with an emerging situation, to the members involved, and to the religious institute as a whole. Congregational policies take different forms and they serve differing purposes.

Policies may simply be internal administrative guides to which the superior can refer as he or she works with an individual religious or a group of religious concerning a matter of some importance but one which is not an everyday occurrence. Policies of this nature often have been developed by the superior or his or her predecessor with the advice of the council and, perhaps, with some input by outside consultants. Such policies might resemble a checklist of questions to be asked or tasks to be done. With the exception of elements which derive from higher authority (e.g., the general administration of the institute, chapter legislation, the constitutions of the institute, or the *Code of Canon Law*) these internal policies bind the superior only to the degree he or she chooses to be bound. Having such policies at hand provides a busy superior with a basic reference or blueprint for organizing or managing a task. Included in this category might be policies for opening or closing a residence of the institute, for certain financial activities, for access to the archives, and the like.

Other congregational policies, named here as institute-wide policies, are more public in nature. Such institute-wide policies may be initiated in a variety of ways — for instance, as a result of action of the chapter, at the request of some person or group (e.g., the personnel board, the treasurer, the council, or the like), or at the initiative of the superior.

---

[1] Margaret A. Stallmeyer, C.D.P. and Richard B. Williams, O.P. contributed to the writing of this chapter.

Often it is desirable that a representative cross-section of the institute with complementary expertise be assembled to think through the various dimensions of the issue and develop a draft of the policy. It may also be helpful to seek advice of outside consultants (legal, organizational, financial, canonical, etc.) who bring different perspectives and objectivity. Depending on the type of policy being developed the superior may ask congregational legal counsel to review the proposed draft for congruence with applicable civil law.

When the policy has been finalized it must be made known to all the members of the institute; this must be done in writing (c. 37) by one with the authority to bind the members and becomes effective prospectively (cc. 7, 9). The superior of the institute or province and the chapter, either general or provincial have the authority to bind the members (cc. 620, 622, 631). In certain circumstances, these policies may be disseminated beyond the members of the institute itself for purposes of information.

In order for an institute-wide policy such as this to be changed, the promulgating authority (i.e., the chapter or the superior) must promulgate a revised policy together with the new effective date. Observation of these canonical formalities is necessary and they also reinforce the serious nature of the matter at hand and the official nature of the policy at hand.

These institute-wide policies are directives for the members of the institute regarding actions to be taken or to be avoided, they lay out for general knowledge procedures which will be followed given a certain set of circumstances, and they constitute a pledge or commitment on the part of the leadership of the community about boundaries, consequences, and reasonable expectations on matters of a serious nature. In formulating these policies it is important that room be left for leadership of the institute to apply the policy in an appropriate manner. Included in this category might be policies for taking a public stand, for initiating a new ministry, or for handling a member suspected of sexual misconduct or substance abuse.

Development of such policies can be a difficult but rewarding process. The effort by the members of the institute to become knowledgeable about a sensitive dimension of community life, the drafting process itself, the manner of promulgation, and the activity which follows upon the promulgation all have educative value. They convey the importance of the matter, reinforce the community dimension of each member's actions, and model gospel attitudes (e.g., humility, solidarity, forgiveness, and justice) and behavior.

When the situation arises the superior, or the person delegated to handle the situation, must apply the policy statements and the accompanying procedures to the particular situation at hand. Adhering to an already established policy conveys a sense of even-handedness. A previously thought-out policy also provides the superior with the benefit of clear thinking without the particularities or pressures of the given situation. A certain amount of discretion must always be available to the person responsible for working with an individual member, but the policy per se should be evident.

Following are some general guidelines for developing institute-wide policies:

- *Root the policy in the institute's deepest values and tie it to its ministry goals.* Policies are not written out of fear but out of commitment to strive for behaviors, environments, and processes which are life-giving to all.

- *Use language which is clear, straightforward, unambiguous.* Policies make clear the congregation's operating principles and procedures describe the manner in which the leadership of the congregation will act. Neither should they attempt to respond to every possible scenario.

- *Write as for a public document.* The tone of the document should be sensitive, non-defensive, and accurate. Identify sources and name authorities and agencies. Even if not intended, the document could become a public text in the event of a crisis.

- *Define terms.* Never assume common understanding of technical terms. A simple glossary is most helpful.

- *Be realistic.* Do not promise a time frame, a type of response, or a behavior which cannot realistically be honored.

- *Make efforts to ensure understanding and receptivity on the part of the membership.* Distribution of the policy to the members provides an excellent time for inservice.

Sexual Misconduct

Recent history and the experience of many dioceses and religious communities make it imperative that each religious congregation has a clear policy regarding sexual misconduct. This may necessitate development of a policy statement, a rewriting of an existing policy, or at least a serious review of one's present policy document.

Components of the policy:

A congregation's policy, if it is attentive to the above writing guidelines, will not be lengthy. However, it ordinarily would contain five main sections:

- *Introduction.* The pastoral tone of the document would be set in this section. It might include such points as the congregation's mission, respect for the dignity of all persons, commitment to prevention, and to a swift, compassionate, just response to any accusation.
- *Policies.* These are the principles governing the community's response to an allegation of misconduct. They should include such topics as who (level of authority) responds to such complaints, compliance with state laws, level and types of care offered to alleged victim and offender, confidentiality issues, criteria regarding continuance in ministry, and the responsibility of each member of the congregation to report suspected misconduct.
- *Procedures.* These give the specifics about how the policies will be carried out. Processes used in the investigation, who conducts interviews, who receives information gathered, timelines, record keeping, how a decision regarding the accusation is reached, future ministry, level of assistance to the victim…all of these need to be addressed concretely in the procedures.
- *Prevention and Education.* Both the method of screening of candidates and the ongoing formation program for members should be included in this section.
- *Glossary.* A definition for each technical term used should be found in the glossary.

Canonical concerns:

- Canon 220 addresses the *right to a good reputation and the right to privacy*. Both of these are concerns in dealing with complaints of sexual misconduct. The privacy of the complainant and the reputation of the alleged perpetrator need to be respected as far as possible. Issues such as official spokesperson, level of evidence necessary for administrative action, interviewing the alleged victim, the persons involved in the investigation, and the like, should be addressed in a manner that the policies and procedures they encompass witness to a desire to protect reputation and privacy as much as possible.

- While several canons speak of the ministry of the religious institute and its members (cc. 673-683), a religious by law does not have the right to be assigned to a particular ministry or to any ministry. Therefore, in cases of alleged sexual misconduct when the nature of the complaint warrants such action, a religious superior has the right to remove the religious from ministry. Often such a response is a protection for the accused as well as the alleged victim. When such action is taken based on the complaint but before validating evidence, the policy statement should state that such action is not a judgment on the accused.

- Canon 221 addresses the *right of the faithful to defend themselves* before an ecclesiastical court. While most cases of sexual misconduct are handled administratively in the church, should a judicial process occur, the religious would have the right to canonical counsel. Similarly, in the event of a civil or criminal case, the individual religious as well as the congregation will need legal counsel. It is the responsibility of the institute to provide such for its members. Generally, the legal counsel for the individual should be different from the congregation's counsel.

Other issues:

- *Former members, associates, volunteers.* In writing their policies, congregations need to give consideration to the handling of accusations against former members, associates and volunteers. Who is responsible for their legal counsel? For psychological evaluations of the victim? Of the accused? What about ongoing responsibility to the victim?

- *Interface with dioceses and/or other institutions.* Another issue to be resolved deals with accusations against members who are ministering in diocesan institutions or in institutions sponsored by another congregation, denomination, etc. – for instance, schools, parishes, offices, agencies. A policy might handle this issue by attaching an addendum specifically addressing the coordination of a congregational and a diocesan (or other institutional) investigation of alleged sexual misconduct. Guidelines regarding communication, roles in the investigation, restrictions regarding ministry, how to respond to criminal investigation and/or civil suit could be part of the addendum.

- *Criminal and civil law.* The policy should state clearly and unambiguously the intent to comply with all applicable laws in the jurisdiction of instance. Criminal and civil law of the fifty states varies considerably regarding such notions as the definition of sexual misconduct, statute of limitations, protected communication, rules of discovery and the like. In addition this body of law changes frequently as it is an active area of litigation. Each religious institute/superior would be well advised to establish a relationship with a good law firm prior to the need for using one, the firm should be put on retainer, educated regarding religious life, and consulted on any problem that could result in litigation.

SUBSTANCE ABUSE

Policies regarding substance abuse are an acknowledgment by a religious congregation of its responsibility to its members. Chemical dependency is a disease which impairs body, mind and spirit. Left untreated it can lead to irreparable harm to the individual as well as to the community and ministry.

Both research and practical experience indicate that a person suffering from the disease of chemical dependency is unable to recognize the symptoms and unwilling to seek help. A congregation's policy must, therefore, give attention to:

- *Education.* Programs which familiarize the members of a congregation with the disease of alcoholism, which seek to identify the early signs of alcoholism, which offer stress management techniques and which stress a common responsibility to help one another are all components of a good education process.
- *Intervention.* Emphasis should be placed on the local community's responsibility to intervene in cases of alcohol or chemical dependency. Resources to assist in such intervention are available and should be referred to in the congregation's policy.

In addition, the policy should address:

- *Treatment options and the congregation's response when a member refuses to enter treatment.* A congregation who responds to its members who suffer from chemical dependency as they would to any member who is seriously ill and unable to make decisions for herself or himself, will not violate the rights of the individual.
- *Reassignment.* The policy needs to acknowledge that alcoholism is an illness, removal from ministry and participation in treatment are never viewed to be punitive. After successful treatment, reassignment should be assured to the rehabilitated member.
- *Aftercare.* The importance of the local community as a support system as well as the member's need for involvement in other support systems, such as AA, is an important component of a congregation's policy.

INTERVENTION

- An *intervention* is understood here as a process wherein an individual (or a group of individuals) is confronted with a pattern of behavior that is destructive to them or to others and asked to undertake a program of therapy or recovery, with an aim to restoring the individual or group to a healthier or more appropriate functioning within the larger community to which they belong. While this definition has a clinical sound to it, it encompasses some very important values which also have canonical implications. The rights of the individuals being confronted, the rights of the community and the nature of the process are the three most prominent areas of consideration.
- Intervention should be one of a number of remedies stated in an institute-wide plan of holistic health care that encompasses a general positive concern of the community for the health and well-being of all its members. Such a policy should be based on gospel values and the particular charism of the institute. Placed in such a perspective, the process of intervention will appear as an extraordinary measure, designed to restore an individual to healthy participation in the community and its ministry. In such a perspective, intervention will appear to a particular member to be an expression of concern and love and not simply as a defensive action on the part of the institute.

- The nature of the intervention process presumes the existence of a pattern of behavior that is destructive. Examples of this could be addictive or compulsive behavior, public or private, (excessive consumption of alcohol, food, drugs; gambling, sexual behavior, etc.) that has a potential for or already has resulted in considerable disruption of ability to participate in the normal life of the religious community or in a given ministry.
- Intervention is essentially a *pastoral* process in which no juridical determination is made of suitability for religious life and ministry. This pastoral determination should be made on the basis of experience of local membership in dialog with the major superior. Such dialog may lead to the necessity for an intervention.
- Because an intervention usually concerns delicate personal and confidential information and the options of the person(s) who are the subject(s) of the intervention are frequently determined by higher authority before the intervention begins, an institute should have a public and written policy that informs all members of the possibility of an intervention in appropriate circumstances. This policy should state the conditions or circumstances which may require an intervention, the parties who should take part, the possible determinations that may result and the requirements of confidentiality.
- The policy should also state the possible *canonical* implications of a refusal to cooperate with the recommendations of the intervention process (for example, immediate enrollment in a treatment program at a given place determined in advance). Canonical implications may include the placing of a person under obedience to take the program, severely restricting the mobility of the member, or even the beginning of a process to dismiss the individual from the institute (cc. 696-699).
- Intervention should take place only when it is clear that the subject is in such a state of denial in regard to their situation that ordinary expressions of concern and challenge have proven to be ineffective. The term used by 12-step programs is "their life is out of control."

- Intervention is usually best performed on a local level with the participation of persons who are valued and trusted by the member. If the member is so alienated or isolated that there are no relationships of trust to bring to bear, then the local superior and persons who are familiar with the situation of the member may take part. Although a mental health professional need not be present, the intervening team should consult one as part of the preparation. The major superior should also be informed. In case the subject of the intervention is a local superior or the major superior, then the next ranking member should be involved if possible — vicar or assistant, etc.

CHAPTER FOUR

Admission of Candidates, Canons 641–645

DAVID M. HYNOUS, O.P.[1]

Although very brief in their exposition of the steps necessary to admit a candidate to the novitiate of a religious institute, these few canons introduce new issues that had never before been considered under canons for admission, e.g., the question of maturity as evidenced not only by letters of recommendation but by psychological testing if deemed necessary. The canons for admission are as follows.

Canons 641–645

- Canon 641 gives to major superiors the right to admit candidates to the novitiate. Whereas, in the past, for most institutes, a pre-novitiate period known as postulancy had been required, no mention is made of any necessary pre-novitiate training. Nor is there any statement about the necessity of a vote of the superior's council.

- Canon 642 lists the basic qualities necessary for admission: sufficient age, appropriate health, suitable disposition, and sufficient maturity. All of these factors may be verified by the use of experts, taking note, of course, of canon 220.[2] A certain amount of discretion is necessary which will depend upon the nature, goals, apostolate, and life-style of the specific

---

[1] Marianne Burkard, O.S.B., James J. Conn, S.J., Bernard Johnson, O.S.C.O. and Gary M. Luiz, C.PP.S. contributed to the writing of this chapter.
[2] This canon protects good reputation and the right to privacy.

community. Is the institute dedicated to the purely contemplative life or the usual combination of both contemplative and active lifestyles?

A certain amount of discussion will be needed to determine whether or not psychological testing is necessary. The canons says "if necessary." Where the candidate is unknown to members of the institute, such testing seems necessary. The willingness to do so must be agreed upon by the individual applying.

- Canon 643, §1, lists six reasons for invalid admission: lack of age; existence of a marriage; an existing bond in another religious institute of consecrated life or society of apostolic life; force; grave fear; deceit about essential elements; or dishonesty, especially about previous incorporation (profession) in another institute. A particular institute may add other impediments even for validity of admissions, in accord with canon 643, §2. There may also be other extenuating circumstances that call for denial or at least postponement of admission, e.g., the care of sick and elderly parents.

- Although there is no mention of invalidity, two additional categories of candidates are admitted only upon the fulfillment of certain conditions. A secular cleric (priest or deacon) must be admitted with the previous knowledge of his bishop. The important phrase is that the bishop must be "informed." He does not have to give "consent." And secondly, candidates with serious financial obligations should not be admitted. Individual institutes will set the "cap" on the limit of an individual's debt as they see fit.

- Finally, canon 645, §§1-4, addresses the required documentation: proof of baptism as a Catholic, reception of the sacrament of confirmation, absence of an existing valid marriage, previous admission (with subsequent departure) from another religious institute or society or seminary, and any other letters of recommendation thought useful (parish priest, employer, etc.).

The Implementation of the Canons

Although the code speaks only of admission by the major superior, each institute or society has been engaged in an admission process that involves a vocation director and possibly a committee. In each instance, the candidate is asked to complete the documentation thought to be necessary. The material is presented to the vocation director, personal interviews are held, and a committee may or may not be involved. The institute or society needs to have a policy about the extent and nature of the confidentiality of the presented material.

For example, the following material generally forms the basis of the initial discussion:

♦ *The institute or society itself:* The candidate is made aware of the history.

The institute's or society's beginnings and its way of life in today's Church.

Its present form of ministry and status of community life in the United States.

The process leading to entrance into the novitiate, first profession, years of preparation and ministry leading either to final profession of a candidate, and (for clerics) studies for ordination to the diaconate and priesthood.

♦ *Criteria for candidates:* The candidate is asked to manifest the following.

Background: personal, religious, educational, social, and family

Why come to this institute or society? (If the community is clerical, why is it that you seek to be a priest or brother with vows?)

What are your strengths or weaknesses, your spirituality and prayer life, your relationship to sexuality?

What is your dating experience? Have you ever been engaged to marry? Have you previously been married?

What background have you come from: are you a neophyte?

What is your educational background?

What relationship have you had with the Church, i.e., your parish or university center?

What are your special interests and talents?

Why have you chosen this community over others? Who did you find attractive about this community? Does anything puzzle or disturb you?

- *Application documentation:* A certain amount of paper work must be presented.

    an application form for admission to the novitiate which is to be accompanied by:

    a most recent copy of your sacramental records: baptism, confirmation, absence of an existing marriage;

    a list of individuals whom you wish to have contacted in order to write letters of recommendation on your behalf;

    a signed psychological evaluation release form so that the results of testing may be studied by the vocation director and admissions committee;

    a financial statement that lists not only outstanding educational loans but any and all other unpaid bills and loans and other financial obligations, e.g., alimony, child support;

    a physical examination report;

    the results of a dental and ocular examinations, and

    a HIV Antibody Test Policy.

- *From the list of documents contained in the above we are interested in the following information which touches either constitutional or canonical matters.*

    Are you a neophyte from another religion? If so, for how long?

    Have you, even after Catholic baptism, practiced a non-Catholic religion?

    Have you been previously married? Has your marriage ended by the death of your spouse or by civil divorce and ecclesiastical annulment? Do you have children; if so, please give the name, age, and address of each.

    The religion of father and mother. Is either of an Eastern Catholic rite, especially your father? Has there been a divorce?

    Are you applying to enter the novitiate freely?

    Have you ever been a diocesan seminarian or ordained for a diocese?

    Have you ever entered another religious community as a novice, been professed, even in a province of the same institute or society?

    Please describe your educational background: school, location, dates, degrees. Were you ever dismissed from school or work?

Is there any financial debt that you are responsible for?

Have you ever been prosecuted or convicted in civil or military court, especially for homicide, procurement of abortion, or other civil accusations?

Does your personal medical history include the presence of any physical or psychological problems, drug or alcohol dependency, attempted suicide? Does any member of your family exhibit any of these problems?

- *Letters of recommendation:* Today's society is wary of such letters. It might be well to ask the candidate to waive his right to review the responses.

    The people who are most interested include: the parents and relatives, the pastor, campus minister, priest/sister/religious friend, members of the community.

    It is strongly recommended that the vocation director personally visit the individual's family.

    The qualifications will include such elements as leadership (ability to inspire others' action and maintain their confidence), ability to engage in teamwork, responsiveness to the feelings and needs of others, emotional stability, characteristic reaction to stress, willingness to serve, and professional ability.

- *Psychological Evaluation Release:* Although the testing may be conducted in a different location, the psychologist should be one who agrees on evaluating a candidate according to the following criteria.

    Psycho-social history

    Wechsler Adult Intelligence Scale for Adults — Revised

    Minnesota Multiphasic Personality Inventory (MMPI)

    Incomplete sentence blanks

    Rorschach Inkblot Test

    Human Figure Drawing

    Miller's Analogies.

- *Financial statement:* The statement needs to include current assets and debts. If the candidate is a minor, the financial status of his or her parents is also relevant.

- *Medical evaluation:* including dental, ocular, etc. At this point, testing for HIV Antibody should be discussed. The testing may be considered as one test in a battery of medical tests. It is helpful for the institute or society to have a policy if it does require testing. Confidentiality should be completely agreed upon but the trend is not to accept anyone with positive results.

Non-Canonical Issues

Among issues which previously existed but have been omitted in the *Code of Canon Law* is that of postulancy or pre-novitiate. Some communities have contributed material for our study of this pre-novitiate experience.

♦ *From a community of Benedictine Sisters:*

> The purpose of the postulancy is to provide an experience of living in the community during which time she will continue to discern her call to Benedictine life in this community. The length of the postulancy varies with the individual but is no less than six months and no more than two years. Admission to the postulancy is granted by the prioress following consultation with the vocation director and the formation board.
>
> The woman being accepted must meet the following requirements:
>
> A practicing Catholic between the ages of 21 and 50.
>
> One who manifests a desire to seek God in prayer, community, and service.
>
> One who has sufficient physical and mental health to live in community, can be involved in service to others, and can form stable and wholesome relationships.
>
> One who has the desire and apparent ability to live the Benedictine monastic life and demonstrates a willingness to embrace conversion as a way of life.
>
> Its purpose is to provide an experience of living in community with the sisters during which time mutual discernment regarding her vocation takes place and, inevitably, to prepare her for entry into the novitiate.
>
> The program takes into account the uniqueness of each individual. It will include prayer, community living, study, ministry, and individual direction.

Following the postulant's request for entrance into the novitiate, a detailed evaluation process is initiated, arranged by the formation director, and the report given to both the council and the chapter.

◆ *From a monastery of Trappists:*

The general principles:

> In accord with St. Benedict, those seeking entry have as their postulancy goals: love of the divine office, an understanding of obedience and of personal trials.
>
> The individual's progress is reviewed regularly by the superior, novice and junior director, and a formation committee in order to maintain good communication and continuity of policy.

The usual documentation is required: certificates of baptism and confirmation, an up-to-date medical certificate, and possibly psychological testing. Canon law will be followed when the candidate is already a priest, seminarian, present or former member of another religious institute or society of apostolic life.

The positive signs of a Cistercian vocation include: sincere desire to embrace the life of the community, a means to union with God; the necessary physical, mental, emotional health. A humble docility making the candidate eager to learn to be open to Cistercian life. The local superior will receive the candidate to the postulancy.

The postulancy itself is a period of initiation and progressive adaptation to the monastic life, particularly in the areas of prayer, divine office, and the *lectio divina*. It assists the postulancy in surmounting the difficulties which will encompass the physical and affective separation from the activities and relationships that were part of the postulant's life before entering the monastery.

The minimum period for the postulancy is determined by each community. On the advice of the novice director, the superior judges that the postulant is ready to begin the canonical novitiate. Having expressed their desire to do so, they are accepted after the council has been consulted.

Conclusion

It has been frequently said over the years that psychologists are not the ones who make final decisions about entry or rejection of a candidate into religious life. That has been the basic purpose of establishing a "committee" of varied members who make the final recommendation or judgment, positive or negative, concerning admission.

The above mentioned procedures as outlined by the canons are conducted so as to assure that the novitiate is not a debilitating experience. There are many other rules and procedures which the canons leave to the individual decision of an institute or society. What is strongly recommended is that institutes or societies and their provinces establish more detailed norms. In a sense, a directory with detailed statutes is the best reference book to have at hand.

SAMPLE
APPLICATION INFORMATION

The following information will help you to fill out the various application forms for entering the novitiate. (For reference, each form is numbered 1 through 9 in the upper right hand corner). If you have any difficulty in completing the forms, please call the Vocation Director (phone number)

To begin the application process fill out the first three forms as quickly as possible and return them to the Vocation Director.

1. *Application for admission to the novitiate.* By filling out and sending in this form you begin your application to the community. The questions on the form are self-explanatory. The references in parentheses are from the constitutions and canon law; by answering these questions you are fulfilling constitutional and canonical requirement. Note that you are to send in your baptismal and confirmation certificate. If you do not have these readily available to you, send the application form in without them and send them to the vocation office as soon as you get them. At your request, a parish will send them directly to the vocation office. Be sure to sign and date the application on the bottom of the last page.

2. *Letters of Reference.* This form indicating the individuals you wish to write letters of recommendation for you should be sent in with the application (#1 above).

3. *Psychological Evaluation Release.* After we receive this signed psychological evaluation release form, we will put you in contact with a psychologist close to where you are living, so that you can have the psychological evaluation that is required for admission. You are responsible for contacting the psychologist and setting up the appointment; the evaluation may take a day. Since the evaluation is required by the community, the cost is paid for by the community.

4. *Autobiography.* The autobiography should cover the four points as indicated on the form. This is your way of introducing yourself to the (wo)men who will be interviewing you during the admissions board process.

5. *Financial Statement.* This form describes your present financial situation. To have educational loans is not a deterrent to entering the novitiate, but personal loans and bills outstanding must be paid up before one enters the novitiate. If there are any questions in this regard, please contact the Vocation Director.

Forms # 6, 7, and 8 should be sent by the doctor and dentist's office directly to the Vocation Office.

6. *Physical Examination Report.* This form should be completed by you (history) and a doctor (physical examination)
7. *Dental Examination.* This form should be completed by a dentist.
8. *Oculist Examination.* This form should be completed by an ophthalmologist (M.D.).
9. *HIV Antibody Test Policy.* This form explains the province's requirement for the HIV Antibody test. Please read this form carefully.

Please note: On the application form you are also requested to submit your high school, college and graduate school transcripts. If you are presently in school, please request that a final transcript be sent to the Vocation Director when your final grades have been recorded or after graduation.

SAMPLE:

Please return to:
Vocation Director
[address]
[City, State, Zip]

Please note: This is not an application and does not obligate you in any way. It is designed to help us to get to know you so we can help you get to know us.

Date:_____

NAME:_____

AGE:_____ PLACE AND DATE OF BIRTH: _____

CURRENT ADDRESS: PHONE: _____

CITY/STATE/ZIP: _____

PERMANENT ADDRESS: _____

PHONE: _____

CITY/STATE/ZIP: _____

Education completed at this time: _____

Name of school attending or last attended: _____

Present occupation: _____

Are you a neophyte to Catholicism:_____ How long?_____

Have you ever applied to, or been refused by another religious community *(for clerical communities: or seminary)*? _____

Have you ever been in a religious community *(for clerical communities: or seminary)*? _____

If yes to either of the preceding two questions, list what community *(for clerical communities: or diocese)* and when: Have you ever been married?

What are your special interests? Do you belong to any clubs or service organizations? Do you belong to a parish or Newman Center?_____
Name: _____

What parish, center, or organizations do you participate in? _____

What college degree do you have? _____

What is/was your college/graduate major field? _____

(For clerical communities: Are you interested in the priesthood or the brotherhood?)
On the back of this page please briefly answer the following questions:

1. How did you become interested in the community; do you know any members?
2. Is there any particular aspect of the life or ministry that attracts you? *(For clerical communities: why do you want to be a priest or a brother?)*
3. What kind of ministry would you like to do?

Thank you for your cooperation.

SAMPLE ADMISSIONS BOARD

The following information will help you to understand the operation of the Admissions Board, especially when you meet with them for your interview.

The four (wo)men who make up the Admissions Board are representatives of the community. The Board is the group that interviews and votes on applicants for entrance into our novitiate. The Provincial or a delegate must then officially accept the decision of the Board. The Vocation Director and the Director of Novices are members of the Board but they do not interview or vote on the applicants.

The length of the Admissions Board meeting depends on the number of applicants that are meeting with the Board. The Board will not last longer than 2 P.M. Sunday afternoon. Transportation back to your place of departure will be provided.

On Friday afternoon or evening the applicants will meet with the Vocation Director for a short time for final directions and to answer any questions about the Board meeting.

The individual interviews with the Admissions Board will begin after supper. Each applicant will meet with two members of the Board for an hour, so there will be two meetings for each applicant.

After all of the applicants have been interviewed, the Board members will discuss and vote on each individual applicant. The Provincial or a delegate then approves the decision of the Board.

Finally, each applicant meets again with the whole Board at which time the decision of the Board is communicated to them and an explanation of the decision is given. Therefore, each applicant will know the decision of the Board before they leave the meeting.

Although this may sound complicated, it is not. Do not worry about the procedure, you will be guided all along the way.

SAMPLE APPLICATION

Paste a recent photograph here

Name: _____
             Last   *First*   *Middle*

Present Address: _____

City: _____ State: _____ Zip: _____

Telephone: (_____) — _____

Permanent Address: _____

City:_____ State:_____ Zip: _____

Telephone: (_____) — _____

(*For clerical communities:* Applying for: Priests_____ Brothers_____)

Date:_____

The following questions are required by church law and the constitutions. Please answer all the questions, putting N/A where the question is not applicable. If you need more room to answer question(s), please use separate sheets of paper.

PLEASE PRINT OR TYPE

1. Date of birth: (c. 643, §1)_____

   Place of birth: _____
   City, County, State, Country

   Present country of citizenship: _____

   Baptism: _____
   Date, Denomination

   _____
   Name and address of church or place of baptism

   Confirmation: _____
   Date, name and address of church

   If you are a neophyte from a non-Christian faith, please indicate the date and place of reception into the Roman Catholic Church.

   _____
   Date, Place

   If you are a neophyte from another Christian faith, in what denomination were you baptized?

   _____
   Date, Place

   Note: Baptismal and confirmation certificates issued within the last six months, along with appropriate certificates testifying reception into the church, must be submitted. Write directly to the respective churches for these certificates (c. 645, §1)

2. Are you or have you been married? Give dates and explain circumstances (*c. 643, §§1 & 2; 1041, §3: 1042, §2*).

_____

_____

_____

Note: Send authentic certificates of marriage and proof of annulment or death of spouse. (c. 645, §1).

Do you have any children? _____

If so, please give the name, address and age of each.

Name   Address

_____

_____

_____

_____

What financial arrangements have you made for them?

_____

Is anyone (including parents, grandparents, children) dependent on you or likely to be dependent on you for their upkeep? (*cc. 285, §4; 644*).

_____

_____

3. Father's full name: _____

   Living:_____ Deceased:_____

   Address:_____

   City:_____ State:_____ Zip: _____

   Occupation (indicate if retired): _____

   Religion: _____

   Is he a member of an Eastern Catholic rite? Yes_____ No_____

   If so please indicate which rite:_____

If a neophyte to the Roman Catholic Church, what was his previous religious affiliation?

_____

4. Mother's full maiden name: _____

   Living:_____ Deceased:_____

   Address:_____

   City:_____ State:_____ Zip: _____

   Occupation (indicate if retired): _____

   Religion: _____

   Is she a member of an Eastern Catholic rite? Yes_____ No_____

   If so please indicate which rite:_____

   If a neophyte to the Roman Catholic Church, what was her previous religious affiliation?

   _____

5. Are your parents separated or divorced? Yes_____ No_____

   If so. please explain briefly:_____

6. Please list, giving full name and age, all your brothers and sisters, both living and dead. List them according to their birth order. Include yourself.

   _____

   _____

   _____

7. Are you applying to enter the novitiate freely, without constraint of any kind? (*cc. 643, §§1 & 4; 645, §1*)

   _____

8. Are you now or have you ever been a postulant, novice, or professed religious of the community, or of any other religious community? (*c. 643, §§3 & 5*)

   What is the name of the community?_____

   Dates?_____

9. Were you ever refused admission to the community, any other religious institute *(for clerical communities: or diocesan seminary)*?

   When? _____ Where? _____

   Why? _____

   _____

10. List all secondary schools, colleges and universities you have attended and the length of time spent in each. Indicate the appropriate degree and major if applicable.

School	Location	Dates	Degree/Major

11. What classical or modern languages have you studied?

    _____

12. Have you ever been a member of the armed forces? Give details of your discharge.

    _____

    _____

    _____

13. Have you ever been dismissed from any school, college, university or place of employment?

    Please explain: _____

    _____

14. Have you any outstanding personal or education debts? _____

    Please explain _____

15. Are you under any work contract or bound to account for any trust fund, etc.? _____

    Please explain (*c. 285, §1*).

    _____

    _____

16. Have you ever been convicted by a civil or military court or are you liable for prosecution before any court? Please explain

    _____

    _____

The following questions are specifically required for ordination but may be helpful for other reasons as well.

17. Have you ever been responsible for homicide? (*c. 1041, §4*)_____

    The procurement of abortion? (*c. 1041, §4*) _____

    Have you ever attempted to take your own life? (*c. 1041, §5*)_____

    If yes to any of the above, please explain: _____

    _____

18. Does your personal medical history indicate the presence of recurrent physical or psychological difficulties or patterns of dependence on drugs or alcohol? (*cc. 1029; 1031, §1*) _____

    Please explain: _____

    _____

19. If you ever joined a non-Catholic religion (c. 1041, §2), including any Masonic, theistic, atheistic, or other secret society, give the name of the organization(s) and the dates of membership.

    _____

    _____

20. Have you ever been a diocesan seminarian? _____

   Dates: What diocese? _____

   What orders or ministries, if any, did you receive? _____

   Are you under obligation to serve a diocese? (*c. 644*) _____

   If you are a diocesan deacon or priest, has your Ordinary been consulted in regard to your becoming a religious? (*c. 644*). (Please include letter.)
   _____

21. Does the medical history of any of your family members indicate the presence of recurrent physical or psychological difficulties or patterns of dependence on drugs or alcohol?

   If Yes, please explain. _____
   _____
   _____

22. Please list in chronological order all employment, including part-time.

   Company   Position   Full-time/Part-time   Dates
   _____
   _____
   _____
   _____
   _____

I have answered all of the above questions to the best of my knowledge and ability, according to the truth and without reservation.

Applicant's Signature: _____

Date: _____

SAMPLE
LETTERS OF RECOMMENDATION

As part of the application process, letters of recommendation are required (canon 1043). The letters required are from the following individuals.

1. Your parents.
2. A close family relative.
3. Your pastor, either of your parish or campus ministry center.
4. Your spiritual director and/or the person who has helped you the most in your decision to enter religious life.
5. One other priest or religious.
6. Either a professional supervisor, if you are presently working, or a teacher/professor/school.

Please fill in the following. The Vocation Director will write to the people you list requesting a letter of recommendation. You may wish to tell them that they can expect a letter from this office.

1. Parents(s)_____
   Phone_____
   Address _____
   CityStateZip _____

2. Relative
   Phone_____
   Address _____
   CityStateZip _____

3. Pastor
   Phone_____
   Address _____
   CityStateZip _____

4. Spiritual Director

   Phone_____

   Address _____

   CityStateZip _____

5. Priest or Religious

   Phone_____

   Address _____

   CityStateZip _____

6. Supervisor or Teacher

   Phone_____

   Address _____

   CityStateZip _____

7.a. Friend

   Phone_____

   Address _____

   CityStateZip _____

7.b. Friend

   Phone_____

   Address _____

   CityStateZip _____

Please Note:
If you have ever consulted a professional counselor, psychologist, or psychiatrist or if you have ever made application to another religious community or diocese, please notify the Vocation Director of this fact. Please do not wait until your autobiography and application papers are ready before returning this list. RETURN THIS LIST AS SOON AS POSSIBLE SO THAT WE CAN CONTACT THESE PEOPLE.

SAMPLE
PSYCHOLOGICAL EVALUATION RELEASE

I, (name), willingly release the contents of the psychological evaluation prepared by the consulting psychologist that the community has assigned to me as part of the admissions process, to the Admissions Board, Formation Team, and Provincial of the community.

I also give them the right to review the contents of all the materials submitted to the Vocation Director for the applications process.

I also waive my rights to review the letters of recommendation which will be included as part of my application to enter the novitiate of the same Province.

Signature: _____

Address: _____

City: _____

State: Zip: _____

Witness Signature: _____

Address: _____

City: _____

State: Zip: _____

Please return to:
Vocation Director
(address)
(city, state, zip)
(phone)

TESTS FOR PSYCHOLOGIST TO ADMINISTER

Psychosocial History

Weschsler Adult Intelligence Scale for Adults–Revised (WAIS-R) or Shipley Institute

Minnesota Multiphasic Personality Inventory (MMPI-2)

Incomplete Sentence Blanks

Rorschach Inkblot Test

Human Figure Drawings

Miller's Analogies

Questions to Ask:

What tests do they administer and why?

Do they administer the Miller's Analogies?

Do they do an Exit Summary or Feedback Visit?

What is the price of the interview and the testing?

Have questions ready about concerns regarding an individual.

SAMPLE AUTOBIOGRAPHY

As part of your application to enter the novitiate, you are asked to write an autobiography. The autobiography will be kept confidential, being available only to the Vocation Director, members of the Admissions Board and Formation Team, and the Provincial. Be sure to keep a copy for yourself; it's handy for future reference. Please submit only a typewritten Autobiography!

a. Please give a chronological list of where you have been in your lifetime, from birth to the present. Include what you were doing or experiencing at each point. Be as specific as possible in your listing.

b. Please sketch experiences and persons you believe were important in your development. What and who helped in making you the person you are today? Within this sketch, you should touch especially on the following:

- ◆ your relationships with parents, emphasizing how those relationships have changed over the years;
- ◆ your relationships with other significant members of the family (the closeness of blood relationship is less important than the significance of the relationship);
- ◆ your relationships with significant friends and acquaintances;
- ◆ experiences which have moved you to consider religious life and/or priesthood;
- ◆ experiences and insights which have influenced your awareness of and acceptance of your sexuality, your self-worth, your ability to love and accept love;

c. Please describe two (2) meaningful successes in your life indicating why these were meaningful to you.

- ◆ "meaningful experiences" are those experiences which helped you to better see the person you are, to give you some purpose in life and to see more clearly how you want to live your life.
- ◆ "successes" are those experiences which led to a feeling of satisfaction within yourself.

These do not have to be earth-shattering events. They may be very simple experiences which, nonetheless, led to some degree of satisfaction within yourself.

d. Please describe two (2) meaningful (as described above) failures in your life and indicate what impact they had on you.

Writing is never an easy task. The creation of your autobiography will require time and hard work. However, your energy will be well used. A carefully and thoughtfully constructed presentation of the requested information will help us come to know you better and will probably clarify your own understanding of some aspects of your history.

>
> Please return to:
> Vocation Director
> (address)
> (city, state, zip)
> (phone)

SAMPLE:

Applicant's Name_____ Date _____

Personal background:

Religious background:

Education background:

Social background:

Family background:

Why this religious institute?

(For clerical institutes) Why priest/brother?

Why community life?

Why celibacy and vows?

Strengths and Weaknesses:

Sexuality:

What future ministry?

Spirituality/prayer

Other options:

Marriage:

Convert:

Other religious community:

Interviewer's Name _____

SAMPLE
FINANCIAL STATEMENT

Name: _____

1. Please indicate the amount of money you currently have on account.

    a. Savings Account: $

    b. Checking Account: $

2. Property you own (its nature and approximate value):

3. Your outstanding debts:

    a. Amount of indebtedness: $

    b. To whom it is owed:

    c. When is payment due on these debts?

    d. What plans have you made for retirement of these debts?

(N.B. Provision must be made in advance for regular payments during the novitiate of any National Defense Student Loans. Novices are not classified as full time students.)

During the novitiate the community will pay ordinary expenses, e.g. room & board, etc., and will provide a small monthly allowance. The community pays for travel during the novitiate year, including one trip home from the place of your novitiate. The community does not pay for the initial trip from your home as you begin your novitiate.

Novices are expected to anticipate clothing needs, medical and dental expenses, and other such expenses during the novitiate. They are to place the money needed for such anticipated expenses on account with the Director of Novices.

Novices are expected to maintain their own medical and hospital insurance during the time they are in the novitiate. If you do not have any other policy (e.g. through your family), adequate coverage must be obtained before coming to the novitiate.

The community asks each novice to contribute $1,000 toward their support during the novitiate year. Payment may be spread throughout the year if necessary. No refunds will be made even if the novice leaves before the completion of the year.

Please indicate if you have any questions.

> Please return to:
> Vocation Director
> (address)
> (city, state, zip)

SAMPLE
DENTAL EXAMINATION

INSTRUCTIONS: This form is to be filled in and mailed directly to the address below by the dentist. It is not to be returned to the applicant or to his parents or guardians.

Name of applicant: _____

Address: _____

City: State: Zip: _____

Condition of Teeth:

    Condition of Gums:

    Remarks and Recommendations:

    Examining Dentist (signed) _____

    Address: _____

    City: State: Zip: _____

    Date of Examination _____

                           Please return to:
                           Vocation Director
                           (address)
                           (city, state, zip)

SAMPLE
EYE EXAMINATION

INSTRUCTIONS: This form is to be filled in and mailed directly to the Vocation Director by the Oculist. It is not to be returned to the applicant or to his parents or guardians.

Name of applicant: _____

Address: _____

City: State: Zip: _____

Sight: right eye _____

             left eye _____

             Accommodation: _____

             Fields of vision:

             Disease or anatomical defects of pupils, lids, etc.:

_____

_____

             Remarks and recommendations:

SAMPLE
HIV ANTIBODY POLICY

The community sees itself as a brotherhood (sisterhood) of apostolic men (women). Since the presence of HIV (Human Immunodeficiency Virus) strongly suggests a diminished capacity for long term ministry and since we are ministerial community, the province requires the HIV antibody test along with other medical information as part of the application process. A false positive result is a possibility upon first testing (the ELISA test). If an applicant tests positive on the ELISA test, the province requires confirmation of this with the Western Blot test which is the common procedure. HIV+ (indication the presence of HIV antibody) precludes admission to candidacy for the province.

An applicant can arrange for testing either through the examining physician, or prior to the medical examination with a separate agency. In the latter case, a copy of the official report is to be forwarded to the Vocation Director upon completion of the test. Further information about testing agencies can be obtained from the Vocation Director or by calling one of the sources listed below.

Although an applicant can terminate or withdraw his application at any time, the Vocation Director guarantees complete confidentiality concerning the results of HIV antibody testing and the province encourages discussion with the Vocation Director about any concerns in this regard.

If an applicant sees the need to talk further with someone other than the Vocation Director, either before or after the testing, the applicant can contact one of the following:

>*Member of the Community*
>(address)
>(city, state, zip)
>(phone)
>
>Anonymous Testing and
>Counseling Departments
>(address)
>(city, state, zip)
>(phone)

SAMPLE
HIV ANTIBODY TEST RELEASE FORM

I, _____, willingly release the contents of the HIV Antibody Test to the Vocation Director, members of the Admissions Board, community Formation Team, and Provincial of the community. I also understand that a positive HIV test result (indicating the presence of HIV antibody) precludes admission to candidacy for the province.

Signature: _____

Address: _____

City: _____

State: Zip: _____

Witness Signature: _____

Address: _____

City: _____

State: Zip: _____

Date: _____

Please return to:
Vocation Director
(address)
(city, state, zip)
(phone)

CHAPTER FIVE

Procedures for Formation: Canons 646–661

ROSE MCDERMOTT, S.S.J.[1]

Erection, Transfer, Suppression of a Novitiate House

Canon 647, §1:

>The erection, transfer, and suppression of a novitiate house are to be done through written decree of the supreme moderator of the institute with the consent of the council.

It should be noted that only the highest superior of the institute (supreme moderator) can erect, transfer or suppress a novitiate. Likewise, this act requires the consent of the council and a written decree.

Unless the proper law of the institute provides otherwise, canon 127, §1 is to be followed with regard to obtaining the consent of the council. The supreme moderator must convoke the council and obtain the consent of an absolute majority of those present for the validity of the act. For example, if there are four councilors present, the supreme moderator must have the consent of three of them. The supreme moderator does not vote with the councilors, nor may he or she break a tie.

The following is an example of a written decree which should be kept in the files of the religious institute:

---

[1] Jonathan DeFelice, O.S.B. contributed to this chapter.

EXAMPLE OF A WRITTEN DECREE

I, _____, supreme moderator (or other appropriate title for highest superior of the institute) of_____ (name of institute), having obtained the consent of the council, establish (suppress) the novitiate house of our institute located at _____ (site of the novitiate), on _____(date).

_____
Supreme Moderator

If the decision is to transfer the novitiate, the written decree should indicate the place from which and the location to which the novitiate is transferred.

The novitiate need not be a separate house; often it is established within the generalate or provincialate of the institute.

Departure or Dismissal of a Novice

Canon 653, §1:

> A novice can freely leave an institute; moreover, the competent authority of the institute can dismiss a novice.

Voluntary Departure

One becomes a member of a religious institute at first profession when one is incorporated into the institute (c. 654). Since a novice is not a member of a religious institute, he or she is free to leave the institute at any time. The decision to depart should not be precipitous, but should be reached through prayer, reflection, and wise counsel from experienced persons, such as a spiritual director, the novice director and/or the major superior who admitted the novice to the institute.

Involuntary Departure/Dismissal

The institute, in the person of the competent authority according to the proper law, can dismiss a novice. Ordinarily this competent authority is the supreme moderator or the provincial superior. The law may require the advice or the consent of the council. Unless the proper law prescribes otherwise, the consent of the council is to be sought according to the process described in the commentary on canon 647, §1. If the proper law requires the advice of the council, the competent superior must convoke the council and seek the advice of all present in order to perform a valid act. Having sought the advice of the council, the competent authority is free to make the decision.

The decision to dismiss a novice should be preceded by prayer, concern for the well being of the novice, and a thorough study of the reports of the novice director, other formation personnel and local superiors. Justice and charity should prompt the superior to advise the novice of the reasons for the dismissal. The novice should depart the institute enriched and encouraged to continue Christian life supported by the experience of religious life. An account of such a departure, whether voluntary or involuntary, should be kept in the file of the religious institute.

Extension of Time in the Novitiate

Canon 653, §2:

> At the end of the novitiate, if judged suitable, a novice is to be admitted to temporary profession; otherwise the novice is to be dismissed. If there is doubt about the suitability of a novice, the major superior can extend the time of probation according to the norm of proper law, but not beyond six months.

If judged suitable, the novice is admitted to temporary profession in accord with canon law and the proper law of the institute. This admission to first profession will be addressed in the commentary on canon 656. The departure and dismissal of a novice is discussed in the commentary on canon 653, §1 above.

If there is doubt regarding the novice's suitability, the proper law of the institute may provide for an extension of the novitiate. The competent major superior (c. 620) in accord with the proper law may decide that additional time and counseling will resolve the issues prompting the reservation(s) to admit the novice to first profession.

Here again, the advice or consent of the council may be required by the proper law. This process is discussed in the commentary on canons 647, §1 and 653, §1 above. The extension of the novitiate, which may not exceed six months, is in addition to the time prescribed for the novitiate in the institute's proper law. If the novitiate is comprised of twelve months, the entire time of the novitiate cannot exceed one year and a half. If the novitiate prescribed in the proper is for a duration of two years (c. 648, §3), the entire time of the novitiate with the extension cannot exceed two and one half years.

It would be wise for the superior making this decision to meet with the novice and explain the reason(s) for extending the time of the novitiate. Likewise, a plan of action addressing the issue(s) delaying first profession should be worked out with the novice, novice director, and other formation personnel for this extended period.

The Validity of Temporary Profession

Canon 656:

> For the validity of temporary profession it is required that:
>
> 1° the person who is to make it has completed at least eighteen years of age;
>
> 2° the novitiate has been validly completed;
>
> 3° admission has been given freely by the competent superior with the vote of the council according to the norm of law;
>
> 4° the profession is expressed and made without force, grave fear, or malice;
>
> 5° the profession is received by a legitimate superior personally or through another.

These five provisions are extremely important, since they are required for the validity of the member's temporary profession. A few comments are in order.

A person cannot be admitted to the novitiate unless he or she has completed seventeen years of age. A novitiate must last at least twelve months. Hence, the person being admitted to temporary profession should have completed the eighteenth year of age.

The person should have had no invalidating impediments (c. 643) to admission to the novitiate. Likewise, he or she should have made the novitiate in the proper place (c. 647, §2) and for the proper time (c. 648) without absences that would invalidate the novitiate (c. 649) in accord with canon law and the proper law of the institute.

The proper law may provide that the competent superior who admits to profession is the supreme moderator or the provincial superior. The vote of the appropriate council may be consultative (advice) or deliberative (consent) in accord with the proper law. See the commentary on canons 647, §1 and 653, §1 above for obtaining this advice or consent of the council.

A novice must make a free and formal request to be admitted to first profession which can be required in writing. The liturgical rite for the order of temporary profession should be followed. Usually, the proper law of the institute contains the formula for profession. Since the act of profession is a contract as well as a covenant, the formula includes: 1) the name of the person making profession, 2) the name of the institute, 3) the time for which the profession is made, 4) an explicit or implicit profession of the evangelical counsels of chastity, poverty, and obedience in accord with the proper law and 5) the name of the competent superior receiving the profession in the name of the institute and the Church.

The proper law should designate the competent superior who receives the profession. It may or may not be the same superior who admits to the profession. For example, the proper law may designate the supreme moderator as the competent authority who admits to profession, while stating that the provincial superior receives the profession. In the event that the competent authority cannot be present, he or she can delegate another religious of the institute (e.g., councilor, superior) to receive the profession in the name of the institute and the Church.

Renewal of Profession/Perpetual Profession

Canon 657, §1:

> When the period for which the profession was made has elapsed, a religious who freely petitions and is judged suitable is to be admitted to renewal of profession or to perpetual profession; otherwise, the religious is to depart.

The member who has made temporary profession in a religious institute is obliged by public vow to fulfill the obligations of profession during the time for which the profession was made. With the completion of the time of profession, the religious is free to leave the institute.

The religious aspiring to renew profession or make perpetual profession requests the same in a free and formal manner. If judged suitable, the religious is admitted to profession in accord with universal law for temporary profession (c. 656,3°) or perpetual profession (c. 658) and the proper law of the institute.

If judged unsuitable for further profession (c. 689, §1), the religious can request to leave the institute immediately (c. 688, §2) or depart with the expiration of temporary profession (c. 688, §1). Exclusion from subsequent profession will be addressed in the commentary on canon 689. An account of the voluntary or involuntary departure of the member in temporary profession should be retained in the files of the institute.

Extension of Temporary Profession

Canon 657, §2:

> If it seems opportune, however, the competent superior can extend the period of temporary profession according to proper law, but in such a way that the total period in which the member is bound by temporary vows does not exceed nine years.

Temporary profession in a religious institute is made for the time defined in proper law, which may not be less that three years nor longer than six years (c. 655). The proper law may provide that the competent superior extend the period of temporary profession in a particular case. But the entire time the member spends in temporary profession cannot exceed nine years. The law of the institute may further require the superior to obtain the advice or consent of the council in order to make this provision. The advice or consent of the council is sought in accord with canon law and proper law as discussed in the commentary on canons 647, §1 and 653, §1 above.

If such an extension of temporary profession is provided in the proper law, it would seem wise to grant the extension for one year at a time. This would afford the competent authority who admits to profession intervals of time to review the progress and suitability of the member after studying the annual reports of those involved in the formation process.

The entire time in temporary profession is not to exceed nine years. This means that if the period of temporary profession according to the proper law is for three years, the extension of a member's temporary profession cannot exceed six years. If the period of temporary profession according to the proper law is five years, the extension of temporary profession cannot exceed four years. In such cases, justice and charity would prompt the competent superior to advise the member of the reason(s) for extending temporary profession.

The Validity of Perpetual Profession

Canon 658:

> In addition to the conditions mentioned in can. 656, nn. 3, 4, and 5 and others imposed by proper law, the following are required for the validity of perpetual profession:
>
> 1° the completion of at least twenty-one years of age;
>
> 2° previous temporary profession of at least three years, without prejudice to the prescript of canon 657, §3.

Besides the conditions of canon 656,3°,4°,5°, canon law prescribes two more requirements for the validity of perpetual profession. The proper law of the institute should be examined, since it may contain additional conditions.

The age requirement for perpetual profession should not be problematic if the member completed eighteen years of age before first profession (c. 656,1°) and has been in temporary profession for the minimal requirement of three years (c. 655).

While temporary profession must be made for at least three years (c. 655), perpetual profession can be anticipated for a just cause, but not by more than three months (c. 657, §3).

Act of Cession Before Admission to Temporary Profession

Canon 668, §1:

> Before first profession, members are to cede the administration of their goods to whomever they prefer and, unless the constitutions state otherwise, are to make disposition freely for their use and revenue. Moreover, at least before perpetual profession, they are to make a will which is to be valid also in civil law,.

Religious life demands the total self-donation of the person to Christ in service to his people. From earliest times this gift of self required a detachment from material concerns and temporal goods. Canon law provides that all religious (whether in institutes of solemn or simple vow traditions) make an act of cession before first profession.

By an act of cession, the person preparing for first profession is to cede or give over the administration of her or his temporal goods to whomever she or he wills. Likewise, the novice is to provide for the disposition of their use and revenue, unless the constitutions of the institute state otherwise. The novice is free to ask the institute to administer his or her goods, and the institute is free to accept or refuse this task. The constitutions of some religious institutes may provide that the revenues from the temporal goods of the member belong to the institute.

It is important to note that an act of cession is not the yielding of the ownership of goods, but rather the appointing of another as administrator of one's temporal goods.

EXAMPLE OF AN ACT OF CESSION

This is an agreement between (legal name of novice), party of the first part, and (legal name of religious institute), party of the second part.

In accord with provisions of admission to first profession by the party of the second part, the party of the first part will depend on and receive the necessities of life from the party of the second part as a professed religious. Canon 668, §1 of the *Code of Canon Law* binds those about to make first profession in an approved religious institute of the Catholic Church, as follows:

1. The party of the first part agrees to render freely his/her service and labor to the party of the second part.

2. The party of the first part retains ownership of all property real and personal. However, provision is made for such property as follows:

    a) The party of the first part cedes the administration of his/her property, real and personal, that he/she owns and that which shall come to his/her ownership during the time of profession and appoints_____ as the administrator.

    b) The use of said property shall be disposed as follows:

    (provisions for use indicated here)

    c) The increment, income and interest of said property shall be disposed of as follows:

    (provisions indicated here)

d) If the profession of vows cease in any way whatsoever, this agreement becomes by that fact null and void.

The parties declare that they intend to be legally bound by this agreement.

_____
Novice/Party of the first part

_____
Major Superior/Legal Representative,
Party of the second part

_____
Secretary of Party of the second part

_____
Notary (Seal)

Date_____

ANOTHER EXAMPLE OF AN ACT OF CESSION

Know All By These Presents, that I, (legal/religious name) of (city, county, state).

In consideration of canon 668, §1 of the Roman Catholic Church concerning the administration of the personal property, its use and usufruct of a member of a religious institute canonically approved by said Roman Catholic Church:

First: Do hereby cede for all the time that I shall be a member of the (legal title of religious institute) the administration of my property to (name of administrator);

Second: Do hereby ordain and declare that, during the same period of time, all the use and usufruct, to wit: the interest, rent, income, annuities, royalties, bonus, etc., shall be disposed of or expended in the following manner (provisions stated);

Third: Do declare and ordain that, if for any reason I shall be refused or rejected as a member for life by what, in ecclesiastical language is called perpetual profession in (religious institute), both the cession of administration of my real and personal property and the disposition of the use and usufruct of said property shall cease, terminate, and be null and void, as if it had never been made;

Fourth: Do solemnly state and declare that I shall never claim or demand directly or indirectly any compensation, remuneration or reward, either in specie or by way of annuity, or pension, or reward, for the service, or work or time I have performed with or for said (religious institute) during the time I may spend or remain there or elsewhere in the name of or upon commission from said (religious institute) knowing full well that the laws of the Roman Catholic Church to which I deliberately and voluntarily submit myself and acknowledge will not uphold or defend any claim of any kind to any wages or remuneration therefore.

In Witness Whereof, I have hereto subscribed my name this _____ day of _____ in the year of Our Lord _____.

_____
Novice (legal name)

_____
Witness

_____
Notary (Seal)

Change of Dispositions of Act of Cession

Canon 668, §2:

> To change these dispositions for a just cause and to place any act regarding temporal goods, they need the permission of the superior competent according to the norm of proper law.

There should be a certain permanence or stability to the act of cession. By its very nature, it frees the religious for total consecration to God, for a common life of sharing with other members and for carrying out the purpose of the religious institute. However, there may be a just cause (significant additional inheritance, illness or lack of integrity on the part of the administrator, serious familial need, more advantageous investment of temporal goods) that warrants seeking the permission of the competent superior of the institute to change the dispositions of the act of cession.

For any such just cause the proper superior as stated in the proper law of the institute can give this permission. The proper law may require this superior (usually the supreme moderator or provincial superior) to seek the advice or consent of the council before giving this permission. See the commentary on canons 647, §1 and 653, §1 for the process of procuring the advice or consent of the council.

Renunciation of Temporal Goods

Canon 668, §4-5:

> A person who must renounce fully his or goods due to the nature of the institute is to make that renunciation before perpetual profession in a form valid, as far as possible, even in civil law; it is to take effect from the day of profession. A perpetually professed religious who wishes to renounce his or her goods either partially or totally according to the norm of proper law and with the permission of the supreme moderator is to do the same.

> A professed religious who has fully renounced his or her goods fully due to the nature of the institute loses the capacity of acquiring and possessing and therefore invalidly places acts contrary to the vow of poverty. Moreover, whatever accrues to the professed after renunciation belongs to the institute according to the norm of proper law.

Renunciation is the act of giving up the ownership of one's temporal goods, both those owned at the time of the act of renunciation and those that come to the member subsequent to perpetual profession in the institute. Not all religious institutes require an act of renunciation before perpetual profession; the proper law of the institute should be consulted.

With the act of renunciation, the member about to make perpetual profession can give the temporal goods he or she owns to whomever he or she desires. The act of renunciation takes effect on the day of perpetual profession. Such a religious is incapable of ownership, and the temporal goods coming to him or her from the time of perpetual profession belong to the religious institute in accord with its proper law.

While the act of renunciation should conform as far as possible to civil law, often civil law does not recognize the renunciation of what is not yet owned.

EXAMPLE OF AN ACT OF RENUNCIATION

I, (legal/religious name) of (legal title of religious institute) diocese, city, state, in consideration of my solemn profession of vows and in accord with canon 668, §4–5 of the *Code of Canon Law* and (article or paragraph) of the proper law of (legal title of religious institute) hereby renounce all of my goods and all goods that I may acquire in the future.

This declaration is to be effective from _____, the date of my perpetual profession and is to remain in effect for as long as I continue a member of the said religious institute.

_____
Date

_____
Signature of Religious

_____
Witness

_____
Witness

_____
Notary (Seal)

Canon 668, §4 also provides that a religious in perpetual profession in an institute that does not require such a renunciation of temporal goods can renounce his or her temporal goods either in whole or in part if the proper law of the institute permits. Note that the member must be in perpetual profession, the proper law must provide for this act of renunciation and the permission of the supreme moderator is required. The proper law may also require the advice or consent of the council. This process is described in the commentary on canons 647, §1 and 653, §1 in this section.

It would seem wise that the proper law provide that the religious be in perpetual profession for a determined number of years before making this request. Such a religious does not make a radical renunciation; he or she does not lose the capacity to acquire and possess temporal goods that may come to him or her subsequent to this renunciation.

LAST WILL AND TESTAMENT OF A RELIGIOUS

Canon 668, §1 provides:

> Moreover, at least before perpetual profession, they are to make a will which is to be valid also in civil law.

Since men and women are entering religious life at more mature ages, it would seem wise that they have made their wills or make them at an opportune time in the religious institute before perpetual profession.

EXAMPLE OF A WILL

I (legal name), a resident of (city, state, county), being of sound mind, memory and understanding, do make and declare this to be my last Will and Testament.

FIRST: I direct that all my funeral arrangements, including time, place, and manner of viewing be determined and financed by (religious institute) in accord with its traditions and customs.

SECOND: I hereby direct that my patrimony, which in accord with canon law includes all assets, real and personal, which I own in my individual capacity and received through inheritances, bequests and, gifts made specifically and unequivocally to me during my life and after my death, be distributed in the following manner:

(Provisions)

THIRD: I hereby acknowledge that all income (principal, interests, royalties, etc.) and assets accrued as a result of my work, work products, and efforts, whether these efforts be in my official ministry or otherwise, rightfully belong to (religious institute). Accordingly, I direct that said assets remain with the said (religious institute).

FOURTH: I hereby acknowledge that my ownership of property, real and personal, is subject to the canon law of the Roman Catholic Church and the laws of the religious institute to which I belong and to civil law.

I direct that my specific intent in the dispositions made in this Will be governed by my general intent to conform to the law of the Roman Catholic Church and the proper law and customs of my religious institute (religious institute).

IN TESTIMONY WHEREOF, I have hereunto subscribed my name and affixed my seal this

_____ day of _____, in the year _____.

_____
Signature of Religious

_____
Signature of Witness

_____
Notary (Seal)

Often the question is raised as to the practicality of a religious who has made an act of renunciation making a will, since this religious has renounced all of the temporal goods possessed and those coming to him or her subsequent to perpetual profession. Since some civil jurisdictions do not accept such an act of renunciation, it seems wise that such a religious make a will providing that all of the temporal goods he or she is given belong to the respective religious institute.

Advance Directives for Healthcare

Membership in a religious institute is acquired at profession (c. 654). It would seem appropriate that part of the preparation for religious profession would be to have a competent person discuss the provisions for advance directives for healthcare with the candidates for religious profession. The institute may already have such a form. For those without such a provision, the Catholic Health Association of the United States has excellent informative pamphlets and a recommended durable power of attorney for healthcare which can be obtained for a minimal fee from the Catholic Health Association in St. Louis, MO.

The laws of states differ in this matter and should be consulted. While the member is free to designate anyone with few exceptions as durable power of attorney for healthcare decisions, he or she should recognize the religious institute as family. Problems can arise for the competent authorities of the institute if the appointed person is deceased, unavailable, or disagrees with the values and opinions of the legitimate authorities of the institute.

The member should realize that the institute is mandated by canon law to provide for its members (c. 670). In giving durable power of attorney for healthcare decisions to the religious who holds the office of major superior (supreme moderator or provincial superior) the member can rest assured that, if and when it becomes necessary, a competent person will be available and act in accord with his or her best interests and Christian values.

CHAPTER SIX

MEMBERSHIP: FULLY INCORPORATED MEMBERS

EMMETT J. GAVIN, O.CARM. [1]

The rights and obligations that flow from definitive membership in an institute of consecrated life or a society of apostolic life are many and varied. This entire handbook, and not just this chapter, is an effort to identify and explain in practical, non-technical terms the canonical consequences that flow from incorporation in such intentional communities.

Consequently, this chapter will address only selected topics that are not dealt with in any detail elsewhere. Those topics are: Rights and obligations of members and activities which are restricted or inconsistent with membership.

RIGHTS AND OBLIGATIONS

Rights and obligations result from definitive incorporation in an institute of consecrated life or a society of apostolic life. In addition, members of such institutes and societies are also subject to and the beneficiary of several other rights and obligations found elsewhere in the code.

For example, by virtue of their baptism and full communion with the church, all the Christian faithful are vested with rights and obligations under the law (cc. 204-205, 208-223). Also, the members of the institutes and societies with which we are concerned are necessarily either laity or clerics and are thereby subject to other provisions of the code which enumerate specific rights and obligations for

---

[1] The two final sections of the chapter, "Right to Privacy" and "Restricted Activities..." were written by Elissa Rinere, C.P.

them as well (cc. 224-231, 273-289). It is not the purpose or intent of this chapter to deal with this broad universe of rights and obligations.

Rather, this chapter will limit discussion to the following topics:

- ◆ Selected General Norms Supporting Consecrated Life;
- ◆ Common Life;
- ◆ Living Outside Community;
- ◆ Cloister;
- ◆ Right to Privacy; and
- ◆ Restricted Activities and Activities Inconsistent with Membership.

SELECTED GENERAL NORMS SUPPORTING CONSECRATED LIFE

Religious Institutes

It is the responsibility of both the individual religious and his or her institute to assure that a lifelong commitment to the vowed life in community can be achieved in a meaningful and fruitful way. The achievement of this goal must take appropriate account of both the charism of the community and the norms of proper and universal law.

As part of this responsibility, the institute must respect and cultivate the gifts of its individual members and foster their apostolic and spiritual growth. To this end, it is incumbent on the leadership of the institute to make adequate provision of time and resources to assure that all members have the opportunity to grow spiritually and professionally and to deepen their vocational commitment.

Canon 670 is the foundational norm governing this requirement. It obligates the institute to provide whatever is necessary under the constitutions to insure that a meaningful vowed life in the institute can be achieved by its members. Since many canons focus on the responsibilities and obligations of members, this norm provides an important balance by clearly emphasizing the reciprocal obligation of the institute and its leadership to provide for the needs of its members, particularly what is required for vocational fulfillment.

Moreover, as stated in canon 670, this obligation is very pointedly grounded in the requirements of proper law. In other words, the requirement that an institute provide what is necessary for the achievement of a member's vocational commitment finds its concrete meaning in the charism and proper law of the institute.

For example, if an institute is dedicated to the teaching apostolate and that focus is clearly reflected in the charism and proper law of the institute, a member would not be justified in relying on canon 670 as a basis for asserting a right to community support to pursue other apostolic or personal priorities. A religious is entitled to receive spiritual and professional training to enable him or her to share meaningfully on an ongoing basis in the apostolate of the institute. While this would include reasonable and regular updating in the skills required to participate in the apostolate of that institute, it would not provide carte blanche entitlement justifying a member to pursue any personal or individual interest.

Other needs embraced within the scope of canon 670, while more generic, are no less important. Specifically, it goes without saying that all religious are entitled to the necessities of life, including not only food, shelter, and clothing but also health care and adequate provision for care in one's senior years.

Equally important is reasonable access to the time and resources to foster one's spiritual life. Again, the requirements of proper law are the best source of what is required, but typically, in accord with the exhortations contained in canon 663 that would, at a minimum, include the opportunity, resources, and time for a well integrated personal spiritual life, including an annual retreat.

In keeping with the obligation that flows from canon 670, proper law should also provide clear guidance to members on the availability of resources to provide for supportive processes such as spiritual direction and, where warranted or indicated, personal counselling. In addition, in keeping with the spirit of canon 670, superiors should regard it as their duty to intervene and require appropriate treatment when a member gives clear evidence of self-destructive behaviors or emotional problems. In these psychologically aware times, such assistance, even when resisted, should be seen as part of an institute's obligation to provide its members with what is necessary for the fulfillment of the individual member's vocation.

It has also been suggested that a policy should be in place in all religious institutes that would enable members to assist close relatives in times of need. To be meaningful, this should include the possibility of time off from the apostolate and, depending on the financial situation of the family and the institute, the availability of some appropriate level of financial assistance.[2]

The need for such a policy is particularly important when a religious is the only family member available to be of help to a needy relative, particularly a parent or a sibling. The ability to be of such help and the peace of mind it affords the concerned religious can arguably be seen as a vocational necessity in the spirit of canon 670.

---

[2] David F. O'Connor, S.T., "Obligations and Rights," in *A Handbook on Canons 573-746*. eds. Jordan Hite, Sharon Holland and Daniel Ward (Collegeville, Minnesota: The Liturgical Press, 1985), p. 189.

At a minimum, however, a policy should be in place in every institute that gives members clear guidelines on these matters. The importance of this is readily apparent because of the need to deal with all members equitably. While individual personal needs, issues, and problems will inevitably differ and will often require individual care and attention, there is nonetheless a serious responsibility on the part of the leadership to give all members as much equal access to the assistance and support of the community as possible. A written policy governing the institute's interpretation of the requirements of canon 670 is, therefore, an important part of assuring that all members can avail themselves of the community's resources on some equitable and consistent basis.

One very important and very sensitive area in which this is clearly a need is in regard to ongoing formation. On this issue, canon 661 is a complementary norm to canon 670. It places the responsibility on the individual religious to make a life long commitment to his or her own ongoing formation. The canon, however, also gives superiors a very direct mandate to assure that individual religious have both the resources and time to fulfill this requirement.

The obligation to pursue ongoing formation applies to all perpetually professed members and is not reserved to a select few. Moreover, it is not something which is to be regarded as an option or as something exceptional or extraordinary. It is intended to be an integral part of every member's religious life.

That is not to say, of course, that the opportunities and programs made available to all members can or should be identical. For example, while sabbaticals have become a significant dimension of ongoing formation in many communities, many factors can and probably should limit their availability. Community priorities, time, resources, and the availability of a suitable opportunity will not normally permit all members to avail themselves of this experience during their years in the community. As long as all can apply and be considered according to known and equitable criteria, however, the obligation to deal evenly and fairly with all would seem to be satisfied.

At the same time it is clear that careful planning and budgeting are required to assure that the overall responsibilities of ongoing formation in the community are properly discharged. Superiors cannot be passive with respect to this obligation. Ongoing training in the spiritual life and the teachings of the Church as well as in areas of professional competence needed in the apostolate cannot be successfully provided without a clear cut plan of action. Each community, therefore, should have an individual responsible for this activity and his or her efforts should be supported with sufficient resources to assure that all members are periodically provided with the opportunities needed to update themselves in their apostolic work and energize their spiritual life.

In 1988 the Holy See issued norms governing this requirement which provide considerable guidance about the expected dimensions of ongoing formation.[3] Among other things, they stress the need in each institute for internal programs and structures to afford members the opportunity to receive ongoing formation. It is stressed that the responsibility for ongoing formation cannot be fulfilled by relying only on outside resources. The vocational health and vitality of individual members depends on the availability of these resources and programs, but so too does the future of the institute and its mission.

It would be very appropriate, therefore, if the proper law of each institute were to set forth the expectations and requirements regarding ongoing formation. The implementation of these norms should then be supported and enforced by provincial guidelines. Members should be apprised of the opportunities the community is providing for ongoing formation and the expectations with regard to participation. This should include the publication and dissemination of information about ongoing formation opportunities within the structures and institutions of the community as well as the availability of access to outside resources.

Canon 661 is at the heart of these requirements and because of that it is a very important specification of the overall requirement contained in canon 670 that a religious institute must provide its members with all that is required under the constitutions in order to achieve the purpose of their vocation.

Societies of Apostolic Life

The obligation to provide members with what is required for vocational fulfillment, although stated with less specificity, is also found in the norms governing societies of apostolic life. Canon 737 provides that incorporation in a society of apostolic life entails reciprocal rights and obligations on the part of the member and the society according to the constitutions. The society has the obligation "to lead the members to the end of their particular vocation...." This responsibility is the functional equivalent of canon 670 and like that canon expresses the obligation in terms of the requirements of proper law. Therefore, just as religious must be provided with all that is needed to allow them to fulfill their vowed commitment, so too members of societies of apostolic life are entitled to the active support of their society in the realization of their vocational commitment.

By analogy, this requirement should be seen as extending to the society's obligation to provide for and encourage the ongoing formation of its members. As

---

[3] *Potissimum instituti* from the Congregation for Institutes of Consecrated Life and for Societies of Apostolic Life, (February 2, 1990) (*AAS* 82 (1990) 470-532; *Origins* 19 [1988-1989] 677-699).

we have seen, canon 661 makes this obligation quite explicit on the part of religious institutes. It is less pointedly stated in the canons governing societies of apostolic life.

Nonetheless, canon 735, §3 does require that proper law should provide for suitable formation for the members of a society of apostolic life "in such a way that the members, recognizing their divine vocation, may be fittingly prepared for the mission and life of the society." The spirit of the canon clearly points to the need to provide for more than initial formation because otherwise the ongoing spiritual and apostolic needs of the society and its members would be neglected.

To be suitably trained and prepared for the "mission and life of the society" is, by its very terms, the agenda of a lifetime and as such requires the nourishment and support of an ongoing formation program. Therefore, while the language of canon 735, §3 is clearly a much less pointed and specific requirement than that articulated in canon 661, the spirit of the two norms would seem to require an equivalent effort to assure the ongoing vocational development of their members.

Secular Institutes

A more limited and focused obligation regarding ongoing formation is also addressed in the code to the moderators of secular institutes. Canon 724, §1 provides that after a member has made his or her commitment in the institute "formation is to be continued according to the constitutions."

The central and determinative role of proper law is once again highlighted by this requirement. Paragraph 2 of canon 724 helps clarify this obligation by explicitly requiring that the "moderators of the institute are to have a serious concern for the continued spiritual formation of the members."

This mandate, although more limited and focused, is clearly in the spirit of the canons discussed above regarding religious institutes and societies of apostolic life. Like them, it makes it clear that the law of the Church is concerned that those who commit their lives to the service of the Church and the People of God by entering into some form of consecrated life are entitled to the help and support of their sponsoring communities in the realization of their vocational goals. These requirements, of course, differ according to the nature of the commitment taken and the nature and proper law of the community in which the commitment is made.

Common Life

In Church law, institutes of consecrated life fall into two categories, religious institutes and secular institutes. They are very different in many ways and particularly so with regard to the requirements and characteristics of common life.

Life in common is normative for religious and integral to the nature of virtually all religious communities. The opposite is true for secular institutes. While a form of common life exists in some secular institutes, it does so only by way of exception. The vast majority of members of secular institutes live apart from one another and quite independent of any form of common life.

The requirement and experience of common life among members of societies of apostolic life, on the other hand, often closely mirror the common life as lived by religious. However, the constitutions of such societies generally allow for more variation and flexibility than would be typically true of the constitutions of religious institutes. More leeway both in the obligation to live a common life and in the style of common life that is permitted normally characterize the proper law of societies of apostolic life. The code itself provides for greater flexibility in this regard as well.

Religious institutes

Canons 602; 607, §2; and 665, §1 provide the principles which govern and define the obligation of members of religious institutes to live in common. The requirements which flow from these canonical norms are generally reflected in the proper law of most religious institutes. Typically, they are quite explicit with regard to the obligation of members to live in community in religious houses of the institute.

At the same time, however, as a practical matter these obligations today are often tempered in practice by the current and evolving realities of the apostolate and the contemporary demands on religious and religious life. Those demands are demonstrably very different from those that gave birth to the norms enshrined in the law of the Church and in the proper law of religious institutes. Therefore, at this point in history any discussion of common life and its requirements must necessarily include the creative and sincere efforts of many religious institutes today to adapt the spirit of the law governing common life to contemporary realities.

Canon 602 is one of the norms common to all institutes of consecrated life (cc. 573-606). Therefore, because it is applicable to secular as well as religious institutes its reference to "vita fraterna" as a norm of life must be properly understood. The term should not be construed as referring to life in common as such. Rather, it is meant to describe a life of shared ideals and commitment which, for members of religious institutes, finds its most authentic expression in the context of community life.

On the other hand, the obligation of religious to live in common with other members of the same institute is reflected quite explicitly in canons 607, §2 and 665. Life in common is specified in those canons as one of the defining characteristics of religious life.

At the same time, while traditional common life is clearly the ideal and expectation held up by the law of the Church as the defining norm for religious life, where necessary, efforts are being made today in many religious communities to be open to redefining the lived experience of "common life" in ways that further the apostolic priorities of the community. This new openness is also an effort to allow room for creative experiences of communal involvement and accountability. For example, it is not uncommon today that some members of an institute may be living on their own in proximity to their individual apostolic commitments and coming together only on some periodic basis with other members of the community for prayer, discussion, and community business and sharing.

In other instances, some such sharing is also done today on an intercommunity basis. At times, this may be in lieu of more regular involvement with members of one's own community. Practical issues such as distance and expense may dictate some of these arrangements but they may also come about because of common apostolic commitments. These variations on more traditional communal living arrangements are growing more common, especially among religious women. Today, frequently because of financial necessity, many women religious work in individual apostolates rather than working together in institutional ministries with other women of their institute. The dispersion of personnel that is reflected in such a shift in apostolic priorities often necessitates such creative living and communal relationships. In this era when religious life is evolving and its future directions and dimensions are so uncertain such innovations and variations of traditional common life are probably not only inevitable but necessary.

It must be acknowledged, however, that the Holy See and some canonical commentators have noted disapprovingly that there is a growing incidence of members of religious institutes living apart from their communities, often on an open-ended basis and for reasons unrelated to apostolic or communal needs or traditions. The consensus of these commentators is that this growing trend is an unhealthy aberration that is at odds with the traditions of the Church and the explicit requirements of the law, including in all likelihood the proper law of the affected institutes themselves.[4]

That excesses exist in this area is undoubtedly true. The avoidance of that and the need to maintain careful ongoing supervision of non-traditional expressions of "common life" urgently require, therefore, that norms governing such living arrangements be developed in all communities that permit members to live and form community in non-traditional ways.

Such norms should, with appropriate canonical advice, take due account of the spirit and letter of universal and proper law. They should also include clear criteria of accountability on the part of members and superiors and provide for regular, periodic reassessment. Every effort must be made in such norms to maximize both the opportunities and the requirements for regular moments and occasions of traditional experiences of communal life.

Common life remains integral to religious life. There is a clear need today to preserve the best of its traditional values and structures. At the same time, creative innovations that retain the values and ideals that give meaning to religious life must not be stifled, lest the ability of the life to adapt and grow in a changing world is foreclosed.

Secular institutes

If common life is normative for religious, just the opposite is true for members of secular institutes. Secular institutes grew up in the Church to give recognition to the reality that some individuals are called to profess the evangelical counsels, but to do so while working and living in secular society.

Thus, by design and purpose, the vast majority of members of secular institutes live independent lives, either on their own or with their families, and give witness to their consecration in the context of that lifestyle and in the midst of their daily lives in the workplace.

Normally, the common life to which a member of a secular institute is called by the proper law of his or her community is defined only in terms of a communion of ideals and spirit (c. 716, §2). Even so, this recognition that some form of common life is characteristic of secular institutes, underscores the validity of the basic principles governing institutes of consecrated life as set forth in Canon 602, namely, that it is a life of shared values in Christ.

Typically, this expectation that every secular institute is to be characterized by a communion of ideals and spirit among its members is best fostered by ample

---

[4] See *CLD* 9:446-452; *Origins* 23, 693-712; *The Canon Law: Letter and Spirit*, pp. 331, 335.

opportunities to come together for reflection and instruction. At the same time, these gatherings are not meant to reflect the traditions and structures of common life as lived by religious.

Canon 714, however, clearly recognizes that in some cases, where proper law provides or permits, one residential option for the members of some secular institutes is a shared living arrangement with other members of the same institute. In those cases, however, it has been clear since the recognition and authorization of secular institutes in 1947 that a shared life among members of secular institutes is not intended to include the communal practices of religious or the holding of goods in common which is so typical of traditional religious.

Nonetheless, practical necessity would suggest and even require that all secular institutes be permitted the option of maintaining one or more communal residences. The need to bring the leadership together for extended periods as well as the need to provide for members who are incapable of caring for themselves might well justify the creation of such communities. Also, the need for periods together for those in formation or those on retreat might well justify the creation and maintenance of such facilities. Their use, however, would typically be by way of exception and only for specified purposes authorized in proper law.

Societies of apostolic life

With regard to the observance of common life, societies of apostolic life tend to closely resemble the lifestyle followed by most contemporary religious institutes. As with religious, life in common is the norm and, indeed, is regarded as an essential element of the vocation. (cc. 731, §1 and 740)

At the same time, it must always be noted that members of societies of apostolic life are not religious; they do not make a public profession of the evangelical counsels. And, as non-religious, the holding of all things in common, which is a key aspect of the life in common characteristic of religious, is inapplicable to them and their communities. Moreover, the obligations and rights of religious generally (cc. 662-665), many of which refer directly or indirectly to the obligations of the common life, also do not apply to them.

Not infrequently the canons governing religious are cited in the canons applicable to societies of apostolic life as providing the model for the members of the societies to follow. With regard to common life, however, that is explicitly not the case. This omission serves to help define and underscore the distinctive character of societies of apostolic life.

That distinctiveness is better reflected in the *Code of Canon Law* than it has been in previous compilations of the law because the societies of apostolic life have been given their own section in the law (cc. 731 -746). In those norms a much clearer demarcation has been made than was previously the case between their style of life and the life of religious.

One of the distinctive characteristics of societies of apostolic life is that they are typically more flexible than religious institutes in their observance of the common life. This is due in large measure to the apostolic purpose behind the creation of these societies. In the eighteenth and nineteenth centuries, when most of these groups were founded, the need to be available to serve the changing needs of the apostolate was seen as requiring less structure and fewer binding norms in regard to common life. To this end, proper law has always played a more central role in defining the style of life observed in these societies than it has in religious institutes.

However, proper law is not the only source of this distinction. The code also provides greater freedom to societies in the structuring of their common life. For example, unlike religious who are normally required to reside in a house of their institute (cc. 665, §1), the norm for members of societies of apostolic life is to live in a house of the institute or a local community established by competent authority (c. 733, §1). In other words, in the case of societies of apostolic life the code allows for proper law to provide for the establishment of local communities apart from cononically created houses. This sets societies of apostolic life apart from religious, who typically are not authorized to live a fraternal life in common outside their own established houses. However, as with the erection of houses, both those of religious institutes and those of societies of apostolic life, the diocesan bishop must give his prior written permission for the creation of such communities.

Again, this flexibility was historically seen as necessary to permit these societies to better achieve their apostolic purposes. The end result is a style of life which, while on the surface closely resembles religious life, nonetheless has important and fundamental differences which set it apart.

LIVING OUTSIDE COMMUNITY

Universal law provides criteria setting forth the terms and conditions that can justify living apart from community for members of religious institutes.(c. 665, §1) Proper law, however, controls in this area with regard to societies of apostolic life. (c. 740)

Exclaustration (cc. 686-687) and a very similar process permitted by canon 745 and applicable to members of societies of apostolic life are, of course, processes that not only allow but require living outside community. They are dealt with in chapter seven on Separation of Members. So too is canon 703 which in particularly serious circumstances permits the major superior to expel a member of a religious institute from a house.

This section, however. deals only with the norms and criteria governing non-communal living for fully incorporated members who are in full and good standing in their communities but who, for a time, are permitted to live apart from the institute or society.

Religious institutes

The authorization of the competent superior must be obtained for a member of a religious institute to be absent from common life. The local superior would normally be the appropriate individual to authorize routine brief absences such as vacations and perhaps even absences of a few months duration for spiritual or apostolic purposes. A "lengthy" absence, however, would typically require the permission of the major superior and his or her council. Under the law (c. 665, §1), such absences are not to exceed one year and require a "just cause."

The determination of what makes an absence "lengthy" and a cause "just" are best addressed in an institute's proper law or can be left to the prudent judgement of the competent superior. Where proper law provides such criteria, however, care should be taken not to be overly restrictive. These are areas where flexibility and the ability to respond to unforeseen circumstances are significant values and proper law should not unnecessarily curtail the discretion of superiors in this regard.

One frequently encountered situation that can justify a lengthy absence is the need for a member to be absent to care for a seriously ill or infirm parent or other close relative. The need for a time apart to discern one's vocation is another just cause that not infrequently arises and that can justify a more prolonged absence. One year, however, is the maximum allowed by the law for such absences. An extension of the absence beyond one year, unless for a reason governed by the three criteria described below, would require either a dispensation from the Holy See or an indult of exclaustration.

An absence of more than one year is permissible for any of three, but only three, reasons enumerated in canon 665, §1: health, studies, and apostolic works undertaken in the name of the institute. The list is taxative. These reasons, especially apostolic work undertaken in the name of the institute, are often the justification for the variations in living arrangements frequently encountered today and discussed above in the section dealing with common life.

However, the health of a member, physical or emotional, can also justify an absence of longer than one year. So too can studies authorized or required by the religious institute. Significantly, no time limits are placed on absences justified and approved under any of these three criteria.

As a practical matter, however, studies and apostolic works undertaken in the name of the community would not normally extend indefinitely. Health, on the other hand, both physical and mental, could well require an absence from traditional community life for an indefinite period. This is a determination left to the prudent judgement of the major superior and his or her council.

When a member is allowed to be absent for more than a year for apostolic reasons, care should be taken to assure that the ministry involved is consistent with the nature and charism of the community and is not simply the private apostolic preference of the member. Not infrequently the personal preference of a member is used to justify an open-ended absence from communal life. Often in such cases the ministry being pursued is primarily a personal apostolic interest of the member, rather than a need of the community, or reflects his or her geographic priorities rather than the best interests of the group at large. Moreover, in such cases it is not uncommon for the ministry involved to be out of harmony with the apostolic priorities and needs of the institute or perhaps even its charism.

It is highly recommended that whenever a member is permitted to live outside a house of the institute either for a *just cause* for up to a year or for reasons of health, studies, or apostolate for more than a year, that an agreement be entered into between the member and the major superior and council governing the terms and conditions of the authorized absence.

Such an agreement should at least include the following:

- the purpose and length of the absence;
- the financial responsibilities of both the member and the institute during the absence, including the disposition of income, budgetary guidelines, or requirements, and insurance coverage;
- the living arrangements agreed to and authorized;
- where applicable, the understanding regarding the use, support, and insurance of an automobile;
- the expected participation in the activities of the institute and required contact with superiors and members of the institute;
- any reporting requirements prescribed by the major superior and council; and
- provision for periodic review of the viability of the member's continued absence and the terms governing it.

Societies of apostolic life

While common life is also generally the norm for members of societies of apostolic life, the criteria governing the practical dimensions of this issue are less restrictive than those applicable to religious. The heavy emphasis on the apostolate that was the origin of most of the societies of apostolic life in the eighteenth and nineteenth centuries was seen as justifying and even requiring a much greater measure of personal and communal freedom in regard to lifestyle.

Typically, therefore, the regulation of the requirements of common life in such societies was then, and is today, left largely to the determination of proper law. The same is true for the criteria governing permitted absences from communal life.

Canon 740 contains the governing principles on this subject in the code. It states that members of societies of apostolic life must live in a house of the society or a local community (c. 733, §1) and observe common life as that is prescribed in the proper law of the society. Absence from a house or community, and therefore from common life, is also explicitly tied to proper law and its requirements. This, in effect, allows each society to craft applicable criteria that best reflect its origins and mission. The end result is a much more flexible and discretionary set of norms governing life in common and absence from the community than would be typically characteristic of a religious institute.

The rather specific and detailed criteria applicable to absences from community for members of religious institutes (c. 665, §1) have no parallel in the canons applicable to societies of apostolic life (cc. 731-746). Moreover, it is also telling that, unlike other provisions in the code governing the lives of members of societies of apostolic life, the law governing religious life on this topic is nowhere cited as a guideline to be followed by societies of apostolic life.

At the same time, a process that is very similar to exclaustration (c. 686) is provided for in canon 745 and it offers the possibility of living outside the society.[5]

In light of the basic principle noted at the outset of this section, namely, that common life is the norm for members of societies of apostolic life, any significant time away from the community should be regulated by an agreement between the member and the major superior. The principles governing such an arrangement in the case of a religious, as enumerated above, are equally applicable here. Together with any suitable guidance to be found in proper law, they would serve as an adequate basis for such an agreement.

---

[5] See chapter seven, on the Separation and Departure of Members.

Cloister

A space apart from the demands of the apostolate and the encroachments of the outside world is regarded as a fundamental right of religious and a necessary component of life in common. Both the individual religious and the community which share a religious house are seen as requiring this assurance of a minimum of separation from the demands and distractions of non-members.

The recognition of this right finds expression in canon 667, §1 which, while deferring to proper law and the character and mission of the institute to determine the specifics of what is appropriate, requires that all religious houses provide for some space not open to non-members. The space so designated should be ample enough to assure that the members of the community can engage in private prayer and rest in an undisturbed atmosphere and also enjoy leisure activity with other members of the community without outside intrusion.

In larger houses this should present no difficulty. In the smaller communities so typical today this canon would seem to require as a minimum that the sleeping quarters of the members be reserved as a private area and also, if possible, a common or recreation room where members can gather in private for community sharing and leisure activities together.

Although societies of apostolic life are not bound to this same requirement by universal law, proper law may well, and probably should, provide for similar rights for their members and communities. Canon 740 calls for common life to be observed as the norm among members of societies of apostolic life and then defers to proper law to define the terms governing this requirement. Given the general importance of some measure of communal privacy as a valued characteristics of all forms of consecrated life, it would be hard to imagine that the proper law of a society of apostolic life would not mandate some requirement governing reserved space for members of the community in its houses.

Such space apart, however, is particularly crucial and, in fact, essential to the nature and identity of the contemplative religious institutes in the Church. The remaining provisions of canon 667 give recognition to this by laying down explicit requirements governing cloister in such communities.

Men's contemplative communities are simply enjoined in canon 667, §2 to observe a "stricter discipline of cloister" than the rather minimalist requirements of canon 667, §1. It is then left to the proper law of such communities to prescribe the nature and restrictions of the "stricter discipline" which is called for.

A different standard is applied to contemplative communities of women religious. Essentially tracking the rather restrictive and highly supervised criteria set forth in the 1969 apostolic constitution, *Venite seorsum*, canons 667, §3 and §4 provide for very little discretion in the observance of cloister in women's contemplative communities.[6]

"Papal cloister" is prescribed for women's communities that are dedicated to the contemplative life. This simply means that the Apostolic See alone is vested with the authority to regulate the terms and conditions of the requirements of cloister in such communities. The actual supervision of the observance of papal cloister, however, is entrusted to the diocesan bishops.

The ordinary of the diocese in which such a monastery of nuns is located and those he delegates to act in his place have the right of access to the cloister of contemplative nuns. For an appropriately serious reason he can also permit others to enter the cloister as well. The need for emergency medical or pastoral services or the repair of monastery facilities would be typically serious reasons justifying entry to the cloister. Again, where the reason is considered to be of appropriate seriousness, such as to receive medical treatment or to exercise the right to vote, the ordinary can also permit the nuns to leave the cloister for whatever period of time is reasonably necessary to accomplish the approved objective.

It is interesting to note, that despite the restrictions governing entry to and departure from the cloister, the code does not prescribe any penalties for violation of cloister. This stands in marked contrast to the 1917 code which prescribed severe penalties, including in some cases excommunication, for the violation of cloister.

RIGHT TO PRIVACY

Any claim a religious might make to a right to privacy within the structure of religious life is not rooted in his or her status as a religious, but in the obligations and rights of all the Christian faithful (see c. 220). Just as a religious does not relinquish basic civil rights upon entering a religious institute, the religious, cleric or lay, does not relinquish claim to the obligations and rights of all the faithful. Consequently, what follows concerning privacy applies to all individuals in religious institutes, societies of apostolic life, or secular institutes.

Within the context of this volume, the right to privacy might best be discussed as confidentiality.[7] For instance, an individual has the right to expect confidentiality in relationships with medical or mental health professionals. Information from these professionals concerning individual religious may be given to superi-

---

[6] AAS 61(1969) 674-690.

[7] For a more thorough treatment of this topic, see Elissa Rinere, C.P., "The Individual's Right to Confidentiality," *Bulletin on Issues of Religious Law* 11 (Washington: LCWR, 1995).

ors only with permission. This permission from the individual religious is usually given in writing and for a specific purpose.

Once such permission is given, the religious should know how and with whom the confidential information is shared. There should be clear limits on how long such information is kept in one's personnel file, what the disposition of such information is once the leadership personnel for whom it was intended leave office, or when the purpose for which the information was released is no longer pertinent. For instance, if confidential information was released in order that a psychiatrist or psychologist might issue an evaluation on the suitability of a religious for a particular assignment, policies should be clear on the destruction of the confidential materials once the assignment question is resolved.

A right of all the faithful which is related to confidentiality is the right to one's good name (see c. 220). Considering the issue in this light, an individual can expect privacy concerning personnel records, letters of recommendation, and any other sensitive material related to past activities. Institutes are well advised to have policies on how long sensitive or incriminating materials are retained in files and who oversees their removal and destruction. For instance, if a religious had a substance abuse or mental health problem in his or her past, but successfully underwent treatment and rehabilitation, stated policies providing for the removal of all mention of this history from the files ensure freedom and privacy for the individual.

As is true with all rights within the structure of the Church, there are limits. Difficult decisions must be made when the rights of the individual come into conflict with the common good, either of the the institute or the larger society. In certain circumstances, because an individual might present a danger to others, sensitive or confidential material might be shared. These situations must be evaluated on a case by case basis and the rights of all parties carefully considered and respected. A religious with an active substance abuse problem or uncontrolled and debilitating psychiatric problems cannot demand a right to privacy and good name at the expense of unsuspecting people who are potential victims. In 1993, a document was published by the NCCB which outlines a recommendation process utilizing silence; that is, lack of comment or disclosure, as a means of trying to protect privacy as well as the common good.[8]

The right to confidentiality is sometimes seriously transgressed in religious life, not maliciously, but out of a lack of awareness of what the right entails. The right is usually respected in situations where personal and institutional boundaries are clear and relationships between members and leaders are mature and honest.

---

[8] This pamphlet, *"Proposed Guidelines on the Assessment of Clergy and Religious for Assignment"* is available from the NCCB. A sample letter of recommendation is included as part of the text and it is noted the "(f)ailure to provide such a statement is sufficient reason for delaying or denying appointment...."

Restricted Activities and Activities Inconsistent with Membership

In its enumeration of the obligations and rights of members of religious institutes, the 1983 Code of Canon Law lists clear restrictions on activity in canons 671 and 672. The first canon is not applied to members of societies of apostolic life or secular institutes. The second is.

Canon 671

For members of religious institutes, canon 671 stipulates the need for permission from the "legitimate superior" before one may accept "duties or offices outside the institute." Among the elements forming the foundation of such a restriction are the nature of the religious commitment, the reality of the vow of obedience, and the obligation and right each religious has to minister according to the mission and charism of the particular religious institute. There is also an underlying and unspoken presumption that members of religious institutes work in institute-sponsored apostolates, thus the required permission covers the extraordinary situation when the individual would not follow that norm.

However, today the number of community sponsored apostolates is declining and permission to accept duties or offices outside the institute is a common request. Through personnel boards or other structures, such requests are carefully evaluated in light of the purpose of the restriction: preservation of the nature of the religious commitment, the reality of the vows, and the nature and mission of the institute.

Canon 672

Religious Institutes

According to canon 672, non-clerical members of religious institutes are obliged to observe the same restrictions on activity expected of diocesan clerics. Although the motivation for holding clerical religious to the restrictions can be attributed to their commonly held clerical status, the motivation for holding non-clerical religious to the restrictions is not as clear. The action is not explained in any source documents on the canons, but one may assume it is related to the nature of the religious commitment which, as with priesthood, involves public ecclesial ministry.

The canons referred to, and which women and men in religious institutes are to observe, are found in the section of the code dealing with the obligations and rights of clerics. Canon 277, §1 requires the observance of "perfect and perpetual continence," which is already accepted by religious as part of the evangelical counsels. The second paragraph of the canon enjoins religious to "prudence" in the company they keep, lest the obligation to continence be endangered or scandal be given to the people.

Although the words here are simple, the issues might be very complex. Individual religious are very different and their ability to tolerate varying circumstances differs. Also, the possibility for scandal or misunderstanding among the people in a specific locale varies according to circumstances and many other factors. It is impossible to set clear rules about which situations are acceptable and which are not. Decisions must be made based on the intent of the law, which is to safeguard continence and also on the fact that members of religious institutes are public ministers in the Church who have certain obligations to their vocations and to the people they serve.

The second canon referred to in canon 672 (c. 285) has four paragraphs, each stipulating a restriction on activity. The first paragraph obliges religious, in accord with particular law, to refrain "from those things unbecoming to their state." The "state" of a religious within the Church is understood to be as an individual in public vows, in public witness to the Church and to the mission and charism of the institute

As stated above, the history of these restrictive canons goes back into the history of diocesan clergy. In that historical milieu, "unbecoming activities" were those which offended against the dignity of the clerical state. Traditional canonical commentators defined unbecoming professions as those held by the "lower classes" of society: actor, inn keeper, gambler, etc. The specific occupations are certainly conditioned by time and circumstance, but the guiding principle was the dignity of the clerical state. Those activities deemed to be beneath its dignity were unbecoming.[9]

The difficulty in applying this canon to members of religious institutes is, of course, that what is determined unbecoming in some way to the clerical state might not be at all unbecoming to the religious state. Certain occupations can certainly offend against the religious vocation, but such a determination must be made on a case by case basis. For some religious, in keeping with their charism and their commitment to the poor, menial occupations are preferred while those with the traditional image of "dignity" are unbecoming. For instance, working as a waiter or waitress in a restaurant might be unbecoming for a religious, but

---

[9] See for instance, T. Bouscaren and A. Ellis *Canon Law: A Text and Commentary* (Milwaukee: Bruce Publishing, 1946) 115-116, or any commentaries on the 1917 *Code of Canon Law* at canon 138.

not those same positions in a soup kitchen or homeless shelter. In dealing with this restriction it is best to say that those activities are unbecoming to the religious state which cloud or detract from the public commitment an individual has made within the Church to the mission and charism of the institute. Unless one considers these elements of the commitment, it is impossible to make a determination about a specific activity.

The second paragraph of the canon under discussion (c. 285) enjoins the avoidance of those things which "although not unbecoming are nonetheless alien" to the religious state. In traditional commentaries on the clerical state the distinction was routinely made between unbecoming and alien activities. While the former offended against dignity the latter were simply incompatible diverting the individual from clerical ministry. Applying this principle to religious life, alien activities are those which divert the individual from public witness and the mission and charism of the institute. The activities traditionally named by commentators are treated and explained in the canons which follow: holding public office, assuming financial liability for others, conducting business or trade for profit, volunteering for military service. By choice or by principle, based on mission and charism, the list for religious may designate these and other activities as alien.

However one understands the words "unbecoming" and "alien," and however they are applied to specific situations, the overriding principle in making decisions is the value being upheld by the law: members of religious institutes are called to live lives of consistency both in word and action; the energies of all the members are focused on and contribute to the clarity of their public profession and the fulfillment of the institute's mission and charism.

The remainder of canon 285, as well as canons 286, 287, and 289 are statements about the traditionally understood "alien" activities. The first, canon 285, §3, forbids the undertaking of any public office which involves the exercise of civil power. This prohibition has a long history in the Church and has been hotly debated at various times.[10] According to the provisions of canon 87, a dispensation from this disciplinary law is possible, but the individual religious and his or her superiors must take into account the very strong statements in favor of the prohibition made by Pope John Paul II.[11]

The final prohibition of canon 285 prevents religious, on their own initiative, from undertaking any financial responsibilities, accounting or debts on behalf of another. Clerical religious must seek permission, as the canon states, from their

---

[10] For some references, see John E. Lynch "Unbecoming Activity," in *The Code of Canon Law: Text and Commentary*, edited James A. Coriden et al. (New York/Mahwah, NJ: Paulist Press, 1985) 221-226.
[11] Ibid.

ordinary. Canon 672 directs members of lay institutes of pontifical right to seek this permission from the proper major superior. The most obvious motivation for this restriction is safeguarding the freedom of the individual religious who, before perpetual profession of vows, according to proper law, either gave up ownership or ceded administration of property and possessions to others. To then, without permission or approval, take on those same responsibilities for others defeats the role the vow of poverty plays in freeing the religious to focus on ministry and mission

It must be emphasized that accepting financial liability for others, although alien to the religious state, is not completely forbidden; rather, there is a requirement for proper permission. For instance, a religious who must assist aging parents or other relatives by taking over their financial matters may seek the required permission. Those designated to give permission must understand the details of the situation, ensuring that the individual has access to the necessary information and resources to undertake the task successfully and that the institute is protected from any mismanagement or other unforeseen events. In other words, permission to accept financial liability for others is not lightly given, nor is it routinely withheld. These same principles apply when religious are asked to act as executors of wills or estates, as guardians for children or disabled adults. In such delicate and sometimes emotionally charged situations, open communication and dialogue between the individual religious and the superior designated to give the required permission contributes greatly to a decision which is mutually understood and accepted.

Canon 285 continues on to include a prohibition against assuming "secular offices which entail an obligation to render accounts." There are differing interpretations on the meaning of "secular offices,"[12] but whatever meaning is given to the phrase, such offices may be assumed by religious only when the requisite permission is obtained.

As in the previous situation, both superior and the individual religious must understand the extent of the responsibility being undertaken and evaluate, within the context of open and honest dialogue, the ability of the individual and the degree of liability, if any, which falls to the institute in case of mismanagement.

Another "alien" activity is treated in canon 286. Religious must not engage in "business or trade either for their own benefit or that of others" without per-

---

[12] For instance, in *The Code of Canon Law: Text and Commentary*, 228 secular office is defined as municipal or public offices not involved with civil jurisdiction, but *The Canon Law: Letter and Spirit,"* 164 defines secular office as any non-ecclesiastical office.

mission from the appropriate superior. For diocesan clerics, this issue of business or trade for personal profit has a long and interesting history.[13] For religious the issue is not as complex since the vow of poverty already excludes any possibility of amassing personal wealth.

In canon 287, §1, religious are obliged to "foster that peace and harmony based on justice" which is sought by all people. In the second paragraph religious are enjoined not to be active in political parties or labor unions unless "legitimate ecclesiastical authority," which is, in this instance, the proper religious superior, judges that such involvement will protect the rights of the church or promote the common good.

Taken as a whole, this canon presents a consistent and understandable principle: religious, committed as they are to the service of all the people, work for justice in a manner that is not fractured or partisan. Political parties or labor unions might be partisan, so such activity is appropriate for religious only when partisan politics is not present.

The last activity considered alien to the clerical state which is also considered unsuited to religious is volunteering for military service without permission from the appropriate superior. As with previous canons, the history of the question is involved with the history of diocesan clergy. The canon pronounces military service "hardly consistent with the clerical state." Its lack of consistency with the religious state is easily understood.

Finally, religious are directed to make use of any available exemptions from "exercising duties and public service offices" which are "alien" to the religious state, whether these exemptions come by law, agreements or customs with civil authority. For instance, if religious profession is accepted in a certain locality as a reason to excuse an individual from jury service, this exemption should be utilized.

In all these instances of restricted activities or activities inconsistent with membership in a religious institute, the guiding principles are always the primary importance of public commitment in the Church, and the protection of the mission and charism of the institute. All decisions, determinations, and dispensations concerning these activities must be grounded in these values.

---

[13] See *The Code of Canon Law: Text and Commentary*, 226-227 for explanation and references.

Secular institutes

Members of secular institutes are not bound by canon 672. The lack of restriction on apostolate is consistent with the nature and charism of these institutes.

Societies of Apostolic Life

According to canon 739, all members of Societies of Apostolic Life are "bound by the common obligations of clerics, unless something else is evident from the nature of the matter." Commentators differ on whether this statement refers only to clerical societies or to all societies.[14] However, the canon itself provides sufficient latitude for each society to make its own determinations, based on its charism, mission, and particular law.

---

[14] *The Code of Canon Law: Text and Commentary,* indicates on page 537 that only clerical societies are addressed, while *A Handbook on Canons 573-746,* p. 299 applies the canon to all members of Societies of Apostolic Life, whether clerical or lay on page 249.

CHAPTER SEVEN

SEPARATION OF MEMBERS FROM THE INSTITUTE

THERESE GUERIN SULLLIVAN, S.P.[1]

Members separate from an institute in one of two ways: transfer, or definitive departure, commonly called secularization, or by *ipso facto*, mandatory or discretionary dismissal. Although not technically separation, this chapter also treats exclaustration. Each type of separation is unique with various subsidiary issues. The following material attempts to highlight the essential elements of each type.

TRANSFER

Definition

Transfer is the change of a perpetually professed member of an institute of consecrated life to another institute institute of consecrated life. The permission of the Apostolic See is required when the transfer is from an institute of consecrated life or a society of apostolic life. The pertinent canons are 684 and 685; 730; and 744, §2.

Mutual Obligations

As with all requests, the petitioner must provide the reasons for a transfer (e.g. the desire for greater perfection, spiritual welfare, etc.).

Permission of the supreme moderators of both institutes, with the consent of each of the respective general councils is to be obtained. In cases of transfers

---

[1] David M. Hynous, O.P., Patrick T. Shea, O.F.M., and Madeline Welch, O.S.U. contributed to the writing of this chapter.

between centralized institutes and monasteries, normally the major superior of the monastery can act as there is no general superior. Proper law is to be observed.

The transfer of a perpetually or temporary professed religious to another institute is a process that requires a timetable and a clear understanding of responsibilities between the two institutes. When the formal period of probation begins the transferring member assumes to live the obligations of the second institute. Salary and expenses then belong to the second institute. During this period, ultimate financial responsibility and accountability remain with the first institute, although an agreement about room and board, medical insurance, etc. will be need to be formulated.

If the member decides to end the transfer process, he/she returns to the first institute. During the period of probation, any patrimony being administered by the first institute remains there.

Time Periods

The transferring member will have a period of probation in which to acquire experiential knowledge of the second institute and to evaluate the decision to transfer to another institute. The minimum for this period of probation is three years. Proper law may require a more lengthy time.

The transfer is granted according to the norm of law: definitive incorporation into the second institute takes place when the member professes vows in the receiving institute. All obligations and duties of the first institute come to an end. Any patrimony or dowry is transferred to the second institute. At the time of transfer a new act of cession of patrimony and dowry are needed.

Procedures

The procedure found in canon 684, §§1 and 2 is to be followed.[2]

---

[2] The transfer of temporary professed members is limited to the monasteries mentioned in canon 684, §3.

APPENDIX 1
PETITION FOR AND APPROVAL OF TRANSFER

To: Supreme Moderator (of petitioner's own institute)
and
To: Supreme Moderator (of institute to which petitioner requests to transfer)

I, (First and last names of the petitioner; Place, day, month, and year of birth; place, day, month, and year of both temporary and perpetual profession) a perpetually professed member of the (Institute name) of (Place) request permission to transfer from the said Congregation to the (Name of institute going to) _____ of (Place) _____. The transfer will be effective upon completion of the requirements of canon law and proper law.

My reasons for requesting a transfer are: (e.g. the desire for greater perfection, spiritual welfare, etc.).

I understand the transfer is granted according to the norm of law and definitive incorporation in the Institute must be preceded by a period of probation according to the norm of the particular law of that Institute, observing the prescriptions of Canon 685, §1. I understand that throughout the period during which the proposed transfer will be discerned I am subject to the Constitution of (Name of institute going to). I further understand that I must return to the Congregation/Order if I do not make profession in that Institute (*c. 684, §2*).

Signature of Petitioner: _____

Dated: _____

This request is approved and formalized as of the date below and by the signatures of the Supreme Moderators of the releasing and receiving religious institutes having the previous consent of their Councils.

Signature: _____
(Supreme Moderator of releasing institute)

Dated: _____

Signature: _____
(Supreme Moderator of receiving institute)

EXCLAUSTRATION

Definition

Exclaustration consists in a member of a religious institute living outside a religious institute for definite or indefinite period of time, with permission granted by legitimate authority, during which time the exclaustrated religious remains a member of the institute but with some alteration of the canonical relationship between the individual religious and the religious institute. This involves a relaxation of some obligations of religious life. The word exclaustration derives from two Latin words, "ex" and "claustrum" and means outside the enclosure.

This canonical institute is limited to members in perpetual vows. Temporarily professed members use a different procedure.

There are several types of exclaustration, two of which are delineated in the code and at least two others that have developed in the practice of the Congregation for Institutes of Consecrated Life and for Societies of Apostolic Life:

Voluntary (or ordinary or simple). This type is described in canon 686, §1.[3] This type of exclaustration may be granted upon the petition of a religious to his or her religious institute.

Involuntary (or imposed). This type is described in canon 686, §3. Exclaustration may be imposed upon a religious by means of a petition of the religious institute made to the Holy See, or to the diocesan bishop in the case of an institute of diocesan right.

Qualified Exclaustration. This is a type of exclaustration given to religious priests who are considering laicization to allow them an environment for discernment in the hopes that they will not seek laicization. Observance of the vows, except the vow of chastity, is suspended as are other obligations of the priesthood; also suspended are certain obligations or rights such as exercise of an apostolate and wearing clerical garb. A priest under such exclaustration is to receive the sacraments like a lay person. Qualified exclaustration has been likened to temporary reduction to the lay state. This type of exclaustration is not frequently granted.

---

[3] Canon 745 seems to provide for a parallel to exclaustration for societies of apostolic life.

Ad Experimentum. This type of exclaustration is granted by the Holy See if a religious priest wants to leave his institute to become a diocesan priest and has found a diocesan bishop willing to receive him on a trial basis.[4]

Exclaustration durante necessitate. It is not clear if this should be a separate type since it is a form of voluntary exclaustration but it can only be granted by the Holy See (or a diocesan bishop in the case of an institute of diocesan right) since its term is indefinite, lasting as long as the reason for which the exclaustration was granted lasts.

Mutual Obligations (Effects of Exclaustration)

Exclaustration involves a freedom for exclaustrated religious from obligations incompatible with their new condition of life. At the same time the religious remains dependent upon and subject to his or her superiors (c. 687). The effects may vary somewhat with the type of exclaustration and the reason for exclaustration. What this means is not always clear. Canon 687 only specifically deals with two effects or rights and obligations: *religious habit* and *active and passive voice*. An exclaustrated member can wear the habit unless the indult of exclaustration provides otherwise. Exclaustrated religious lack active and passive voice.

There are additional items which also require consideration.

Poverty. Exclaustrated religious are freed from many obligations of poverty consistent with community life, especially the need to request certain permissions for ordinary expenses and turn over income. The exclaustrated religious is still expected to request permission for extraordinary or very large expenses. The exclaustrated religious is expected to live a simple lifestyle.

Financial needs. Exclaustrated religious are expected to obtain employment and so they may keep the income that they need for support. Whether a religious can obtain employment may be a factor in determining whether he or she can be granted exclaustration. Since involuntary exclaustration is often imposed on a religious for the benefit of the institute and since the religious on whom it is imposed may have problems that make employment unlikely, an institute may have a higher level of obligation to provide support for such a religious. In any event, if a religious on exclaustration is in need, the institute seems to have an obligation to provide support.

Financial needs can cover many matters. Institutes should consider whether

---

[4] It seems that the Congregation for Institutes of Consecrated Life and for Societies of Apostolic Life

it should provide for: simply a cash gift; continuation on health insurance; provision of an automobile or expenses therefore; a loan. This will be discussed in more detail below.

Obedience. Exclaustrated religious are freed from many obligations of obedience consistent with community life, so they need not ask many permissions that they might have to request if they were living in community. It does seem that the religious would still have to request permissions or dispensations that have nothing to do with community life and/or which cover important matters (e.g., publishing, travel). Other obligations of the institute and individual religious that should be considered are: updates or reports by the religious on progress or situation or changes of address; receipt of community mailings; visits to the community; use of a contact person within the institute.

Relationship with local ordinary. Exclaustrated religious remain dependent upon and subject to their superiors and also to the local ordinary, especially if the exclaustrated religious is a priest. Moreover, in the granting of simple exclaustration of a cleric, the local ordinary where the cleric is to reside must first give consent. This covers a variety of possible situations that might include a religious priest exercising ministry under the general supervision of the diocesan bishop. It would at least seem to involve in the case of a non-ordained religious, advising the local ordinary of the presence of the exclaustrated religious in the diocese.

Chastity. The obligation of chastity is unaffected by exclaustration.

Time Periods

The time periods vary according to the type of exclaustration. There is a limitation on how long a religious institute can grant exclaustration.

With regard to voluntary or simple exclaustration, canon 686 provides that the religious institute can grant exclaustration for a period not exceeding three years. The canon further says that extending the indult or granting it for more than three years is reserved to the Holy See, or the diocesan bishop in the case of institutes of diocesan right. It is not clear whether institutes can grant extensions in situations in which the institute made the initial grant for less than three

---

has been granting exclaustration with specific time limits to religious who wish to found new institutes or who seek to become virgins or hermits; therefore, the condition of these would not properly be *ad experimentum*.

years and the extension and the initial grant will not exceed three years; commentators have interpreted this provision both ways and a number of institutes follow the practice of granting exclaustration in periods of less than three years, as long as the total grants do not exceed three years. The indult might provide another limitation on the term; it might state that the indult lasts for a certain time period but only as long as the motivating cause for the exclaustration lasts.

In cases of involuntary exclaustration, the exclaustration lasts as long as the situation that requires the imposition of exclaustration lasts. Thus, the term is indefinite.

Qualified exclaustration has a term of only one or two years and this is not commonly extended.

In cases of exclaustration *durante necessitate* or any grant of exclaustration that is granted as long as a condition exists, this must be granted by the Holy See or the diocesan bishop, even if it is likely that it will last less than three years, since it could last longer than three years. Ordinarily this type of exclaustration is granted only after a religious institute has granted exclaustration for as long a period as it could do so.

Voluntary (Ordinary) Exclaustration

PROCEDURE
PETITION

- ♦ Formalities:

    First and last names of petitioner;

    Place, day, month, and year of birth;

    Place, day, month, and year of temporary and solemn profession;

    Whether petitioner is a cleric or lay religious;

    If petitioner is a cleric, place, day, month, and year of priestly (or diaconal) ordination;

    Principal ministries of petitioner or his curriculum vitae in the apostolate;

    Petition signed by religious and perhaps essential part of request in his or her handwriting.

- ♦ Purpose or reason:

    Written request by petitioner giving reason;

    The reason must be a grave or serious reason. Such reasons could include: vocational discernment, support or care of aged or infirm parents, personal health problems, doing pastoral or diocesan work, business ventures. It might be noted that some of these matters could also be handled under permission to be absent from the community (c. 665, §1).

- Permission of local ordinary, if petitioner is a cleric;

  A document from some local ordinary is needed in which the bishop agrees to accept the religious cleric during the period of exclaustration.

- The length of time for which exclaustration is sought (i.e., one year, two years, three years, or as long as the need exists);

- Information and a votum from the major superior and the council according to the proper law of the institute or its practices or procedures

GRANTING AUTHORITY

- Supreme moderator of the institute with the consent of the council, if exclaustration is for three years or less;

- Diocesan bishop, if it involves an institute of diocesan right and if the term of exclaustration exceeds three years, is an extension beyond three years or is indefinite;

- Holy See, i.e., Congregation for Institutes of Consecrated Life and for Societies of Apostolic Life, if it involves an institute of pontifical right and if the term of exclaustration exceeds three years, is an extension beyond three years, or is indefinite.

INDULT

- Formalities: in the form of a decree, signature of the supreme moderator and general secretary at the bottom, date and place of execution, stamp or seal of the institute;

- The day on which exclaustration takes effect and the date on which exclaustration ceases;

- The fact that the member requested exclaustration;

- The serious reason(s) for granting exclaustration;

- A recitation that the Supreme Moderator and the council consented to the exclaustration

- If the member is a cleric, a recitation that the consent of the named local ordinary has been obtained;

- The means by which the local ordinary of the place of residence of the member has been or will be informed of the presence and status of the exclaustrated member;
- That the exclaustrated member will not have active or passive voice in the institute during exclaustration;
- Whether the exclaustrated member may wear the habit of the institute or any other insignia or otherwise identify himself or herself as a member of the institute;
- The ways in which the member will be dependent upon the institute during the time of exclaustration: e.g., use of a contact person, frequency and type of contact, etc.;
- The duty of the exclaustrated member to return to the institute immediately if the superior recalls him or her during exclaustration;
- The right and duty of the member to return to the institute if the reason for which exclaustration was granted should cease;
- Whether the member during the time of exclaustration may visit house(s) of the institute, and if so, the member's duty of informing the major superior or other contact person before so visiting.

Involuntary Exclaustration

PROCEDURE

The code provides no procedure, but the Congregation for Institutes of Consecrated Life and for Societies of Apostolic Life has indicated that the procedure for dismissal should be followed but with less rigor. This would seem to involve the competent authority:

- collecting or completing the proofs;
- warning the religious once in writing or in the presence of two witnesses about the behavior in question, delineating the expected conduct or modification of conduct and the possibility of imposed exclaustration;
- permitting the religious ample opportunity to respond to the warning and to defend himself or herself; and
- obtaining the consent of the council with regard to requesting imposed exclaustration after fifteen (15) days from the formal warning;

- advising the religious of the request for imposed exclaustration and his or her right to present a defense to the supreme moderator

PETITION OR REQUEST FOR IMPOSED EXCLAUSTRATION
- Formalities:

    first and last names of religious

    place, day, month, and year of birth

    place, day, month, and year of temporary and perpetual profession

    whether religious is a cleric

    if a cleric, place, day, month, and year of priestly or diaconal ordination

    principal ministries or curriculum vitae of ministries

- explanation in detail of the situation composed by the competent authority delineating the serious reason(s).

    This type of exclaustration is ordinarily used in the case of a religious who is troubling or has serious problems living in community and a recitation that the competent authority advised the religious of the request for imposed exclaustration and his or her right to provide a defense for himself to the supreme moderator;

- if the case involves a religious cleric, the statement of some local ordinary in which he states that he will accept the religious during the period of exclaustration;

- a request for any special provisions to be placed in the decree of imposed exclaustration, with regard to habit, return to a religious house during the time of exclaustration, etc.

GRANTING AUTHORITY
- Diocesan bishop, if it involves an institute of diocesan right;
- Holy See, i.e., Congregation for Institutes of Consecrated Life and for Societies of Apostolic Life, if it involves an institute of pontifical right;

Termination of the Decree and Return to the Institute — since imposed exclaustration is at the discretion (*ad nutum*) of the Holy See or the diocesan bishop, then a petition must be made to the Holy See or diocesan bishop to end the exclaustration because the reason for which exclaustration is imposed is no longer applicable; it is not enough that the exclaustrated religious and the institute agree that the exclaustration should end.

Some Civil Law Considerations.

The status of exclaustration raises some civil law concerns. The institute will wish to maintain some ties and give some assistance to the religious departing on exclaustration. On the other hand, since the institute has less control over the religious, it may wish to decrease the likelihood that the institute will be responsible for the debts of the religious or be liable in tort for the misconduct of the religious. There is no sure way to avoid liability. Essentially the more ties that the religious has to the institute, the more likely that a court might find that the exclaustrated religious is an agent or employee of the institute; the less ties that an institute retains, the less it fulfills its assistance to a religious who may have served the institute for many years, and the more likely that the exclaustration will turn into a more permanent departure. There is no definite test for liability, there is no limitation on the number of factors (e.g., five out of ten factors); the test will be a rather subjective balancing test.

- *Agency.* There should be a provision in the indult and in any accompanying agreement that the exclaustrated religious is not an agent and has no power to bind the institute and the institute is not responsible for the actions of the exclaustrated religious.

- *Debts and Obligations.* There should be a statement in the indult and in any accompanying agreement that the institute is not liable for the debts or obligations of the exclaustrated religious unless it has accepted liability in writing.

- *Credit Cards.* If exclaustrated members have credit cards of the institute, they may be perceived as agents of the institute with regard to the use of the card; thus, the religious departing upon exclaustration should surrender institute credit cards to the institute. If the institute helped a religious to obtain a credit card by giving the issuer some sort of guaranty of payment, then the institute should advise the issuer that it no longer makes any such guaranty for the member departing on exclaustration. An institute may also wish to advise any merchants that has regularly extended credit to members that the institute is no longer responsible for credit extended to that member.

- *Automobiles.* Provision of the exclaustrated religious with an institute owned automobile makes the religious seem more like an agent, especially when driving. An exclaustrated religious should usually obtain his or her own automobile or it should be titled in the name of the religious. If an exclaustrated religious has an institute car, then the accompanying agreement should make it clear that car insurance must be provided and who will provide the insurance.

- *Health Insurance.* Such insurance is becoming a necessity in this society. The institute is obliged to help an exclaustrated religious in case of need, and a major illness could constitute such a need. On the other hand, such insurance is usually provided by employers, and it would seem that an exclaustrated religious should find employment that provides this benefit. Provision of this insurance can be construed as one mark of an employer-employee relationship, and so, one more tie between an exclaustrated religious and an institute.

- *Retirement.* This is another benefit that employers usually offer to employees. Some institutes may have formal plans that will determine eligibility and so reference should be made to that in any agreement. Other institutes may have a more informal fund for the care of elderly or infirm members, such that there is no right to accrued benefits. It would seem that there is little need for such institutes to make contributions for an exclaustrated member since the member makes no financial or apostolic contributions to the institute. If there is a decision not to make such contributions, that should probably be stated in any agreement. The ultimate decision may depend upon whether the exclaustrated member is likely to return and live out retirement in the institute; there may also be reason to make such contributions where the religious is on imposed or indefinite exclaustration since that religious may not have a job and may be more dependent on the institute during retirement.

- *Social Security.* Some religious institutes have elected Social Security coverage for all members; institutes seem to consider members who work outside the community and have funds withheld by their employers as not being part of this special coverage, but as employees of their outside employers rather than fictional employees of the religious institute. It would seem that the institute should treat religious on exclaustration as it would any member working outside the institute. The case may be different, however, for religious on imposed or indefinite exclaustration since they might not have employment and they may be more dependent upon the institute.

- *Income Tax.* Since religious on exclaustration have control over their income, the IRS would probably consider them liable for income tax. Moreover, exclaustrated religious are less likely to work for a Catholic organization.

- *Professional Counseling.* The institute paying for counseling of an exclaustrated religious may be another tie to the institute suggestive of benefits supplied to an employee or agent. Yet there may be good reason to do this, especially in the case of members on imposed or indefinite exclaustration, where a psychological condition is part of the reason for exclaustration.
- *Liability Insurance.* If an exclaustrated religious is involved in a business venture or if he or she earning money as a professional, the institute should advise them to obtain the appropriate liability or malpractice insurance.
- *Release of Claims.* Religious institutes should be concerned not only about civil-law claims brought by third parties but also lawsuits by the exclaustrated or departed members for past services, for other obligations allegedly owed them, or for personal property that the institute retains. The institute may wish to insert in any agreement a provision that the religious departing on exclaustration acknowledges that they have in possession all their personal property and effects and they release the institute and all organizations affiliated with it from any claims against the institute and affiliated organizations for all claims that they may have against the institute and affiliated organizations, especially for compensation for services.

Enforceability of Accompanying Agreement. Any agreement between the religious and the religious departing on exclaustration will not bind a third party who did not sign the agreement. An agreement is a helpful description of the relationship set out before any litigation arises.

The foregoing checklist is meant as helpful instrument, but it is not an exhaustive, nor can it cover every unique situation. Checklists and sample forms are no substitute for the advice of an attorney.

Definitive Departure: "Secularization"

Individuals are free to depart an institute at the completion of the time of temporary vows. Such a departure is legitimate and would qualify for readmission according to canon 690. All rights and obligations entailed by profession cease. Wills, cession of administrative documents, and dowry (if any) are returned to the person departing. The one departing may not claim remuneration for any work done while a member of the institute. The institute must observe equity and charity in dealing with the former member.

Temporary Professed Member

- At expiration of vows (c. 688, §1)

    The expiration of vows is at the time of the anniversary of the profession of vows. The individual is free to leave the institute. The request should be in writing and is actually a statement of intent. No further action is required. The departure is legitimate and would qualify for readmission according to canon 690.

- During temporary vows (c. 688, §2)

    If the person departing wishes to leave the institute during the period of temporary vows, the norms of canon 688, §2 are to be followed. The request for an indult to leave the institute should be in writing stating the reasons for it. The departure is legitimate and would qualify for readmission according to canon 690.

    The supreme moderator must act upon the request with the consent of his or her council. In the case of institutes of pontifical right, no further action is required. In cases of institutes of diocesan right and in monasteries mentioned in canon 615, the indult must be submitted to the diocesan bishop of the place where the religious is assigned for his confirmation. Without the confirmation of the diocesan bishop the act is invalid.

    The indult of departure mentioned in canon 692 consists of the request with the affirmative response or the request with affirmative response and the required confirmation. It is subject to the specifications and effects of that norm.

- Exclusion from subsequent profession (c. 689)

The major superior competent to admit to profession should be indicated in the proper law of the institute. Canon 689, §1 states the competent major superior is to act after hearing his or her council. Hearing the council constitutes a consultative vote.

Canon 689 states that just causes are required for exclusion from subsequent profession. The canon seeks to insure charity and justice by requiring the opinion of an expert to evaluate the person's suitability for the life of the institute. An exclusion based on health should include the opinion of an expert (unless incurred through institute's negligence or while engaged in an institute's work).

Perpetually Professed Member

The seriousness of the departure from the institute of a person perpetually professed is emphasized by the wording of canon 691 which states the perpetually professed is not to seek an indult to depart without very grave reasons weighed before the Lord.

The petition for an indult is to be submitted to the supreme moderator who is to transmit it with a personal opinion and that of the council to the competent authority. For institutes of pontifical right the Apostolic See reserves the right to grant the indult. In institutes of diocesan right the diocesan bishop of house of assignment can grant the indult.

The request for an indult of departure should contain: brief statement of the concrete reasons for the request; specific resources which were used in the attempt to resolve the difficulties mentioned in the request including spiritual, psychological, and medical resources; curriculum vitae of the person involved. The opinion of the supreme moderator and the council should be objective and state their approval or disapproval.

APPENDIX 1
INDULT OF EXCLAUSTRATION

In accord with canon 686, §1 of the Code of Canon Law and in response to his (her) written request, and after having obtained the consent of my council, [and after having obtained the consent of the local ordinary where he will reside (in the case of a cleric)] I, the Supreme Moderator of the Religious Institute (hereinafter "Institute"), hereby grant an indult of exclaustration to _____(name)_____ (hereinafter "Religious") for the period of _(number)_ of year(s) [months] effective from the time of his (her) acceptance of this indult (or effective on the __day of_____, 20_ _ and expires on the _____ day of _____, 20_ _).

This indult is granted for the following serious reason(s):

In accord with canon 687, during this period of exclaustration, Religious is free from those obligations incompatible with his (her) new condition of life except that he (she) shall remain bound to chastity and shall ultimately be responsible to the supreme moderator (provincial). The right of the Religious to active and passive voice is suspended. Moreover, he (she) may not wear the habit of the Institute, or other identifying insignia or identify himself (herself) as a member of the Institute.

Religious may not act as an official agent of the Institute apostolically or contract debts or obligations on behalf of the Institute. Religious shall keep the Supreme Moderator (Provincial) informed of his (her) residence and telephone number (both home and work) and contact the Supreme Moderator (Provincial) (named contact person) at least every ___months. Religious is responsible for his (her) own finances according to the attached agreement; Religious can in his (her) own name, work, earn, retain and dispense funds necessary to provide for his (her) personal needs. The religious understands that he (she) shall be required to comply with all civil laws common to all persons who are not members of a religious institute, which include but are not limited to federal and state income tax laws.

The Institute will inform the local ordinary where Religious is to reside of the granting of this indult, will send Religious the regular Institute communications, and will fulfill the financial obligations of initial assistance and the like, according to the agreement attached.

For the duration of this indult, Religious may not return to the Institute without first consulting Supreme Moderator (Provincial). This indult may be revoked by the Supreme Moderator for a just cause. This indult will also terminate if the serious reason for which it was given ceases. At least ___ days prior to the expiration of this Indult, Religious shall advise the

Supreme Moderator (Provincial) of his (her) intention either to return to the Institute or to seek an extension of this Indult or an indult of departure. At the expiration of this Indult, Religious must return to the Institute, unless further arrangements have been made in accord with canon law;

Granted on this _____ day of _____, 20_ _ at the General Curia of the Institute in the City of _____, State of _____.

Signature: _____
Supreme Moderator

Attest:

Signature: _____
Secretary

I, ___(name)___, understand and accept the terms, requirements, conditions, and consequences of the indult of exclaustration which I have accepted. I also understand and accept the terms, requirements, conditions and consequences of the financial agreement which I have entered into with the Institute and which is attached hereto as "Exhibit A" and made a part hereof as though fully set forth herein.

Date: _____
Date of Profession

Signature: _____
Religious Legal Name, if necessary

Witnesses:

_____

_____

APPENDIX 2
LETTER OF CLERIC SEEKING TO LEAVE WITHOUT LAICIZATION FOLLOWING PERPETUAL VOWS

Dear_____

I am writing to seek your assistance in obtaining my voluntary departure from the Congregation/Order of _____.

As you know, I have not been functioning as a priest now for several years. I do not intend to function as a priest in the future. At one time, I had been on exclaustration, but that has also come to a close, and I do not intend to return to the Congregation/Order.

Thus, I am writing to request an indult to leave the Congregation/Order. I am not requesting a dispensation for priestly celibacy. However, I do wish to clarify my relationship with the Congregation/Order, to make it clear that I am not a member of the Order, and to indicate that I will not be functioning as a priest.

At present there is no bishop ready to accept me for priestly service into a diocese. Nor am I actively seeking such a bishop at this time. At present, I simply wish that my separation from the Congregation/Order might be permanent. While separated from the Congregation/Order, and without a bishop, I have no intention of functioning as a priest.

I would appreciate it if you could send this letter with any such information that would be necessary to the proper authorities in order to facilitate my voluntary departure. Thank you very much for your assistance.

Sincerely yours,

The signed letter, together with a letter from the major superior supporting their petition is sent to the Congregation for Institutes of Consecrated Life and Societies of Apostolic Life.

APPENDIX 3
LETTER FROM SUPERIOR SUSPENDING FACULTIES

Having received the petition of (Name), a religious priest of _____, to initiate the case for his laicization and dispensation from priestly celibacy, considering the content of the Instruction *Per Litteras* of the Congregation for the Doctrine of the Faith, of October 14, 1980, and the procedural norms contained therein; by this document and in virtue of my office, I prohibit *ad cautelam* (Name) the exercise of all ministerial activities corresponding to his priestly state, while he is awaiting final resolution of his case. This prohibition, nonetheless, according to the norms of canon 1335, is suspended as often as it is necessary to care for the faithful in danger of death.

Given in (City, State) in (Place), under the seal of the Congregation/Order, (Date).

(Name) _____
Supreme Moderator/ Provincial

(Name): _____
Secretary

Dismissal

Definition

Dismissal of a member from an institute is an action taken by the competent authority which imposes on a professed member permanent departure from the institute. See canons 701; 729; and 746. All rights and obligations arising from profession are dispensed.

There are three types of dismissal. 1) *ipso facto* dismissal is dismissal from the institute of a member who has notoriously abandoned the Catholic faith or has contracted marriage or has attempted it, even only civilly. 2) mandatory dismissal is dismissal for the offenses listed in canons 1397, 1398, and 1395 when those offenses are proved and the member has been given the opportunity of self-defense; 3) discretionary dismissal is the dismissal of a member for other causes, provided they are grave, external, imputable, and juridically proven.

The competent superior first needs to determine whether any delicts have been committed. This process for making this determination is in Book VI of the code. Since those procedures are beyond the scope of this present work, the superior must consult a canonist for instruction on how to proceed.

MUTUAL OBLIGATIONS

Dismissal procedures are subject to strict interpretation according to the norms of canon law because they are connected to penal legislation. The rights of the individual member as well as those of the institute are to be protected.

Proof of grave, external, imputable offenses toward the church or religious community are to be documented.

TIME PERIODS

Upon consideration to begin the process for dismissal the competent superior is to write a letter to the member informing him or her of this process. The letter should indicate the member has the right to defend himself or herself. A time limit is set in which the defense is to be given in writing. After this initial indication of intention, the superior enters into the formal process presented below.

Upon the advice of his or her council, the superior then sends the member the two canonical warnings mentioned in canon 697 at least fifteen days apart. These are sent certified mail with a request for a return receipt. Essential contents of both warning letters are: 1) an explicit threat of subsequent dismissal unless the member reforms, 2) the cause of the dismissal is to be clearly indicated and 3) the member is to be given the full opportunity of self-defense.

Upon the completed time for the warnings the acts of dismissal is prepared by the council. The acts of the case, with two signatures are sent to the supreme moderator with the following: curriculum vitae, report of misdeeds, attempts by major superiors, two canonical warnings, proof of reception of these warnings, defenses given by religious, acts from the council meeting wherein the dismissal was decided, summary and review of the case by the major superior.

It is only after the collegial vote that the supreme moderator issues the decree. The lower council does not actually decide the dismissal. It is to be noted that the diocesan bishop makes the decision in the case of monasteries as described in Canon 615

PROCEDURES

For *validity*, there must be a council of four in addition to the supreme moderator. The decree itself is an act of the superior, but the decision is made by secret collegial vote. The decree, the cover letter, or an excerpt from the council minutes should make clear that the required number were present and whether the vote was unanimous.

For *validity* the decree must contain a summary of the cause of dismissal in fact—the actions of the religious, and in law-showing that the violations were contrary to universal and proper law and are of a type and gravity considered in law, grounds for dismissal.

For *validity*, the decree must contain notice that the religious has ten (10) days from the receipt of notification within which to appeal. The notification is not communicated to the individual before it has been confirmed.

Particular Tpes of Dimissal
IPSO FACTO

The automatic penalty described in canon 694 is applied in the case of a member who has publicly abandons the Catholic faith or attempts to contract marriage. The use of this penalty is to protect the institute from the action of a member whose behavior is directly and publicly contrary to the nature of consecrated life.

The behavior of the member effects the penalty. The canon directs the competent superior to collect the proofs and issue a declaration of the fact so the dismissal is established juridically. Standard rules for proofs apply here. The superior must obtain either documentation; e.g. a certified marriage certificate, or testimony from reliable witnesses.

Mandatory

The competent superior must judge the facts and the imputability of the matter and collect proofs of both the facts and the imputability. The accusation and the evidence must be made known to the member and the member must be given the opportunity of self-defense.

The competent superior is the major superior, such as a provincial if there is one at a lower level than the general superior.

Because of the seriousness of the matter and the complex nature of penal law, qualified experts should be consulted before using the provision of this canon.

If the case involves the causes in canon 695, there are no canonical warnings, but rather an emphasis on proofs of fact and imputability.

Discretionary

The other causes mentioned in canon 696 for which a member may be dismissed from the institute are to be grave, external, imputable, and juridically proven. These reasons for dismissal can be related to the fundamental obligations of consecrated life. They need not be specified in the proper law of the institute but should constitute repeated behavior on the part of the member.

All prescriptions of the process of dismissal must be observed including the right to self-defense and to recourse. If all procedures are not carefully carried out the dismissal process may be nullified for lack of proper procedure. The decree of dismissal does not take effect until confirmed by the Holy See to whom all the acts of the case must be sent. In the case of diocesan institutes, the confirmation is by the diocesan bishop of the house of assignment.

APPENDIX 1
PROCEDURES FOR DISMISSAL

- Consult with council about feasibility of beginning dismissal procedures
- Initial warning to member that dismissal procedures are likely to begin
- First formal warning in writing by certified mail or with two witnesses after consulting council
- Second formal warning after fifteen days in writing by certified mail or with two witnesses
- After fifteen days, council votes on forwarding acts of dismissal to superior general
- General council votes on dismissal
- Member notified of dismissal

APPENDIX 2
DECLARATION OF DISMISSAL *IPSO FACTO*

We, the undersigned Supreme Moderator and members of the Council of the (Name of institute) _____ with headquarters in (Place) _____, (number of) ____ in number, duly assembled at (Place) _____, on the (date) have thoroughly reviewed the proofs and have determined that (NAME), a perpetually professed member of this institute, has attempted civil marriage. We, therefore, declare that the above mentioned member is automatically dismissed from the Congregation in accordance with c. 694, §1, 2°.

An authentic copy of this declaration is being sent to the same member on (DATE).

The documentation pertinent to this case is appended.

Councilor: (Name) _____

Councilor: (Name) _____

Councilor: (Name) _____

Councilor: (Name) _____

Supreme Moderator: (Name) _____

[SEAL]

Secretary: (Name) _____

APPENDIX 3
FIRST CANONICAL WARNING

TO: (Name) _____

FROM: (Name of Supreme Moderator or Provincial) _____

You will recall that on (date) _____, _____, and _____, I wrote you inviting you to return to fraternal life within the (name of province or local house) _____. This followed oral invitations for you to come back to our community. While you have written me and talked with me on the telephone about some of the issues you have been dealing with in your life at the present time, and you have assured me that you have been meeting periodically with (name of contact person for the institute) _____, the time for your official leave of absence has expired with no indication of your intention to return to our community life. In that sense, you have neither responded to nor complied with my pastoral invitations.

Now therefore in accord with canon law and the law of our Congregation/Order, you are hereby given the first canonical warning required by canon 697.2 and article (cite article number) _____ of our Constitutions prior to being dismissed from the (name of institute) _____.

You have been unlawfully absent from the Congregation/Order and community life for more than six (6) months. As noted above, you have failed to respond to various invitations to return and again take up religious life.

I must advise you that your unlawful absence from the institute for more than six (6) months is an imputable offense which subjects you to dismissal from the Congregation/Order under canon 696.1 and article (cite number) of our Constitutions.

Having heard the advice of my Council, I hereby declare that you will be dismissed from the Congregation/Order unless you:

return to the (place) _____ within fifteen (15) days of receipt of this first canonical warning to take up immediately religious life as a member of the Congregation/Order.

If you fail to comply within fifteen (15) days of receipt of this first canonical warning, I will issue a second canonical warning. If you fail to respond to a second canonical warning, and I with my Council determine that your actions demonstrate incorrigibility and that you have offered an insufficient defense, I will proceed with dismissal by submitting evidence to the

Supreme Moderator and his/her Council, who will decide the case and submit it to the Apostolic See.

You have a right under canon law and the law of order to self-defense, including a canonical counsel in this matter at all stages. You have the right to present your defense to me, in person or in writing against this first canonical warning and proposed dismissal within fifteen days of receipt of this warning. You also have the right to communicate with and offer a defense directly to the Supreme Moderator.

Please be advised of the seriousness of this matter.

GIVEN AT: (place) _____

Signed: (Supreme Moderator) _____

Signed: (Secretary) _____

CERTIFIED MAIL - RETURN RECEIPT REQUESTED

APPENDIX 4
SECOND CANONICAL WARNING

TO: (Name) _____

FROM: (Name of Supreme Moderator or Provincial) _____

You will recall that on _____, and _____ I wrote you inviting you to return to community life (place) _____. This followed oral invitations to you to return. On (date) _____, I issued you a First Canonical Warning. You have neither responded to, nor complied with my pastoral invitation. or my more formal canonical warning.

Now therefore in accord with canon law and the law of our Congregation/Order, you are hereby given the second canonical warning required by canon 697, 2° and article (cite number) _____ of our Constitutions/Statutes prior to being dismissed from the Congregation/Order.

You have been unlawfully absent from the Congregation/Order and community life for more than six (6) months. As noted above, you have failed to respond to various invitations and a canonical warning to return and again take up religious life.

I must advise you that your unlawful absence from the Congregation/Order for more than six (6) months is an imputable offense which subjects you to dismissal from the Congregation/Order under canon 696.1 and article (cite number) ____ our Constitutions/Statutes.

Having heard the advice of my Council, I hereby declare that you will be dismissed from the Congregation/Order unless you:

return to the (place) _____ within fifteen (15) days of receipt of this second canonical warning to take up immediately religious life as a member of the Congregation/Order.

If you fail to comply within fifteen (15) days of receipt of this second canonical warning, and I with my Council determine that your actions have demonstrated incorrigibility and that you have offered an insufficient defense, I will proceed with dismissal by submitting evidence to the Supreme Moderator of the Congregation/Order of _____ and his/her Council, who will decide the case and submit it to the Apostolic See.

You have a right under canon law and the law of order to self-defense, including a canonical counsel in this matter at all stages. You have the right to present your defense to me, in person or in writing, against this second canonical warning and proposed dismissal within fifteen days of receipt of this warning. You also have the right to communicate with and offer a defense directly to the Supreme Moderator at (address, phone number, FAX) _____.

Please be advised of the seriousness of this matter.

GIVEN AT: (place) _____

Signed: (Supreme Moderator) _____

Signed: (Secretary) _____

CERTIFIED MAIL - RETURN RECEIPT REQUESTED

APPENDIX 5
DECREE OF DISMISSAL

The undersigned General Superior, having proceeded collegially with the General Council on (date) to weigh the proofs, arguments, and defenses in the case, and in the same manner having moved to a decision by secret ballot, decrees that Sister NN, a (perpetually) professed member of the (Congregation) is hereby dismissed, for the following reasons.

According to the proper law of this Institute (Constitution nn.) and the law of the Church (cc) religious are obliged to _____ Canon law also recognizes that failure in this matter constitutes a cause for dismissal, stating among other causes "_____" (c. 696, §1).

In the present case, despite various efforts to correct the situation, including two formal canonical warnings issued (date/date) Sister NN has persisted in the behavior which violates the above religious obligations. (Brief resume of factual violations which merit dismissal in the case.)

This decree takes effect following its confirmation by the Holy See. Sister NN then has ten days, following receipt of notification of the confirmed decree within which she may have recourse to the Holy See.

_____
General Superior
Date

[SEAL]

_____
General Secretary

APPENDIX 6
DECREE OF DISMISSAL

(Name)_____ a member of our Congregation/Order is dismissed from the Congregation/Order, according to the norm of Canon ____ of the Code of Canon Law and of Article (cite number) ____ of the Constitutions/Statutes, because of the delict of unlawful absence from a religious institute.

After having left the religious house lawfully, he remained outside the structures of religious life for more than one year. Numerous informal invitations to return met with a negative response. Formal canonical admonitions and invitations to return to obedience were sent by the Provincial/Supreme Moderator on _____ and _____. There was no response to either admonition, although certified mail receipts indicate and prove that the admonitions were received.

Therefore, since a year has elapsed since the cessation of his/her permission to live outside the religious house this declaration is authorized, according to which (Name) _____, is declared lawfully dismissed from the Congregation/Order of _____.

This declaration is supported by the accompanying copies of letters and admonitions which indicate clearly the reasons for dismissal.

Councilor: (Signed) _____

Councilor: (Signed) _____

Councilor: (Signed) _____

Councilor: (Signed) _____

Councilor: (Signed) _____

Councilor: (Signed) _____

Supreme Moderator: (Signed) _____

Secretary: (Signed) _____

Given at (place) _____ on (date) _____

Special Provisions

Readmission to the same Institute

This canon applies to any religious who has legitimately left after profession. Legitimate departure includes departure at the conclusion of novitiate according to canon 653, §2; at the expiration of temporary profession according to canon 688, §1; by an indult granted to a religious in temporary profession according to canon 688, §2; by exclusion from subsequent profession according to canon 689; by an indult granted to a perpetually professed religious according to canon 691 and by dismissal according to the various categories and procedures of canons 694-703.

Readmission to the same institute would depend on the present condition of the person involved and the judgment of the competent superior acting with the council and in accordance with the norm of proper law. The reasons for the departure would also need to be evaluated.

Canon 690

> §1. The supreme moderator with the consent of the council can readmit without the burden of repeating the novitiate one who had legitimately left the institute after completing the novitiate or after profession. Moreover, it will be for the same moderator to determine an appropriate probation prior to temporary profession and the time of vows to precede perpetual profession, according to the norm of cann. 655 and 657, §2. The superior of an autonomous monastery with the consent of the council possesses the same faculty.

Institutes' responsibility for those who have left

Canon 702 legally excludes the right of an former member to remuneration for work done while a member of the institute. In a spirit of charity and equity institutes should assess the needs of the former member and provide assistance. Institutes that have policies providing for the assistance of former members are in a good position to attend to those people with such charity and equity.

APPENDIX 1
FORM FOR RELEASE OF MEDICAL RECORDS

RELEASE OF MEDICAL INFORMATION

I, _____ do hereby authorize any hospital or doctor, from whom I have received medical services of attention, to release to _____ any and all information from records or personnel which may he in their possession. Such release of medical information shall apply to all organizations and persons who may have medical knowledge concerning my physical and mental health. I further authorize such persons having knowledge about my case to discuss all aspects of my physical and mental health with any representative of (name institute) _____.

Dated: _____

Sworn and Subscribed before me (date) _____,

Signed: (Secretary/Notary) _____

APPENDIX 2
AGREEMENT FOR ABSENCE FOR HEALTH REASONS

MEMORANDUM OF AGREEMENT FOR HEALTH LEAVE

(Name) _____ will begin a health leave at (name of institution or program) _____ on (Date) ___. This leave for reasons of health will last for (state duration) _____ but may be extended. On successful completion of this program of treatment, (Name) _____ will resume his/her ministry as (cite ministry) _____ at (place) _____.

During this health leave, expenses will be paid by (Name of institute, diocese) _____.

Signed: (Name of person on leave) _____

Signed: (Superior) _____

Date: _____

APPENDIX 3
BASIC FACT SHEET

FACT SHEET OF THE CONGREGATION FOR DIVINE WORSHIP AND DISCIPLINE OF THE SACRAMENTS
(To be filled in and transmitted with the other documentation)

Congregation for Divine Worship and Discipline of the Sacraments

ORDER: _____

Province:

First and Family Names of Petitioner: _____

Date of Birth: _____

Place and Country of Birth: _____

Date of Priestly Ordination: _____

Date of Defection: _____

Date of Leave / Exclaustration: _____

Principal ministries exercised by Petitioner:

Liberal Arts studies, and other studies, completed:

Reasons for petition, existing either before or after ordination:

Juridical Status of Petitioner: _____

Current Activity (job) of Petitioner: _____

Whether Petitioner has attempted civil or religious marriage:
Date of marriage: _____ Status of the woman
(i.e. never married: previously married, or divorced: former religious): _____
Children: (names and ages) _____

Votum of local diocesan ordinary of place where the Petitioner is currently residing, as to the absence of scandal if the petition is granted:

Votum of Major Superior:

Place:_____ Date:_____

Signature (of Instructor of the Case): _____
(Seal of the Province, or Congregation/Order)

CHAPTER EIGHT

APOSTOLATE

BEVERLY K. DUNN, S.P.[1]

INTRODUCTION

Of the various dimensions of religious life, the apostolate probably involves an individual religious the most directly. Religious institutes participate in the mission of the Church by their very nature. This participation comes about through two agencies. Individual members do so by virtue of their baptism (c. 204). Religious institutes undertake the mission in a new and more stable manner through their members' total consecration by the profession of the evangelical counsels and the life of prayer and penance (c. 573). The witness of consecrated life itself serves as the primary apostolate of a religious. For members of contemplative institutes, the apostolate consists in their sacrifice of praise leading to a life rich in holiness (c. 674). Apostolic institutes participate through apostolic action in service of others which proceeds from union with God and is conducted in communion with the Church (c. 675).

The law always uses the word "apostolate" to designate the lay faithful's participation in the mission of the Church distinguishing it from the term "ministry," which it uses for ordained clergy. The code came at just the time when Catholic language was changing. Often "apostolate" will refer to the same concept as "ministry" in today's common usage. Interestingly, the early 20th century saw precisely the same progression regarding the term "apostolate."[2]

---

[1] Kathleen Ann Bierne, P.B.V.M, Joyce Hoben, S.N.D.N, and Kevin D. O'Rourke, O.P. contributed to the writing of this chapter.
[2] Richard A. Hill, S.J., "The Apostolate of Institutes: Canons 673-683," in *A Handbook on Canons 573-746*, edited by J. Hite, T.O.R, S. Holland, I.H.M, and D. Ward, O.S.B, (Collegeville: The Liturgical Press, 1985), 197-198.

Today, many apostolic institutes exercise their apostolate both through sponsoring institutions of education and charity and through the works of their individual members. The code addresses the topic of apostolate primarily in terms of the institute's corporate works (cc. 673-683). However, it also recognizes the works of individual religious (for example, see cc. 665; 671; 682).

A religious institute's constitutions, rules, and policies will give more detailed directives concerning the apostolate than the general ones given in universal law. Thus, the following considerations must always be read in that light.

Apostolate of Religious Institutes as Part of the Apostolate of the Church

Conciliar documents and the code treat the apostolate of religious institutes in a two dimensional manner, as an integral characteristic of religious life and as part of the mission of the Church (c. 675).[3] The apostolate's integral character allows religious institutes to enjoy a just autonomy of life and governance concerning their apostolic works subject to the authority of the diocesan bishop (cc. 586; 673; 678, §1). Some institutes enjoy the privilege of exemption, removing them from the jurisdiction of the local bishop for the greater good of the universal Church (c. 591). Concurrently, religious institutes, including exempt religious institutes, participate in the life of a diocese in communion with and under the authority of the diocesan bishop.

Mutual Relationship between the Bishop and Religious Superiors in the Apostolate

The overlapping authority of religious superiors and bishops leads to the necessity for both to proceed by means of mutual consultation and acknowledgment of each other's role (c. 678, §3). The law singles out certain areas requiring particular care regarding this coordination.

---

[3] *LG* 12; *PC* 8; *CD* 33-35; *AA* 20d, 23.

Preaching

Baptism and religious profession charge religious to proclaim the gospel in a variety of ways (cc. 211; 758). At the same time, they are subject to the bishop and to the norms given by the episcopal conference regarding how that preaching is to be carried out in a particular diocese. This particularly applies to lay preaching in churches. The bishop can both restore and take away the right of a particular religious cleric from preaching in the diocese (cc. 386, §1; 764).

Catechetical and Liturgical Formation

Catechetics, which includes liturgical formation, should play a part in the apostolic life of all religious, according to the requirements of the character of their institute and the apostolate itself (c. 776). Bishops are to issue norms concerning catechetical matters in his diocese which also bind religious (c. 775).

Public Exercise of Divine Worship

All religious are subject to the diocesan bishop in the "public exercise of divine worship" (c. 678, §1). Generally, this refers to the exercise of divine worship involving many people, open to all and known by many, as opposed to non-public, private, individual, or small group exercise of divine worship. The difference between a community Mass and a parish Mass would illustrate this point. However, all exercise of divine worship must conform to the general liturgical norms of the Church. Because of the public nature of even private worship, such as devotional practices, these too fall within the power of the bishop if they are not beneficial to the "proper care of souls," or do not conform with truth (cc. 834, §2; 846, §1). In practice, this area requires the utmost dialogue and respect for both autonomy and authority on the part of major superiors and bishops.

Catholic Schools and Religious and Moral Education

Canon 804 directs the bishop to see that teachers of the Catholic religion follow correct doctrine, witness to Christian living, and possess pedagogical skill. He may name, move, or remove them or demand their removal if such is required for reasons of religion or morals (c. 805). This can obviously cause many difficulties if he does it without respect for due process. The major superior's role consists in seeing that policies are in place and followed, particularly in institutions sponsored by the institute. The superior also must assure a level of dialogue that handles problems prior to major difficulties, generally by clear contracts and job descriptions, as well as identifiable criteria for both hiring and employment severance.

Even institutes or societies whose mission is education require the diocesan bishop's permission to establish a school (c. 801). This permission may also extend to other means of providing religious education or catechetics.

Media Apostolate

The Church encourages its ministers to make use of the instruments of social communication (cc. 822-832). It calls on national episcopal conferences to establish norms for the participation of both clerics and religious in radio and television programs which deal with questions concerning Catholic teaching or morals (c. 831, §2). In 1984, the NCCB determined that each bishop would establish guidelines for his own diocese.[4] Canon 832 requires religious to receive permission from their major superiors to publish works in the written media on religion or morals. Some cases require the permission of the bishop, namely in publications that are customarily inimical to the Catholic faith (canon 831, §1).[5]

Apostolic Works of an Institute

The law approaches the apostolate of religious as activities of a religious institute and most often locates those activities within the structure of a religious house. The term "religious house" designates a formally founded, stable community under the authority of a superior. A religious house differs from a number of religious working and living in a local area. It indicates an institute's ongoing commitment to the mission of the Christ and the Church in a local area. A religious house or local community may only be founded with the written permission of the bishop (c. 609, §1).

Works Proper to an Institute

Institutes must strive to preserve their spiritual patrimony, including their mission and proper works (c. 677, §§1-2). The founders and early members undertook these works, or they were introduced as a result of signal events in an institute's history. The constitutions contain reference to them (c. 578). At the same time, religious institutes must adapt to changing circumstances (c. 677, see also c. 631). Once a religious institute establishes a house in a diocese, it may undertake the full range of its proper works by right, unless the permission of the bishop to found the house includes a restriction on its range of works (c. 611, 2°).

---

[4] National Conference of Catholic Bishops, *Implementation of the 1983 Code of Canon Law: Complementary Norms*, (Washington, D.C.: United States Catholic Conference, 1991) 9.

[5] Congregation of the Doctrine of the Faith, instruction, "Supervising the written media," in *Catholic International*, (1992) 756-776.

The permission to found a house also entitles clerical religious institutes to have a church within which they may conduct sacred ministries (c. 611, 3°). Since this church is not as such a parish church, the clerical religious must uphold parochial rights, observing the law concerning faculties for hearing confession and marriages, as well as any diocesan norms on preaching (cc. 966-976 and 1109-1112). Additionally, they need the bishop's permission concerning the particular place of building it (c. 1215, §3).

Apostolic Works Entrusted to a Religious Institute

The diocesan bishop may entrust apostolic works such as a parish, a school, or a social service agency to a religious institute (cc. 681, 790). In these cases, the bishop and the competent superior of the institute are to make a written agreement, including, among other things:

- The work to be done;
- The members to be assigned; and
- Financial arrangements.

This agreement does not include the permission to engage in the full range of works proper to the institute as in canon 611. A work may be entrusted to an individual religious rather than the religious institute. This arrangement requires both the consent of the religious superior and a written agreement (*Eclesiae sanctae* I, 31). When the work involves the conferral of ecclesiastical office, the diocesan bishop makes the appointment (c. 602).

Religious institutes or individual religious conduct the entrusted works under the authority and direction of the bishop or his delegate, perhaps a pastor. For example, the chancery, rather than religious superiors, would process indults of alienation for such a work. However, this organization does not prejudice the authority of religious superiors with regard to their own members. Neither does it excuse superiors from the duty to exercise vigilance over the work, lest the institute be held responsible for mismanagement by their members in charge (cc. 681 and 1289). Thus, superiors may inspect the financial accounts of entrusted works.

If a parish is established within a clerical religious institute's church, a proper agreement should be made between the diocese and the institute. In these cases, the institute maintains ownership of its property while the property of the juridic person of the parish is separate from that of the institute. The agreement may regulate such matters as the disposition of free-will offerings to the parish, etc.

Organized Collaboration

Canon 680 restates numerous calls for an organized cooperation among religious institutes and between them and the secular clergy in planning for the apostolate of a diocese, under the direction of the bishop.[6] Institutes may not invoke just autonomy or exemption to justify choices in the apostolate conflicting with the organic communion called for in a healthy ecclesial life of a diocese.[7] Various kinds of actions can respond to this call, such as a diocesan organization of religious institutes which would promote communication and understanding among them. Religious institutes may participate in diocesan pastoral planning processes. In some regions, coalitions of religious congregations are pooling their resources to initiate new apostolic works in response to new needs.

New Apostolic Works

The experience of the last thirty years has led many religious institutes to re-evaluate their proper works, as canon 677 directs. Many have withdrawn from traditional works and initiated new ones. Frequently, these new endeavors have come about through the initiative of individuals. Any new apostolic action must remain consistent with the constitutive elements of an institute's way of life, such as:

- Its understanding of its proper works;
- The vowed status of its members, including the obligation to common life;
- Discernment of the members' gifts and abilities; and
- The common good of the individual, of the institute, of those served, and of the Church

If a religious institute decides to begin a new work, it does so with a commitment to that work's future beyond the involvement of its founders. However, that commitment may not guarantee the institute's own members as future staff. Rather, it may entail such resources as governance or association

---

[6] *CD* 35-36; *AG* 32-33; *MR* 21, 62-66.
[7] John Paul II, apostolic exhortation, *Vita Consecrata* 49, 25 March 1996, in *Origins*, 25 (1995-1996), 697.

with other established works. Nor will the new work necessarily become part of the institute's proper works. Before instituting a new work, the institute should ask itself some *fundamental questions*:

- Is this new work in the best interests of those served?
- Does it contribute to the mission and public witness of the institute and of the Church?
- How will the new work relate to the bishop?
- Is this new work an appropriate response to the needs, given the resources available?
- How will the institute and the participating individual members live up to their mutual responsibilities of:

    Dependence, limitation of use, disposition of goods?

    Supervision, evaluation, guidance, mutual support?

    Sharing of common life?

    Commitment for the future of this work?

If the institute does decide to initiate the new work, it then must attend to some *practicalities*:

- Building broad-based support among the members of the institute;
- Determining the civil and canonical structural arrangements;
- Developing a strategic plan;
- Formulating a written agreement, acceptable to all parties if the enterprise is a collaborative venture, including:

    Clear lines of accountability and periodic reviews of the work for the purpose of protecting the mission and assuring proper functioning;

    Financial responsibilities, including liability protection;

    Personnel policies, including qualifications, hiring and firing procedures for their own members;

    Means of ending the work and distributing the assets;

    Identifying the personnel to work in the new venture and the scope of their involvement.

Modifying an Apostolic Work

As needs and resources change, religious institutes may find themselves in need of changing the character of their apostolic works. Three principles may guide these choices:

- Religious institutes are to remain true to the mission and the works proper to the institute, while continually adapting them to today's needs (c. 677, §1);
- The bishop coordinates the works of the apostolate in his diocese in mutual consultation with religious superiors (cc. 394, §1; 678, §3);
- Religious superiors must obtain the consent of the bishop in order to change the purpose of a work located in the context of an established religious house/community (c. 612).

The law does not define what constitutes a change of apostolate. Some changes; such as the addition of new degree programs to a college or university, or the addition of a hospice program to an acute care hospital; can indicate growth and development, rather than change. A true change in the apostolate would involve a change of activity producing a new service in the apostolic life of the diocese. In the long run, it is critical to involve the diocesan bishop in the consultation with religious superiors in the development or changes in apostolates.

The process of changing from one apostolate to another differs, depending upon the canonical designation of the apostolic work in question. A work *entrusted* to a religious institute requires the bishop to change its nature (c. 681). However, he must consult with the religious superiors on the matter (c. 678, §3).

A work *proper* to an institute enjoys greater latitude insofar as changing an apostolate is concerned. Permission to establish itself in a diocese gives an institute the right to carry out its proper works (c. 611). Even then, religious institutes have a serious responsibility to consult with the bishop who coordinates the apostolic activity of the diocese before making substantial changes. An apostolic work associated with an established religious house requires his consent to change its nature (c. 612).

Termination of or Withdrawal from an Apostolic Work

If circumstances indicate that the viability of a particular work has ceased, an institute may deem it best to terminate it or withdraw from it. Major superiors can suppress a proper work of an institute not associated with a legitimately established religious house (c. 611). But again, they are to do so in consultation with the bishop as coordinator of the apostolate of the diocese. The supreme moderator can suppress a legitimately established house and its associated works after consulting the bishop (c. 616).

The termination of a work entails the necessity to distribute its assets. If the work is owned by an entity of the religious institute, the assets revert to the next highest level, for example the province or general administration level, always keeping in mind the intentions of the donors of the assets (c. 123). If the work received civil incorporation, then its distribution of assets would be governed by civil law and the articles of incorporation, which could have stipulated that they go to the institute as a whole, or one of its units.

In other circumstances, the work's viability may remain strong but the institute may determine that withdrawing its personnel and resources for distribution elsewhere would better serve the needs of people. The work continues but without the involvement of the religious institute which had taken responsibility to assure its mission as part of the Church's apostolate. Under the new arrangements the religious institute no longer maintains this responsibility. As part of the withdrawal process, the institute needs to help the new directors of the work make the transition by answering some *fundamental questions*:

- Will the work remain part of the Church's mission?
- If yes, who is going to take responsibility for assuring that mission?
- What kind of structural relationship to the Church will this new entity take?

In the case of withdrawal from a work rather than its closure, the institute usually can claim only those assets for which it can prove prior claim, such as unpaid salaries, loans, etc. The institute needs to attend as well to the transfer of ownership through the sale of the work if this action was not taken previously.

Apostolate and Individual Religious

Often the challenge for religious institutes today lies in the re-articulation of their traditional values and expectations into what may appear as radically individualistic ministry or employment environments.

Ecclesiastical Offices Entrusted to Individual Religious

A bishop may entrust an ecclesiastical office to a member of a religious institute (c. 682). Or he may entrust to an institute a work which by definition includes an ecclesiastical office, as in the case of a parish with its office of pastor. Canon 145, §1, defines an ecclesiastical office as any function constituted in a stable manner by divine or ecclesiastical law to be exercised for a spiritual purpose. The code identifies a number of offices reserved to priests, such as vicar general, pastor, and parochial vicar. Other offices, including tribunal collegial judge, chancellor, and finance officer, do not require ordination. In addition, a bishop may establish ecclesiastical offices for his diocese by decree. A bishop may entrust these offices to individual religious.

Canons 682 and 145-96 present some basic principles concerning ecclesiastical offices and religious:

- A bishop may appoint a religious to an ecclesiastical office either on presentation by or with the approval of the religious' competent superior (c. 682, §1). Thus, a religious superior does not appoint a pastor of a parish. He presents a candidate to the bishop, who appoints him.
- Most dioceses require testimonials from major superiors concerning a candidate's suitability and moral character before conferring an office on a religious;
- Either a bishop or the religious' competent superior may remove a religious from an ecclesiastical office. Each must notify the other, but neither requires the other's consent (c. 682, §2). The removal must be made in writing (c. 194, §4). Financial obligations may not necessarily cease with removal from office.

Though this canon does not require a statement of cause by either the bishop or the religious superior in the removal of a religious, the bishop would be bound by canon 193, §3, which requires a just cause for removal. By profession of obedience, the religious is at the disposition of the religious superior for works of the apostolate. However, justice would indicate making a statement of cause, especially if culpability were involved. Canons 1740-1752 on the removal or transfer of pastors do not apply to religious priests. A religious may appeal removal from an ecclesiastical office through the usual appeal processes (cc. 1732-1739). Provision of ecclesiastical office is also governed through provisions of the law (c. 194):

- The candidate for an ecclesiastical office must be in communion with the Church and qualified (c. 149);
- Offices entailing the full care of souls may only be held by priests (c. 150);
- An office which is not vacant cannot be conferred on another (c. 153, §1);

- A promise of an office, no matter by whom it is made, has no juridic effect (c. 153, §3);
- The provision of any office must be made in writing (c. 156);
- The loss of an ecclesiastical office is to be communicated in writing (cc. 186; 193, §4).

A number of positions in the diocese and parishes are considered administrative positions, rather than offices, for example, staff assistants, secretarial staff, etc. Diocesan personnel policies may address these positions. Otherwise, the law could be applied in these instances in a way analogous to its provisions for the diocesan level offices. At the same time, the Church, as an employer, must meticulously observe the civil laws pertaining to labor and social policy including paying its employees a just and decent wage (c. 1286).

Individual Religious Initiating New Works

An individual religious rather than an institute may initiate a new apostolic work. In these cases the institute supports the work through its approval and support of the religious but makes no further commitment to the work's future. The religious together with the institute must undertake a discernment of *fundamental questions*:

- Is this new work an appropriate expression of the institute's mission and apostolate?
- Is this new work good for the individual religious?
- Is it consistent with the apostolate of the local Church?
- Is it good for those served?
- How will the individual religious and the institute live out their mutual responsibilities?

It must also attend to some *practicalities*:

- Careful planning by the individual made in dialogue with the institute's leadership;
- Communication with the institute's membership and the bishop about the scope and appropriateness of the individual's new work;

Formulation of a written agreement among the relevant parties concerning:

- Clear lines of accountability and periodic reviews of the work for purposes of protecting the mission;
- Financial concerns;
- A means of assuring the professional growth of the religious;
- Financial and legal responsibilities, including such items as: sources of income, insurance, taxes, liabilities, agency, licenses, supervision, relationship with the institute's civil corporation(s);
- Any necessary legal contracts and documents ensuring an arms-length relationship between the religious congregation and a separate corporate entity.

The institute, which has discerned that the new work relates to its own mission, gives a mandate to the individual religious. It also recognizes the individual's continued commitment to the vows and the common life.

Governance of Apostolic Works

Apostolic works of religious institutes operate as part of the apostolate of the local Church. Their governance falls under the authority both of the bishop and of the superiors of the institute (cc. 586; 678; 806, §1). However, the law only gives directives to the bishop about governing works of the apostolate.

The Responsibility of the Bishop

FOSTERING AND COORDINATING THE APOSTOLATE

The bishop fosters the various forms of the apostolate in his diocese, as much as possible assuring a balance of services to a broad range of people in all parts of the territory (c. 394). Religious institutes are to contribute to the apostolate according to their spiritual patrimony and discipline (cc. 677, §1; 678, §2).

VISITATION

The bishop exercises oversight of apostolic works through visitation. At least every five years he is to visit persons and Catholic institutes, including churches, oratories, schools open to the public, and other works of the apostolate (cc. 397, §1; 683, §1; 806, §1).

CORRECTION OF ABUSES

If the bishop becomes aware of abuses concerning apostolic works of religious, he is to issue a warning to the superior. If this proves in vain, he can deal with the situation by his own authority (cc. 392, §2; 683, §2). The generality of these canons poses one of the greatest potentials for conflict between bishops and religious. Situations require mutual respect and delicacy of procedure. If an individual religious or an institute feels wronged in such an action, it can appeal to the Holy See.

FORBIDDING AN INDIVIDUAL RELIGIOUS TO RESIDE IN A DIOCESE

For the gravest reasons, a bishop may enact the drastic measure of forbidding a religious to reside in his diocese (c. 679). He must have informed the religious superior beforehand of his intent and the reason for it and not have received a satisfactory response. The bishop must immediately report the action to the Holy See. Some questions go unanswered in this case. For example, what happens if the religious belongs to an autonomous monastery or to a congregation with no houses outside the diocese in question? Furthermore, a priest in such a situation would lack faculties to absolve sins and to preach. The individual religious can appeal the decision to the Holy See.

FORBIDDING A RELIGIOUS INSTITUTE TO CONDUCT
AN APOSTOLIC WORK IN THE DIOCESE

The law makes no specific provision allowing a bishop to prohibit a religious institute to continue to conduct its proper work in his diocese once a religious institute has been established. He is the coordinator of the apostolate of the diocese. He may withdraw an entrusted work from the care of religious institute according to the provisions of the original written agreement. If conflicts between bishops and religious institutes reach this very serious state, they can be referred to the Holy See.

The Responsibility of the Religious Superiors

Canon law makes rather extensive provisions for the administration of apostolic works.[8] However, it says very little about the governance and oversight of apostolic works by superiors of religious institutes. What it does provide concerning the governance role of superiors comes within the context of the governance of members of the institute, rather than apostolic works (cc. 617-630). Canon 678 directs that religious are subject to their superiors in the exercise of the apostolate. The

---

[8] See *Code of Canon Law*, Chapter V, "The Temporal Goods of the Church."

traditional model for the governance and administration of apostolic works consisted of the superior of the local community also serving as the administrator of the associated apostolic work. One rarely finds that model today.

If the responsibility for governance and oversight of an apostolic work does not reside in the superior of a local community associated with the work, then it resides in a higher level, that of major superiors on the general or provincial level. Chapters also have a governance role to play in apostolic works. Since the law does not provide information about the authority of these superiors regarding apostolic works, one can propose the following in parallel to the functions outlined for a bishop. These considerations assume that superiors work in conjunction with their councils and chapters.

SUPERIOR OF MEMBERS OF THE INSTITUTE PARTICIPATING IN ITS MISSION

A superior's primary role and concern relates to the members of the institute. Thus, the superior fosters participation by the members in the apostolate of the institute. The superior:

- Encourages members to offer their gifts to the apostolate according to their talents and the needs of the time and place;
- Assigns members to, or at least approves their involvement in, a particular work;
- Assures that the members are professionally qualified for their apostolic works.

COORDINATOR OF APOSTOLIC WORKS

Religious institutes can offer only a finite number of personnel or other resources to the mission of the Church. Superiors must make choices concerning the allocation and coordination of those resources in the face of the urgent needs of people. This may entail determining the kinds of works, or the places in the world that an institute will focus its resources. It may involve determining the decision-making process that an institute and its members will use in assigning its personnel. While a bishop coordinates the apostolate of the diocese, an institute coordinates its involvement in the apostolate of Church, often in several dioceses.

RESPONSIBLE FOR OVERSIGHT AND VIGILANCE

An Apostolic Work

An institute's commitment to an apostolic work brings with it an obligation for its oversight. Failure to exercise adequate oversight can leave an institute legally liable for misadministration of the work or worse. Some of the means superiors may use for oversight can include:

- Assessment of the work's participation in the institute's mission and response to the needs of people;
- use of reporting processes;
- approval of some categories of decisions, such as purpose, policies, etc;
- visitation.

An Individual Religious

If an individual religious is employed in a work of the religious institute, major superiors possess the same obligation of oversight of the member as they do for other employees and works of the institute. The same would hold true regarding members who participate in a work where the institute's leadership has decision-making power over its assets and philosophy.

Major superiors do not possess an obligation for oversight of particular apostolic actions of members employed in other settings. Rather, the superior's concern would revolve around the question of how such activities facilitate a member's participation in the mission of the institute.

Correction of Abuses

The obligation for oversight and vigilance over apostolic works and individual members brings with it the need to be able to correct abuses. Some methods could include:

- reassignment of members.
- hiring and firing key personnel in an apostolic work.
- enforcement of policies.

In all their actions, superiors must be mindful of due process for all and their members' rights in both civil and canon law.

Apostolic Works in Civil Society

Members of religious institutes exercise their ministry and operate apostolic works in civil society as well as the ecclesial society. Thus they must follow civil law as well as canon law in the apostolate. The institute and the individual religious have a responsibility wherever possible to arrange civil structures to honor the obligations of religious life and the apostolate. Very often, the interaction of canon law and civil law becomes relevant in the areas of finances and liability.

Remuneration

In virtue of their vow of poverty, everything a religious acquires through personal labor or on behalf of the institute by way of gift, offering, stipend, fee, salary, pension, insurance settlement, or similar manner, belongs to the religious institute and not the individual religious (c. 668, §3). The vow of poverty includes any work and its royalties. Copyrights should be held in the name of the religious institute. If religious are dispensed from their vows and leave religious life, social security benefits and the like accompany them and no longer belong to the institute.

Religious institutes must follow IRS regulations in order to maintain their non-taxable designation. These include: 1) religious working in an apostolic positions as mandated by their superiors; and 2) turning the control of their income over to the institute.[9] Even though institutes may be exempt from taxation, an individual religious might be subject to paying taxes. One should consult an attorney expert in taxation.

In light of current Catholic social teaching and the needs of the institute, religious need to work toward the goal of just compensation for their services:

- ♦ Religious seeking employment in diocesan-sponsored work should make themselves aware of the compensation package appropriate to their positions. Ordinarily they should not negotiate for less without approval of their leadership. The packages vary from diocese to diocese.

    Religious seeking employment outside the diocesan structure should seek a compensation package commensurate with their experience, education, and level of responsibility;

---

[9] Due to the complexity and changeable nature of IRS regulations, they cannot be included here.

In some institutes those who seek employment in positions of direct service to the poor which cannot provide just salaries may apply for partial subsidy or grants from designated ministerial funds from the institute if such is provided;

- Those who free-lance services or manage independent apostolates are accountable to their leadership and their finance offices for the financial parameters of their remuneration.

If an apostolic work is recognized as Catholic by the diocesan bishop, it may be listed in the *Official Catholic Directory* and use the IRS group tax exemption granted to the Catholic Church.

Liabilities

Religious Institutes and Incorporated Works

Traditionally charitable institutions could not be sued. However, that protection ended decades ago. In response, many apostolic works civilly incorporated as non-profit corporations. Incorporation provides the benefit of civilly separating the assets of the work from those of the institute and thereby limiting the institute's liability. A non-profit civil corporation possesses a legal identity separate from those who govern it. As a result, governing boards have limited personal liability for the corporation's debts, as long as they are acting only in their corporate capacity (as employee, officer, director) without intention to defraud.

The religious institute must take care to respect the reality of the separation of the incorporation, lest the corporation be interpreted as mere formality and the institute lose its protection from liability. An institute can demonstrate the separation through different names, assets, logos, addresses, and boards of directors. An institute can also lose its protection if it gains economically from the corporation beyond fees for services rendered or if it exerts undue control in the governance of the corporation. A religious institute can structure the separately incorporated work in such a way that those responsible for the religious institute assure the work's fundamental purposes and integrity.[10] Canonical commentators vary in their opinions about the effect of civil incorporation on the works' canonical status in terms of governance. An institute needs to consult a canonist when structuring a civil corporation for a work.

---

[10] A.J. Maida and N.P. Cafardi, *Church Property, Church Finances and Church-Related Corporations: A Canon Law Handbook*, St. Louis, MO, The Catholic Health Association, 1984, pp. 189-215.

Religious Institutes and Individual Religious

The individual religious and the religious institute and its civil law corporation are separate legal entities. There is nothing in the relationship between the individual and the institute that automatically renders the congregation liable for all the actions of its members. Rather, the vows create a canonical relationship with canonical obligations. Permission to engage in an apostolate is a canonical, religious affair and does not create an employment relationship between the individual and the institute. Nor do the vows render all actions of the individual as works of the institute. On the other hand, there are questions concerning agency and *respondeat superior*. When the possibility of such questions can arise, the institute should consult its attorney.

Membership in a religious institute does not alter the position of an individual before the civil law. Individual members of religious institutes have exactly the same rights and obligations before the civil law, as well as exposure to liability, as do any other individuals. The major difference lies in the fact that a member of the Catholic Church operates under two legal systems: canonical and civil.

Because being subject to canon law does not deprive individual religious of any personal civil rights regarding third parties, they maintain the civil law right to enter into contracts, to sue and to be sued, to acquire and dispose of property. Although generally the individual religious must obtain permission from the canonical superiors to exercise these rights (c. 639), the civil law validity of the exercise is not affected by the failure to obtain the permission.

SPONSORED WORKS

In the last few decades, the relationship between many religious institutes and the institutions they founded has changed due to a number of factors, such as new needs, a redistribution or diminishment of personnel, etc. Many institutions of charity have evolved into large, complex social institutions serving as an integral part of the public social service system. This has led to new forms of governance of institutions and a complex of structural relationships to religious institutes, described by the term "sponsorship."

Sponsorship is neither a canon law nor a civil law term. It has developed as a practical response to new realities, permitting religious institutes to provide stable governance for charitable and educational institutions, while assuring their primary mission of continuing the Lord's saving action toward people. The sponsoring religious institute may not be able to take part in all the activities of the institution, but it does provide its name, oversight, and control in critical areas of the institution's life. Sponsors can serve to guarantee an institution's Catholicity.

Relationship to the Religious Institute

Religious institutes may participate in the institution's life in a wide range of degrees, from close involvement to only the matters of governance. The institutions, in turn, may operate as part of larger systems or coalitions of institutions. Not all of the components of these systems need to relate to the sponsoring religious institute. The relationships of the sponsoring religious institutes can be categorized in three broad categories.

Governance Relationship

A governance relationship describes the situation in which a religious institute retains primary responsibility for an institution's governance. The institute may hold the institution as part of its own assets and govern it as part of itself. On the other hand, the institution may have received separate incorporation, where the articles of incorporation and the by-laws place the responsibility of its governance ultimately in the hands of the superiors of the religious institute. Some of the various ways of formulating the civil documents to accomplish this situation could include:

- Identifying the major superior and council as the board of directors of the institution.
- Requiring that the institute's members, appointed or approved by the major superior, comprise a certain percentage of the board of directors of the institution.
- Using a membership corporation structure, where certain decisions, such as approval of the board of directors, the mission statement, certain financial activities, etc., are reserved to a panel of persons (the members of the corporation) appointed or approved by the institute. The major superior and council or others appointed by them could comprise the panel. In this category of relationship, the ultimate responsibility for governance rests with the religious institute, which assures the Catholic identity of the institution.

An Influence Relationship

A religious institute may participate in the sponsorship of an institution or an aggregate of institutions, while acting in partnership with others, Catholic or not. The institute enters into such a partnership by means of a formal agreement on the issues of purpose and structure, which cannot violate fundamental Catholic values. If the institute holds a position of major partner, then it can exert considerable influence on the formulation of that agreement and the handling of new issues as they arise. For example, if a religious institute sponsors a school, a hospital, or a healthcare system and enters into equal or majority member partnership with other education, or healthcare institutions, the religious institute can exercise considerable influence over the governance decisions of the new entity. Usually, the greater the holdings of a partner, the greater potential for influence. The resultant new entity may or may not retain a Catholic identity, as determined by the formal agreement and the approval of the bishop.

An Advocacy Relationship

At other times, collaborative agreements may result in a religious institute sponsoring a minor component of a larger entity. Again, such a partnership requires a formal agreement, which cannot violate fundamental Catholic values. In this case, the institute usually can exercise only a reduced level of authority. Its role becomes one of advocacy to assure that the new entity never forget its responsibility to justice and the poor. For example, if a religious institute sponsors a healthcare or social service agency that joins a larger system comprised of a number of components, the institute may not be able to exercise major influence in governance decisions. However, it can always raise the issue of attending to Gospel values in making those decisions. Again, the formal agreement and the approval of the bishop would determine any Catholic identity of the new entity.

Catholic Identity

Sponsorship concerns Catholic identity, among other things. Since the Catholic identity of institutions relates primarily to the mystery of the Church, no single formulation can completely capture its essence. However, all expressions recognize that Catholic institutions participate in the mission of Jesus, which includes two kinds of elements: the internal faith response to Jesus Christ and the external practicalities of belonging to a visible Church with institutional structures. The Second Vatican Council expresses this as communion.[11] Communion finds its source in relationships, which by their nature can never remain static, implying the possibility of various levels and degrees.

---

[11] *LG* 1, *passim*. See also, John Paul II, apostolic exhortation, *Christifideles laici* 30, 30 December 1988, in *Origins*, 18 (1988-1989), p. 575.

Faith Dimensions of Catholic Identity

While no comprehensive presentation of the faith dimension of all Catholic institutions exists, one has been formulated for a Catholic institution of higher education, which states that:

> By institutional commitment it brings to its task the inspiration and light of the Christian message. Catholic ideals, attitudes and principles penetrate and inform its activities. It operates as an institution in which Catholicism is vitally present and active.[12]

Structural Relationships in the Church

A variety of forms of structural relationships between the Church and people and organizations of the apostolate are possible. Apostolic works may have begun as the proper works of a religious house. However, in many cases the house has been suppressed, while the work continues with fewer, if any religious, present. What, if anything, happens to the status of these works? Other works may have been established with no reference to a religious house or with no long-term commitment of a religious institute. What status in the Church's apostolate do these works possess? Answers to these and other questions are still evolving.

JURIDIC PERSONALITY

Catholic entities may receive juridic personality which gives them rights and obligations in the Church, similar to physical persons (cc. 113-123). This personality compares quite closely to corporations in civil law. The law itself recognizes some organizations as juridic persons: dioceses, parishes, seminaries, religious institutes, their provinces and houses, etc. Ecclesiastical authority, i.e., the Holy See, the conference of bishops, or the diocesan bishop, can establish other juridic persons by decree (c. 116). A juridic person participates in the mission of the Church and is recognized as Catholic. It in turn must maintain communion with the Church and is subject to some degree of oversight by ecclesiastical authority.

The law recognizes two kinds of juridic persons, public and private (c. 116). A public juridic person fulfills a specific allotted spiritual or temporal role congruent with the mission of the Church and acts in the name of the Church. This role includes, works of piety, of the apostolate, or of charity, whether spiritual or temporal (c. 114, §2). As a public entity of the Church, its goods are ecclesiasti-

---

[12] John Paul II, apostolic constitution, *Ex corde Ecclesiae* 14, 25 September 1990, in *Origins*, 20 (1990- 1991), p. 269.

cal goods governed by canon law (cc. 1254-1298). It is more closely subject to the authority of the bishop or the Holy See than a private entity. A private juridic person acts to further the mission of the Church in its own name. It does not act as an agent of the Church (c. 116). Its goods are not ecclesiastical goods, so are not as subject to canon law. A private juridic person is less closely governed by a bishop than a public juridic person.

The Congregation for Institutes of Consecrated Life and Societies of Apostolic Life (CICLSAL) has been granting juridic personality for health care systems that cross diocesan boundaries and which currently or historically have belonged to individual or consortiums of religious institutes. Such requests are usually 3-4 pages long, spelling out the background history, the reasons for the request, and the consequences. A request for an institution operating completely within the boundaries of a single diocese should be directed to the diocesan bishop.

RECOGNITION AS CATHOLIC

A bishop, by means of a public document, may recognize an organization or institution as Catholic without establishing it as a juridic person (cc. 216; 300; 803; 808). The entity publicly participates in the mission of the Church while it remains a private endeavor under private governance. Since the entity's continued recognition depends on the bishop's ongoing acceptance of it as Catholic, it could serve both parties well to identify some basic elements for making the grant.[13]

Ecclesial Structures of Sponsored Institutions

Catholic institutions of the apostolate may receive a variety of forms of structural relationship with a religious institute and the Church. Religious institutes may be involved in the operation, management or governance of any of the following structures.

---

[13] An example of this kind of institution would consist of a school established by private individuals who run it as a Catholic school, have received public recognition of it by the bishop, but who have not sought to receive juridic personality for it.

Institutions with formal juridic ties to the Church

Institutions with formal ties to the Church would fall into one of three major categories:

- Institutions operating under a public juridic bond, either:

    Through participation in a public juridic person, such as a religious institute or a diocese. Most Catholic schools and healthcare institutions fall in this category, as well as many other institutions sponsored by religious institutes.

    Through their own public juridic personality obtained by virtue of their establishment by ecclesiastical authority.[14]

- Institutions operating under a grant of private juridic personality by ecclesiastical authority.

- Institutions recognized by ecclesiastical authority as Catholic.

Catholic entity managed under Catholic auspices, while owned and operated within a larger secular institutional framework

A Catholic campus within a largely secular hospital or school would illustrate this case. Contractual and civil law documents, as well as the local bishop, would specify the extent and manner of the unit's relationship with the Church. A religious institute could contract to manage or to operate the unit.

An institution which operates in the Catholic tradition and which incorporates that commitment into its civil law documents and policies but which does not possess formal juridic bonds to the Church

An institution's articles of incorporation may commit it to teach a Catholic curriculum, follow Catholic healthcare ethical guidelines, or require representation on its board of directors from a religious congregation. In this category, the facility would not possess juridic standing in the Church, because it is not integrated into a juridic person, such as a religious institute, nor has it received juridic personality from ecclesiastical authority. Canon law would not directly regulate such an institution but it would regulate individual Catholics involved. The facility

---

[14] For example, Catholic Healthcare Initiatives (CHI), headquartered in Denver, CO, a national healthcare system, includes healthcare institutions founded by over a dozen religious institutes. The system has obtained public juridic personality on its own and the original sponsoring institutes have withdrawn sponsorship from the component institutions. In return, the institutes provide members of the board of directors.

would require the bishop's permission to use the name Catholic (cc. 216, 803, §3, and 808). Many Catholic universities and other schools in the United States operate under this model. The board of directors could contract with a religious institute or with individual religious to operate, manage, or govern the institution.

An institution which operates in the Catholic tradition, but which possesses no civil or juridic bonds to the Church

In this category, the institution has not bound itself in either the civil or ecclesiastical sphere as a Catholic institution. The personal commitment of the governing authorities and staff maintains the ecclesial connection. Canon law would not apply to the facility itself. However, Catholics involved would be subject to some canonical regulations, such as the need for the bishop's permission to call the facility Catholic (c. 216). As in the previous example, the institution could make contractual arrangements with a religious institute or individual religious for its operation, management, or governance.

A secular institution, i.e., non-ecclesiastical institution, under the management of an ecclesiastical entity, such as a religious congregation

A non-ecclesial institution may contract with a religious institute to operate, manage or govern it. The agreement establishing this arrangement would regulate the situation, not canon law. Members of religious congregations, in the manner of all Catholics, would be bound by the obligation to maintain communion with the Church, as well as by their own proper law. An example of this arrangement could include a contract by a Catholic institution to manage an on-site food service.

Conclusion

As this chapter has shown, the apostolate remains an integral component of religious institutes. At the same time, its form and organization is undergoing rapid and dramatic change. A number of decades ago, most works of the apostolate consisted of works associated with established houses of religious. Today, religious engage in many different kinds of activities organized and governed in many different ways. New forms and relationships appear every year. While the law cannot be expected to anticipate these developments, it has proven flexible enough to accommodate their creation.

ASSIGNMENT FROM CONGREGATION

Date

Major Superior
Dear Member:

This letter assigns you (confirms your assignment to) ———— for the year ————.

[Closing remarks]

_____
Signature

_____
Major Superior

TESTIMONIAL LETTER OF PERMISSION TO A BISHOP

Date

Major Superior

Dear Bishop N:

I am writing to certify the suitability of ———, a member in good standing in ——— Institute.

She/He has permission to serve at (name of apostolic work) from ——— to ———.

Furthermore, I have carefully reviewed the personnel records which we maintain, and I have consulted with some who served with him(her) in the works assigned under our authority. Based on these inquiries, I testify to the best of my ability and assure you that ——— is a person of good moral character and reputation, and is qualified to serve in an effective and suitable manner in your (arch)diocese. In addition, also based on inquiry and to the best of my knowledge, I assure you that nothing in his/her background would limit or disqualify him(her) from assignment or cause serious scandal. (This would include such improper behaviors as: untreated problems with substance abuse, violations of celibacy, sexual impropriety, physical abuse, or financial impropriety.)

I hereby grant him(her) permission to minister in your (arch)diocese under your authorization.

A curriculum vitae including name, date of birth, place and date of profession of vows/ordination, formation/seminary, and previous assignments is enclosed.

_____
Signature

_____
Title

AGREEMENT BETWEEN A RELIGIOUS INSTITUTE AND A BISHOP CONCERNING MEMBERS WORKING IN AN (ARCH)DIOCESE

Parties to the Agreement: In accord with c. 681, §2, this agreement is entered into between the ——— Institute and the (Arch)diocese of ——— for the services of the following members of the Institute (list of members).

Duration of Agreement: The agreement for services shall begin ——— and extend through ———.

Terms of Service: (Listing of mutually agreed upon conditions of service.)

Compensation: The (Arch)diocese agrees to pay the Institute remuneration for services rendered under this agreement by members of the Institute as follows: (terms of agreement).

Termination: This agreement may be terminated or altered by mutual agreement of the parties. Termination can apply to one or more of the members listed or to all members who serve under this agreement. (details of notification process.)

Signatures of the Contracting Parties

By: _____ for _____
       Signature   (Arch)diocese

_____ for _____
       Title   Date

_____ for _____
       Signature   Institute

_____ for _____
       Title   Date

OUTLINE OF AN INTER-INSTITUTE AGREEMENT TO JOINTLY SPONSOR A WORK

Introduction
Parties to the Agreement

Provisions
Statement of Purpose of the Work
Governing Structure/Officers of the Work
Funding, Including Contributions by Participating Parties
Evaluation Structure
Dissolution Mechanism and Distribution of Assets

Signatures, Titles and Dates

CHAPTER NINE

TEMPORAL GOODS

DANIEL J. WARD, O.S.B.[1]

INTRODUCTION

The canonical norms regarding temporal goods would be entitled "the law of property" in American law. The law of property generally is concerned with the legal relationships between and among persons with respect to things. It includes the rights and the non-rights, the privileges and the duties, the authority and the non-authority with respect to things.

In the law of property, there are differences between categories and terminology between canon law and American law. Canon law categories property as *movable* and *immovable*, *fixed* and *free*. American law categories property as *real* and *personal*. While the categories of canon law and American law are generally equivalent, there are certain differences.

In American law, real property includes fixtures which are things built on, growing upon or fixed to land. A house is real property and the furnace in the house is a fixture and thus part of the real property. The canon law equivalent, immovable property, includes as fixtures only those things which are intended to be permanent and if removed would result in damage to the land. Thus a chandelier would be a fixture in American law, but not necessarily a fixture in canon law.

In American law cash is personal property while in canon law cash is not considered under property law unless it is formally designated by a competent authority or donor for a set purpose as fixed capital.

It is important when considering the canonical norms governing temporal goods to be aware of the differences in language and definition between canon law and American law.

---

[1] The author is grateful for the cooperation, comments and suggestions made by Sister Margaret Modde, OSF, Father Francis Morrisey, OMI, and Father Kevin Seasoltz, OSB, in the writing of this chapter.

ACQUISITION OF TEMPORAL GOODS

General Principles

Religious institutes, secular institutes, and societies of apostolic life are to follow the provisions of Book V on "The Temporal Goods of the Church" for acquiring, possessing, administering, and alienating temporal goods (cc. 635, 718, 741, §1). Most of the canons of Book V regulating the acquisition of temporal goods concern donations, bequests, taxation, fund raising, and prescription (cc. 1259-1272). The more important canons for an institute or a society are the canons regulating donations and bequests. While the canons parallel American law regarding the obligations attached to donations and bequests, the canons require approval of the person-in-charge for any donation or bequest that has a condition attached or has been given for a specific purpose (cc. 22, 1290, 1299, §2). The canons require authorization from the competent authority to conduct business or trade in the name of the institute or the society (cc. 286, 672).

There are specific canons governing alienation and business transactions having an adverse affect on the patrimonial condition of an institute or a society (cc. 638, 1292, 1295); however, these are treated below under Alienation since canon law considers alienation and such business transaction under a different title.

Particular Issues

PROPER LAW

Each institute or society may establish its own norms governing the acquisition of temporal goods as long as these norms are not contrary to canon law (c. 1257, §1). For example, an institute or a society could establish its own procedures for the purchase of property and the acceptance of donations and bequests beyond those stated in the *Code of Canon Law*.

THE TITLE *CATHOLIC*

The mere fact that an institute or a society acquires a non-Catholic institution does not mean that the acquired institution would be considered by the fact of the acquisition to be Catholic in canon law. The acquiring institute or society would have to decide whether or not the acquired institution is to be included in its patrimony. If it were to be included, then the acquired institution would be considered ecclesiastical goods according to canon law and would be considered Catholic. However, the acquired institution could only use the term "Catholic" in its title with the consent of the competent ecclesiastical authority (c. 216). While the canons do not define "competent ecclesiastical authority," the preferred opinion of the commentators is that in most instances the competent ecclesiastical authority would be the diocesan bishop.[2]

If the acquiring institute or society decides to "manage" the acquired institution but not to include it in the patrimony, the acquired institution does not become ecclesiastical property and is not subject to canon law.

THE AUTHORITY OF THE DIOCESAN BISHOP

The diocesan bishop has authority in certain instances when an institute or a society acquires property. If the institute or the society is already established within a diocese with the consent of the diocesan bishop, then the institute or the society has a right to engage in works proper to the institute or the society without further consent of the diocesan bishop unless the original consent limited the works of the institute or the society within the diocese (cc. 611, 733, §1). If the acquired property were in a diocese in which the institute or the society was not already located, the consent of the diocesan bishop would be required if the property were to become a religious house or an apostolate of the institute or the society. If the property were neither of these, but, for instance a vacation cabin or real property for investment purposes, the consent of the diocesan bishop would not be required since it would not be a religious house or an apostolate.

GRANTING CANONICAL JURIDIC PERSONALITY

If temporal goods acquired by an institute or a society become part of the patrimony of the institute or the society canonically the acquisition becomes ecclesiastical goods of the juridic person even if the acquisition were a separate civil entity.[3] However, the competent authority through a decree could grant the acquisition its own canonical juridic personality (cc. 114, §1, 116, §2).[4] This canonical separation would not be considered an alienation if the new juridic person remains subject to the same ultimate authority of the institute or the society.[5]

---

[2] See *The Code of Canon Law, A Text and Commentary*, Coriden, Green, and Heintschel, editors, New York: Paulist Press, 1985, p 120, canon 216.

[3] See the discussion under "The Title 'Catholic'" above.

[4] The competent authority would be the diocesan bishop or a congregation at the Apostolic See. The Congregation for Institutes of Consecrated Life and Societies of Apostolic Life holds that an institute or a society cannot grant the juridic personality.

[5] For instance, when an institute is divided into provinces by a decree, although each new province is a new juridic person, the new provinces remain under the same supreme moderator. Therefore, there is no alienation of the stable patrimony of the institute.

Administration of Temporal Goods

Introduction

This section covers the norms concerning administration of ecclesiastical good of an institute or a society. It does not directly consider "sponsorship" of an apostolate since this is covered in chapter eight.

General Principles

The structure of governance for an institute or a society consists of a superior, a council with both advise and consent duties according to law, and administrators responsible to the superior. Generally, canon law leaves the area of administration of temporal goods to the particulars of the proper law of each institute and society. However, there are a few requirements established in the code itself. First, each institute or society must have a financial administrator who is distinct from but who works under the direction of the superior (cc. 636, §1, 718, 741, §1). Second, since the institute or the society is a public juridic person, it must also have a financial council (c. 1280). Third, all administrators are to take an oath of office to perform their duties with diligence and care (c. 1283). The diligence and care is similar to the fiduciary obligations American law imposes on administrators (cc. 1284-1286).

Canon law has two categories of financial administration for an institute or a society: ordinary and extraordinary.[6] However, the law leaves it to each institute and society to define what is ordinary and what is extraordinary administration. Therefore, the proper law of each institute or society must specify when an administrator may act on his/her own in financial matters (ordinary administration) and when the administrator must receive the consent of another person or body[7] before acting (extraordinary administration).

While financial transactions such as a mortgage, an indebtedness, or a refinancing are not considered within the categories of ordinary or extraordinary administration but rather under the title of contracts and alienation (see below), note must be made here about such financial transactions. If such a financial transaction could adversely affect the patrimonial condition of the juridic person, the written permission of the competent superior with the consent of his/her council is required. If the transaction exceeds the amount set by the Apostolic See for the country in

---

[6] Canon 1277 creates a third category of administration for a diocese, namely acts of major importance.

[7] Often the body is either the council of the superior or a chapter of the institute or the monastery.

which the transaction is to take place, the approval of the Apostolic See is required (cc. 638, §3, 1292, §1). Each case must be examined individually to determine if it could have an adverse affect. As a general rule, however, all indebtedness would be considered to have an adverse affect. The conditions and procedure for obtaining the permissions and approval are considered below under "Alienation."

Issues

Civil Corporate Structures

While canon law does not mandate a particular civil structure to parallel the canonical juridic person's structure, it does require that the ownership of ecclesiastical goods be protected through civilly valid methods such as a corporation, a foundation, a trust, etc. (c. 1284, §2,2°). However, it is necessary to keep in mind a few canonical provisions when setting up the civil structure:

- The civil and the canonical structures should parallel one another as closely as possible to avoid having two widely divergent governing and managing structures. This can be a problem in establishing board structures and the officer of the civil entity. The role of the superior and council must be taken into account in the civil structure since canonically they are responsible for the governance and the management of the temporal goods of the juridic person.

- The internal management structures need to ensure that the canonical procedures for ordinary and extraordinary acts of administration, alienation, and business transactions adversely affecting the patrimonial condition of the juridic person are followed.

- Care must be taken not to alienate the stable patrimony of the institute or the society when constituting the governing board and its powers. If the make-up of the board and its powers results in the institute or the society losing effective control, this would be an alienation. In such a case, the procedures for alienation must be followed.[8]

A canonical alienation can be avoided in many instances by a carefully structured civil entity. At times a membership corporation with reserved powers and composed of members of the institute or the society can insure that the property or the institution is not alienated contrary to canon law. While the laws of the jurisdiction of incorporation must be observed, in most jurisdictions it is per-

---

[8] See the section entitled "Alienation of Ecclesiastical Goods."

mitted to reserve to the members at least the authority to approve various actions of the board of directors/trustees. If there are to be reserved powers they should include the approval of indebtedness, of amendments of the articles and the bylaws, of the transfer or the mortgaging of property, of the merger or the dissolution of the corporation, and of the mission statement along with the right to appoint at least some of the directors/trustees.

The Authority of the Diocesan Bishop

Generally the diocesan bishop does not have authority in the internal management of an institute or a society and its temporal goods. The exceptions are:

- A monastery which is autonomous AND is not associated juridically with a monastic congregation, federation, or confederation must give a yearly account of administration to the local ordinary[9] (cc. 615, 637). The consent of the local ordinary also is required for acts of extraordinary administration (c. 638, §4).
- The local ordinary has the right to be informed of the financial affairs of a religious house of diocesan right (c. 637).

---

[9] The term "local ordinary" is broader than the term "diocesan bishop." For the purposes of canons 637 and 638, local ordinary refers to a diocesan bishop, an administrator of a diocese, those who govern territories or communities which are similar to a diocese, vicar generals, and episcopal vicars c. 134).

Alienation of Ecclesiastical Goods

General Principles

The alienation of part or all of the stable patrimony[10], the alienation of goods donated to the church through a vow or goods which are especially valuable due to their artistic or historical value, and any business transaction which could adversely affect the patrimonial condition of a juridic person are subject to special canonical procedures (cc. 635, §1, 638, §3, 718, 741, §1, 1291, 1292). In such cases, the written consent of the competent superior with the consent of his/her council must be given. Proper law could require additional consents or approvals. If the amount of the alienation or business transaction exceeds the amount set by the Congregation for Institutes of Consecrated Life and Societies of Apostolic Life for the institutes and societies of the region the approval of the Congregation is also required.[11] When the approval is given by the Congregation, a tax may be charged for the approval. There is no set tax. The tax for an indebtedness approval is generally minimal, but the tax for an alienation approval could be higher, especially if the income from the alienation is not

---

[10] Stable patrimony is not defined in the *Code of Canon Law*. However, canon 1291 requires the stable patrimony of a juridic person to be so designated. designation may be explicit or implicit. Explicit designation is accomplished by an institute or a society specifically listing the properties as stable patrimony. Commentators disagree on implicit designation of stable patrimony.

In the *New Commentary on the Code of Canon Law* (CLSA, 2000, pp. 1495-1496), Robert Kennedy states that real property by its nature is part of the stable patrimony unless it has been explicitly designated not to be. On the other hand, in *The Church Finance Handbook* (CLSA 1999, pp. 249-252), Nicholas cafardi states the use or designated purpose determines whether or not real property is part of stable patrimony. cafardi concludes: "It has been the consistent praxis of canon law that those assets that are necessary to a public juridic person in order to accomplish the ends for which it was established are part of the stable patrimony of that juridic person and may not be freely alienated." (p. 252).

The author does not believe that it is possible to make a universal determination on what is included in stable patrimony except for those properties that have been explicitly so designated. Therefore, when an institute or a society decides to alienate property, it is necessary to make factual determination whether or not the property is part of its stable patrimony and subject to the norms of alienation.

To alleviate the dilemma, an institute or a society could establish canonical principles setting forth what will not be considered part of the stable patrimony. based on these principles, the institute or the society would designate future-acquired property as part of or not part of its stable patrimony

[11] The amount may or may not be the same as the amount set by the Congregation for Bishops for dioceses of the region. The United States presently has the same amount, $3 million, for dioceses, institutes, and societies.

needed by the institute or the society for a special purpose, such as the care for the elderly or payment of a debt or liability. In each case it is indicated in a separate bill attached to the approval. The payment of the tax should be sent to the Congregation for Institutes of Consecrated Life and Societies of Apostolic Life.

Procedures

- For both an alienation and a business transaction adversely affecting the patrimonial condition of the juridic person, the written consent of the competent superior with the consent of his/her council is required.
- In the case of an *alienation* which requires the approval of the Apostolic See, the following documentation is required:

   A petition addressed to the Congregation, signed by the competent superior and including the following:

   the request for approval to alienate a described property or fixed capital;

   the reasons for the alienation (c 1293, §1);

   the proposed use of the income, especially if it will be used for a need of the institute or the society;

   the portions or parcels which have already been alienated if the property is divisible (c 1292, §3);[12]

   an explanation if the property is being alienated for a price below the evaluation given by the experts (c 1294, §1);

   a statement that the consent of the council has been given.

   The opinion of two experts giving their evaluation of the property to be alienated (c. 1293, §2).

   The opinion of the diocesan bishop in whose diocese the property to be alienated is located.

   Any other pertinent information regarding the economic condition of the institute or the society.

---

[12] The inclusion of those parts which have previously been alienated must be mentioned; otherwise the approval by the Congregation is invalid (c. 1292, §3).

- In the case of a transaction which adversely affects the patrimonial condition of a juridic person, such as indebtedness, the following documentation is required:

    a petition addressed to the Congregation, signed by the competent superior, and including the following:

    the request;

    the reasons for the transaction;

    the financial condition of the juridic person;

    the effect of the transaction on the juridic person;

    the means of repaying the indebtedness (if applicable);

    the use of the money from the loan or bond issue (if applicable);

    a statement that the consent of the council has been given.

    the written estimate of two experts (if applicable);

    any other documents which may support the viability of the request.

- For both an alienation and a business transaction the documentation is to be addressed to the Congregation:

    The Congregation for Institutes of Consecrated Life and Societies of Apostolic Life
    Piazza Pio XII, 3
    00193 Rome, Italy

    If the institute or society has a procurator general or generalate at the Apostolic See, the documentation should be sent to the procurator general or the appropriate generalate official for presentation to the Congregation. It is best to send the packet by FedEx, UPS, or other private carrier rather than by international mail to insure prompt and accurate delivery.

If the institute or the society does not have a procurator general or a generalate in Rome, the documentation packet may be sent directly to the Congregation or through the courtesy of the Apostolic Nunciature. If the packet is sent through the courtesy of the Apostolic Nunciature the following procedures should be observed:

> place the documentation in a sealed envelop addressed to the Congregation;[13]

> address a letter to the Pro-Nuncio requesting that the enclosed packet be sent by diplomatic pouch to the Congregation. In the letter, state the contents of the packet, e.g. permission to sell a hospital;

> send the sealed envelop with the letter for the Nuncio to the Nunciature. This may be sent by regular mail. In the United States the address is:

>> The Apostolic Nunciature
>> 3339 Massachusetts Av NW
>> Washington, DC 20008

There is no charge by the Nunciature for use of the diplomatic pouch. This service of the Nunciature assures speedy and correct delivery of the packet.

Issues

The Amount Requiring the Approval of the Apostolic See

The amount of an alienation which triggers the need for the approval of the Apostolic See is the *valuation* of the property, not the amount to be received. If the valuation is less than the amount set for the region, but the offered price is greater, the approval of the Apostolic See is not required.

The valuation of the property is the net value, that is, the value after deducting all debts and liabilities on the property.[14]

---

[13] Some Nunciatures, such as in Canada, prefer that the envelop remain unsealed. It also may be left unsealed in the United States.

[14] Not all canonists accept the interpretation that the evaluation may be based on the net value of the property. It should be noted, however, that there is no authentic interpretation, and, therefore, a person may choose the most favorable interpretation.

In the case of indebtedness, the amount requiring approval may be based on the net indebtedness, that is the intended debt minus the fixed assets set aside to cover the debt.[15]

If the approval is received from the Congregation for an indebtedness, it is not necessary to seek additional approval for indebtedness until a new indebtedness, which would exceed the previous approval by the amount set for the region, is to be incurred. For example, if approval is received for a debt of $4 million and the amount sent for the region were $3 million, a new approval would not be required until a new indebtedness of $3 million would be incurred.

The approval, however, for the indebtedness is usually an approval for a stated reason such as a new wing to a hospital or a new classroom building. The approval is usually based upon the ability of the institute or the society to pay off the debt within a stated period of time. It is not a general approval to raise the amount at which future approvals must be sought.

Experts

There is no definitive answer as to who may or may not be an expert. Since the opinion of at least two different experts is required, the practical determination of who should be an expert must be considered in light of the cost factor. The Apostolic See has accepted as experts the financial auditors of a juridic person if the auditors have had a long history with the juridic person. The local property tax valuation should be acceptable if this is given at the fair market value or the percentage of the fair market value is stated.

The Time to Seek the Approval

In the case of alienation, the approval may be sought prior to or after the agreement to alienate property or fixed capital has been made. In either case, the agreement should be made subject to the required canonical approvals. If the approval of the Congregation is sought before the final purchase price has been agreed upon, all the other available information may be sent to the Congregation which then often gives "approval in principle." When the final purchase price has been agreed upon, it can be faxed to the Congregation for final approval. In such cases, the final approval is often received within a matter of hours since the Congregation has had the opportunity to study the matter beforehand.

---

[15] See footnote 13. The practice of debt financing while having sufficient reserves set aside to cover the debt has been an important practice for institutions of higher learning. These institutions have been able to receive public financing at an interest rate lower than the earnings which can be made from investment of an equivalent amount of capital.

In the case of indebtedness, approval may also be sought before final agreement has been reached. This is particularly important when an institution is seeking financing through tax-exempt bonds.

Corporate Reorganization as an Alienation

If the effect of a corporate reorganization were effectively to end the control by the institute or the society of an entity which is part of its stable patrimony, this would be considered an alienation.

A Lease

Since a lease of stable patrimony is a conveyance of an interest in real property, a lease would be an alienation. Further, in some cases a lease of any temporal good could have an adverse affect on the patrimonial condition of juridic person. However, because of the complications of making universal norms for lease arrangements, the *Code of Canon Law* leaves to each episcopal conference the right to establish the norms governing leasing (c. 1297).[16]

It would seem advisable that each institute or society establish its own norms governing leasing. The norms should include the approvals required within the institute or the society, especially in the cases of long-term and indefinite leases since these type of leases tie up property beyond the present circumstances of the institute or the society.

Charitable Trust

Alienation refers to the transfer of property or of rights over property from a person or a juridic person to another person or juridic person. It applies when the transfer involves real property or fixed capital. Since in many cases the trust is created with money or its equivalent such as securities, stock or bonds which have not been formally designated as fixed capital, the creation of the trust does not involve an alienation. If, however, the creation of the trust involves the transfer of real property or fixed capital which is part of the patrimony of the institute or the society, an alienation could result depending upon the control over the trust retained by the institute or the society. Since each civil jurisdiction has its own laws concerning trust and the amount of control able to be retained by the institute or the society as donor, each trust document must be examined on its own terms to determine whether or not the creation of the trust results in an alienation.

---

[16] As of 2001 the episcopal conference for the United States has not made any norms regarding leasing.

The transfer of money or its equivalent to a charitable trust could be a business transaction which could adversely affect the patrimonial condition of the institute or the society. However, since the purpose of the charitable trust would be to protect the assets of the institute or the society, it would seem that it should not be considered to have adverse affects. It would be important to structure the trust so that it is clearly the intent and the actuality to protect the assets of the institute or the society. Again, each trust must be examined on it own merits to determine whether or not its creation adversely affects the patrimonial condition of the institute or the society.

Definitions[17]

Acquisition: the act of becoming the owner of specific property. Acquisition may be by purchase, by a gift, by inheritance, by trade or barter, by prescription, or by natural accretion (crops, change of natural boundaries). In canon law, acquisition also includes exercising dominion over temporal goods, that is authority or control which is less than ownership.

Alienation: in the strict canonical sense, the conveyance in any manner of an interest in or title to real property or fixed capital to another party.

Assets: temporal goods or cash which can be made available for the payment of debts or liabilities.

Ecclesiastical goods: the temporal goods of a public juridic person such as a religious institute, a secular institute, or a society of apostolic life.

Extraordinary administration: an act of administration, as determined in the proper law of the institute or the society, involving expenditures and financial matters beyond the daily management of a juridic person. The act requires the administrator to receive the consent or approval of another person or body.

---

[17] The definitions are based on both canon and civil law. Where there is a difference, and it is not evident from the text, the difference is noted.

Fixed capital: money or its equivalent (securities, stocks, bonds, certificates of deposit) which have been formally designated by the competent superior or by a donor for a set purpose. Business or auditing account designations are usually not fixed capital.

Immovable goods: real property. In canon law it does not include fixtures unless the fixture is intended to be permanent and removal would result in damage to the property.

Patrimonial condition: the temporal goods, the heritage and the matters which are constitutive to an institute or a society.

Proper law: the law which is specific to the institute or the society. It includes constitutional norms which are approved by the Apostolic See and secondary norms.

Ordinary administration: expenditures and financial matters which are for the daily needs of the juridic person as determined in the proper law of the institute or the society.

Stable patrimony: in the strict canonical sense, the immovable goods and the fixed capital of a juridic person.

Temporal goods: property which can be acquired, retained, administered, and alienated.

Title: the means whereby a person has legal ownership of property.

CHAPTER TEN

JUDICIAL PROCESSES

VICTORIA VONDENBERGER, R.S.M.[1]

RESOLUTION OF DISPUTES ABOUT RIGHTS

Boards of Reconciliation

In the Church and within religious congregations and societies of apostolic life, persons have rights which must be protected. It is helpful if a congregation has some kind of reconciliation or appeal process in which rights are safeguarded. In such a process, conflicts of interest even when rights are not involved can be resolved and conflicts of rights can be conciliated, mediated, and/or arbitrated. Such a process is designed to facilitate better relationships among members of a congregation. A reconciliation or appeal process is a way to deal with situations when religious need assistance in their interactions with each other: those occasions when personality differences interfere with conflict resolution as well as the perceived violation of rights. It is assumed that healthy adult relationships are both the goal for religious communities and the basis for such reconciliation procedures.

Credibility of witness to the Gospel demands fidelity to justice among religious themselves (Mt. 18: 15-17). A reconciliation process exists to defend *human rights* based on the dignity of the human person, *ecclesial rights* from baptism as Christians, and *ecclesiastical rights* related to rights of office when other appeal processes are not in place for these. Any reconciliation process must recognize the limitations on the independent exercise of power by persons in authority. Far from undermining authority, this limitation does much to win respect for it and thus to enable persons to govern more effectively.

---

[1] Paulissa Jirik, S.S.N.D. and David M. O'Connell, C.M. contributed to this chapter.

There are many and varied models for the resolution of disputes about rights. A composite rather generic plan is presented here to help congregations develop plans fit to their specific resources and needs. Such procedures are not part of the *Code of Canon Law* but become part of the particular law of institutes and societies when properly established by them.

Any professed religious may refer a matter to the reconciliation process. The matter referred must be a perceived injustice (not merely a breach of charity), the violation of a right generally accepted as granted by membership, or an instance where human dignity has been violated.

Both parties to the dispute must agree to participate in the process. Good will on the part of all those involved is essential if the process is to be efficacious.

A violation of confidentiality in the process is a serious failure of trust and immediately terminates the process. Discretionary consultation among the members of the board of reconciliation is not a violation of confidentiality. Preliminary step: a religious contacts a member of the board of reconciliation for informal, preliminary counsel about the process. The board member helps the religious see if the matter is proper for the process and explains the options the person has.

Option one is conciliation

Conciliation is a process of compromise between disputing parties to settle a controversy. The board of reconciliation member is an objective listener to each party. The goal is to assist both parties in understanding the issue, to clarify perceptions and feelings and to bring about resolution or reconciliation.

The initiator contacts a member of the board by phone or mail and requests that person to serve as conciliator. The initiator provides a written and signed statement describing the nature of the difficulty.

The conciliator sends a copy of the initiator's statement to the other party involved requesting the other party's written and signed statement (usually within two weeks). The process is considered terminated unless the conciliator has written and signed statements from both parties.

The conciliator meets with each party separately to provide an opportunity to express feelings and clarify concerns and expectations concerning the outcomes of the conciliation procedures. Such a meeting is held in a place of privacy and usually limited to no more than one hour.

Within two weeks the conciliator prepares a written summary of his/her observations for both parties and encourages them toward reconciliation or reminds them about further options in the appeal process.

Records of the conciliation process are signed and sealed by the conciliator and kept in a confidential file in the province (regional, area) offices of the congregation, open to further steps of the process (mediation or arbitration) *only* with the written consent of *both* parties and destroyed after a period of three years. No one else has access.

Option two is mediation

In mediation, the board of reconciliation member is a facilitator for a meeting of the parties pursuing reconciliation. The goal is to bring the parties together with a third person to facilitate settlement of the issue in a simple, informal manner.

Either party may pursue mediation usually within two weeks of the end of conciliation procedures. This is an option only when level one (conciliation) is completed and found to be inadequate. The second level initiator selects a member of the board of reconciliation as a mediator. Both parties must agree to mediation and to the mediator. This could be the same person who handled the conciliation for these parties. If the parties cannot agree on a mediator, the process cannot go forward and so is terminated.

The mediator arranges a meeting with both parties in a private setting with a usual time limit of one hour. Each has the other's written statement of the issues. The mediator first checks for any needed clarification about the content of the statements. The mediator might request access to the conciliation file.

The mediator facilitates both parties speaking in the first person and taking responsibility for their own actions, feelings, etc. as well as helping each understand the actions and feelings of the other. Gently but firmly the mediator tries to move both toward decision or action explaining the options of giving/receiving forgiveness, requiring a second session with the mediator rather than unduly prolonging the first, seeking professional assistance for the issue/interaction, and pursuing arbitration (reviewing those procedures). The mediator assists both parties to communicate with each other.

The mediator prepares a summary report giving copies to both parties and placing a copy in the confidential file with the same restrictions about access *only* with the written consent of *both* parties and only for possible arbitration as well as destruction after three years.

Option three is arbitration.

Arbitration is a last resort designed to resolve a controversy through voluntary agreement of those concerned to abide by the decision made by a panel of three impartial parties. Three members of the board of reconciliation function as objective evaluators whose majority decision will settle the dispute. The goal is to bring the dispute to settlement.

This is an option only if levels one (conciliation) and two (mediation) have been completed with the issue still unresolved. One must be sure the matter is appropriate for arbitration and both parties must consent or the process is terminated. This is a formal process and it is important that all steps be followed carefully.

A panel of three persons from the board of reconciliation serve as evaluators. Each party selects one arbitrator from the board of reconciliation and those two choose a third board member who serves as chairperson. It is highly recommended that the third panel member be acceptable to both parties.

Both parties agree to accept the judgement of the panel before the arbitration process begins or the process is terminated. The panel chairperson arranges a meeting of the three arbitrators and the parties. Each party has one half hour to present each position. Panel members ask questions for clarification. The panel may choose to have one or more meetings with the parties. Within two weeks of the final meeting the chairperson delivers the decision. A written summary prepared by the chairperson is given to both parties and placed in the confidential file dated and sealed to be destroyed after three years.

Further appeal is possible to a central or general board of appeal for larger institutes and always to the institute major superior. If an institute has, for example, seven units such as provinces, each unit would have a reconciliation board and each unit would select a certain number of members for a central or general board of reconciliation especially for issues in which those concerned are from different units or provinces. Such a board would be approached if both parties seek further review, if there is not a unit board in place for some reason, if the process was terminated for a reason other than that the initiator's willingness to cooperate, if unit directives refer the issue to the central board, or if the religious involved in the dispute are not members of the same unit.

The general administration of the institute designates one member of the central board as the facilitator for the board. This person selects three persons acceptable to both parties. A hearing is held within thirty days of selection and acceptance of the panel. Prior to the hearing the central panel arbitrators review all materials from the provincial process released by signatures of both parties. Within ten days of the hearing both parties are notified of the panel's decision. All maintain professional confidentiality. By mutual written agreement of the parties involved, opinions reached as a result of the central appeal process may be communicated to appropriate persons or made public. Records are kept in the central administrative offices and destroyed after three years.

Board Members number at least ten with three alternates to replace a member or complete an unfinished term. These religious are nominated by all the religious they could serve and elected from a slate of those willing to accept the role. The term of service is whatever time period parallels the chapter or administrative team term. No members of the province (regional, area, institute) administration may be members of the board. At least once in every term there should be an evaluation of the processes and pertinent recommendations.

Matter appropriate for appeal through the reconciliation board would include perceived injustice involving two members of a unit (province, region), a member and a group of members such as a local community (represented by a designated spokesperson unless the issue is within the group when all would participate in the process) or a decision of unit (province, regional) administration. There is no appeal for a disagreement of a member with a decision of community authority where there is not a perceived injustice except through the usual appeal to a major superior. Inappropriate matters are those which involve institutions (sponsored or not), parishes, schools, staffs, dioceses who may employ religious (the member should use the channels of due process of the place of employment), decisions about admission of members to stages of incorporation, or decisions about religious in perpetual profession for which canon law or particular law makes provision such as imposed exclaustration or dismissal.

Rights of the Parties Involved

In recognizing the right to due process, the Church says explicitly that people have the right to be informed of proposed actions which affect their own rights, the right to be heard in defense of their rights, the right in the face of accusation to confront their accusers and the right not to be judged by their accusers. (*Protection of Rights of Persons in the Church*; Washington, D.C., Canon Law Society of America, 1991).

A religious brought to a process of conciliation, mediation, or arbitration as well as a canonical trial would certainly have at least the rights which church law affords a respondent in a marriage case. These include the following:

- The right to appoint an advocate and procurator (c. 1477, c. 1481);
- The right to be summoned (c. 1507, §1, c. 1686);
- The right to know the allegation(s) (c. 1508);
- The right to name witnesses (c. 1551);
- The right to know the other witnesses usually before they are heard (c. 1554);

- The right to inspect the acts of the case, all documents and testimony with careful safeguarding of the right to defense even in matters which concern the public good where some part of the evidence may be shown to no one (c. 1598, §1);
- The right to propose new evidence and proofs after reviewing the acts (c. 1598, §2);
- The right to reply to any further statements or pleas of the other party (c. 1602);
- The right to know the contents of the decision (c. 1614);
- The right to appeal (c. 1628 and 1687) or propose a plea of nullity (c. 1626).

If a penalty may be imposed as a result of a process of reconciliation, more rights need to be safeguarded. A main underpinning of penal law is canon 18 which insists on very strict following of procedures with regard to penalties and penal trials. Penalties must be a last resort for handling problems (cc. 1317, and 1341) and should be designed to restore justice, repair scandal, or reform the accused. No one is to be punished through church procedures except strictly according to law (c. 221, §3).

The code presents three distinct levels or stages that should be pursued before any penalties are imposed:

1. Preliminary investigation (cc. 1717-1719) about the imputability of the one accused of misconduct to determine if an offense truly occurred and if the accused can be help responsible for that offense. Care must be taken to protect the good names of those involved. There must be the highest degree of confidentiality.
2. The penal process (cc. 1720-1728) where the accused must be fully informed and have the opportunity to respond to the allegations. There can be a canonical trial only for offenses listed in canons 1364-1398 or in the particular law (cc. 1315-1320). The accused must have a capable advocate. The accused must be given the right to write or speak last in the process and is never bound to confess.
3. The victim's right to seek repair of damages (cc. 1729-1731) sustained due to an offense.

Canon law has a history of concern for the guaranteeing of rights and has affirmed the availability of a judicial remedy for the protection of rights (cc. 1732-1739).

A religious would also have the right to defend legitimate canonical rights through a Church court (c. 221). Such rights as presented elsewhere in this book would include the following:

- the rights of all Christians (cc. 208-223),
- the rights and obligations of laity (cc. 224-231) or of clergy (cc. 273-289),
- and the specific rights of religious (cc. 662-672,
- plus various others gleaned from canons 598 ,607, 618, 620, 627, 631, 635, 643, 653, 654, 656, 657, 659, 660, 661, 675, 676, 678, 680, 681, 682, 683, and 684-704, 737, 738, 739).

PENAL PROCEDURES

Dismissal of a Member of a Religious Institute or a Society of Apostolic Life

The rights and obligations of a member of a religious institute or a society of apostolic life cease when membership is terminated either voluntarily through legitimate departure or transfer or involuntarily through a process of dismissal initiated by legitimate authorities with ultimate confirmation by the Holy See.

Dismissal is a serious action taken by competent ecclesiastical authority through which permanent departure is imposed on a member with resulting dispensation from vows and from all rights and obligations arising from profession or incorporation. This juridic procedure is initiated by legitimate authority only for the most grave causes which must be external, imputable and juridically proven. What applies to institutes of consecrated life also applies to societies of apostolic life unless otherwise noted in the appropriate universal or particular law (c. 746).

Dismissal is a penal procedure and so is subject to strict legal interpretation regarding exact procedures according to canon 18 as has been repeatedly demonstrated by the Congregation for Institutes of Consecrated Life and for Societies of Apostolic Life.

The rights and obligations of a member of an institute or society cease when membership is terminated by legitimate dismissal (c. 701) which occurs as a voluntary choice of the individual with approval from competent ecclesiastical authority (cc. 686-693), by proper canonical transfer (cc. 684,485) or involuntarily. For involuntary dismissal, a careful process must be observed (c. 699) and confirmed by the Holy See (c. 700).

There are three types of dismissal described in the Code of Canon law: automatic (c. 694), compulsory (c. 695), and facultative (c. 696).

Automatic dismissal occurs when a member either has notoriously abandoned the Catholic faith or has contracted or attempted marriage, even only civilly. The major superior with council is to collect proofs and issue a declaration of the fact so that the dismissal is established juridically.

Notorious rejection of the Catholic faith must be an irrefutable, public act as in the case of heresy, apostasy, or schism (c. 751) and not merely a matter of personal or private disagreement with the Church and its teachings. In addition to automatic dismissal, such rejection warrants automatic excommunication (c. 1364). Attempted marriage by a member, whether a cleric (c. 1087) or not, is also cause for automatic dismissal as well as for other appropriate canonical penalties (c. 1394).

Compulsory dismissal (c. 695) results from kidnaping, homicide, mutilation and serious wounding of a person (c. 1397), procurement of an abortion (c. 1398), or external violations of the sixth commandment (c. 1395) unless the major superior determines otherwise. In the case of external sexual misconduct, obviously incompatible with religious life and its obligations, the major superior must carefully balance the harm done to the victim, the rights of the accused and the good of the Church seeking Gospel justice. There may also be civil and other canonical consequences of these actions.

Facultative dismissal (c. 696) includes grave, external, immutable, and juridically proven offenses such as habitual neglect of serious obligations associated with religious life, repeated violations of sacred vows or bonds, grave disobedience of lawful prescriptions of superiors in serious matters, grave scandal from culpable behavior, holding or spreading doctrines condemned by the magisterium of the Church as well as adherence to ideologies infected by materialism or atheism, unlawful absence (c. 665) from the institute or society lasting six months, and other similar serious causes.

The habitual neglect of serious religious obligations includes neglect of the observance of the Gospel, the law of the Church or of the institute or society (cc. 662-672; 573). There must be genuine evidence of these offenses and not mere accusation or presumption. If there is a question of disobedience, it must be demonstrable, stubborn rejection of serious matters prescribed by a lawful superior. If there is a question of other culpable behavior, it must be the occasion of scandal, leading another to evil or sin (*Catechism of the Catholic Church*, 1994).

As causes for dismissal, adherence to teachings condemned by the magisterium or to materialistic, atheistic ideologies must be pertinacious and unyielding on the part of the offending member. Regardless of the canonical category in which a cause for dismissal is classified, the process of dismissal itself requires the most careful discretion and observance on the part of ecclesiastical authorities concerned (c. 696, §2).

Dismissal may be initiated by the legitimate major superior (c. 697) after having heard the council. Consent of the council is not required but consultation is necessary (c. 127) and the superior should not act contrary to a consensus of the council unless there be an overriding reason. The major superior must: collect proofs and inform the member; warn the member explicitly either in writing or in the presence of two witnesses regarding the consequences of the action and of the dismissal process; give the member the opportunity for an appropriate self-defense and for reform and, if needed, provide a second warning in the same manner as the first. Fifteen working days must elapse between the initial warning and the second (c. 201). Another fifteen working days must pass before the major superior must transmit all acts of the dismissal process signed by a notary, along with the signed response of the member, to the supreme moderator (c. 697). Throughout the process, the major superior must inform the member of the right to communicate with and offer a defense directly to the supreme moderator (c. 698). If the member is a cleric, the notary in this process must be a priest (c. 483, §2).

Once the acts of the case are transmitted to the supreme moderator, she or he must proceed collegially with at least four councilors for validity, weighing the proofs and defenses presented. A secret ballot yielding an absolute majority decision precedes the drafting of a decree of dismissal by the supreme moderator which must express the motives for dismissal in law and fact for validity (c. 699). In the case of autonomous monasteries (c. 614), the diocesan bishop fulfills the role of major superior (c. 699, §2).

The decree of dismissal for members of pontifical institutes or societies does not take effect until it is confirmed by the Holy See, having received all the acts of the case. If the institute concerned is of diocesan right, the diocesan bishop of the house to which the member is assigned issues this confirmation. For validity, this decree must indicate the member's right of recourse to the Congregation for Institutes of Consecrated Life and for Societies of Apostolic Life. This recourse has a suspensive effect upon the decree and must be exercised within ten working days of the notification (c. 700).

Once ultimately confirmed by the Congregation or diocesan bishop, the decree of dismissal communicated to the member terminates the member's vows, rights and obligations as a member of an institute or society (c. 701). She or he can request nothing from the institute or society for past service although the code encourages the institute to observe charity and equity toward the dismissed member (c. 702). If the member is a priest, the exercise of sacred orders is prohibited until he may be received for priestly service by a diocesan bishop.

The identification of dismissed members is to be included in reports sent by the supreme moderator to the Holy See (c. 704).

Specific Rights of the Accused in a Penal Process

All the rights and obligations which a member of a religious institute or society of apostolic life ordinarily possesses remain intact during a penal process unless otherwise specified in the universal or particular law. The same is true for a member involved in the process of mediation, conciliation, or arbitration mentioned above. The following rights should be specifically protected by all concerned with the penal process:

- The right to a good reputation and to privacy (c. 220);
- The right to vindicate and defend ecclesial rights in an appropriate ecclesiastical forum in accord with the norm of law applied with equity and the right to not be punished except in accord with the norm of law (c. 221);
- The right to know the offense, the accusation and the proofs (c. 694 and 695);
- The right to formal notifications and warnings (c. 695 and 697);
- The right to know the offense and the effects of the action contemplated (c. 697);
- The right to self defense and to reform (cc. 695, 697 and 698);
- The right to confidentiality (cc. 1361, §3 and 1455);
- The right to contact the supreme moderator directly throughout the process (c. 698);
- The right to recourse with suspensive effect on the action contemplated (c. 700);
- The right to strict interpretation of penalties and careful observance of all dimensions of the penal process and any restriction of rights (c. 18).

The penal law of the Church affecting a member of a religious institute or a society of apostolic life goes to great lengths to protect the rights of the accused in a penal process while balancing those rights with the rights and obligations of others in the Church. Major superiors are encouraged to consult with a canonist prior to and throughout any penal process to ensure these rights and this balance are maintained for the protection of all concerned and for the good of the Church.

CHAPTER ELEVEN

THE SACRAMENT OF ORDER

MICHAEL P. JOYCE, C.M.[1]

INITIAL FORMATION FOR THE SACRAMENT OF ORDER

Admission Into Candidacy

This rite is mandated for those seeking the diaconate either transitionally or permanently. Canon 1034, §2 exempts vowed members of clerical institutes of consecrated life and some members of societies of apostolic life seeking the ordained priesthood.

Candidates

While the code does not require vowed members of clerical institutes of consecrated life or societies of apostolic life to celebrate the rite of candidacy before ordination, a close reading of the code makes clear that the rite is obligatory for members of some institutes or societies[2]:

- members of lay institutes of consecrated life (whether bound by vows or promises, etc.). This situation occurs in the case of a brother in such an institute seeking permanent diaconate or priesthood.
- members of clerical societies of apostolic life who do not profess vows but some other form of commitment (oath, promises, etc.).

---

[1] Rev. Vincent B. Grogan, O.F.M. contributed to this chapter.
[2] Canon 1034, §2. Note the phrase "A man who has not been admitted through vows to a clerical institute...." The term *vows* is not modified by the adjective *religious*. (See c. 731, §1 that describes societies of apostolic life.)

Requirements for admission into candidacy

The requirements for admission into candidacy are:

- a minimum age of twenty and the beginning of theological studies for those aspiring to the transitional diaconate;
- specific qualities expected in the candidate: signs of possessing an authentic vocation, presence of suitable moral characteristics, absence of serious mental and physical deficiencies (i.e. disorders or disabilities that would prove a hindrance to the exercise of the sacrament of order), irregularities, and a desire to dedicate themselves to the service of the church;
- a formal written petition to the major superior in which the person indicates explicitly that he is seeking candidacy freely;[3]
- a formal written acceptance of the petition by the major superior with the prior recommendation of the formation team and the local superior.

Celebration of admission into candidacy

The proper minister of the rite in clerical institutes or societies is the major superior (or his delegate). In lay institutes or societies the bishop of the domicile of the member admits to candidacy at the formal written request of the major superior.

Records

A record of the rite of admission (including the name of the celebrant, the place, and the date) is kept in the person's file. A copy is placed in the archives of the religious house where it was celebrated (or in the diocesan archives when the bishop has presided over the rite). A certificate attesting to admission to candidacy is also presented to the individual admitted.

Canonical Effects

There are no canonical effects that follow from this rite. Therefore no dispensation is necessary if the person subsequently decides to leave the institute or society.

---

[3] See the appendix for a sample petition.

Institution into Ministries
Candidates

The code (c. 1035, §1) prescribes that before ordination to the diaconate, the individual must receive the ministries of lector and acolyte. Either or both of these ministries may be conferred on members of lay institutes of consecrated life of men and on lay members in a clerical institute of consecrated life or a clerical society of apostolic life; that is, these ministries are not restricted to candidates for the sacrament of order (see canon 230, §1).

Requirements for installation in ministries

The requirements for candidates to be installed into either ministry of lector or acolyte are:

- minimum age of eighteen;
- suitable preparation and training in the various aspects of the respective ministry;
- a formal letter to one's major superior requesting installation to the specific ministry; the member must indicate that he is seeking it freely and of his own will;[4]
- a recommendation from the person(s) responsible for the candidate's formation mentioning that the required training for the ministry has been given if the individual is in formation for either permanent commitment or ordination;[5]
- formal written approval of the request by the major superior;
- observance of intervals between the installation into each ministry (six months);

---

[4] See the appendix for a sample petition.

[5] If the individual is not in a formation program (e.g., a perpetually professed brother in a institute of consecrated life or a society of apostolic life), the approval of one's local superior is appropriate. The superior needs to make the recommendation and state that the required training has been given.

Celebration of institution

The major superior in clerical institutes of consecrated life and societies of apostolic life is authorized to institute his subjects in the ministries. He may also designate another priest to do so.[6] In lay institutes of consecrated life and societies of apostolic life the local ordinary of the individual's residence institutes the member into the ministries. The major superior needs to request the institution formally of the local ordinary.

Records

A record of the institution including the name of the one who instituted the person in the ministry and the date and place where the celebration took place is retained in the personal file of the member and in the archives of the house or diocese where the institution took place. A formal certificate attesting to the institution is also given to the individual.

Canonical effects

No canonical effects result from institution in the ministries. Therefore if a member subsequently departs from the institute or society, no dispensation from ministries is required. Profession of perpetual vows or promises is not required in order to be instituted in the ministries (as it is for ordination). Temporary vows or promises suffice. Novices, postulants, or aspirants may be instituted in the ministries. However, the institute or society in its best interests may chose to restrict institution in ministries to those related to the institute or society by at least a temporary bond so that the focus of formation in the earlier stages of entrance into consecrated life is not confused with the preparation for ordination.

The ministries may be received in either sequence. Institution into the ministry of lector, however, may be more appropriate before the ministry of acolyte, taking into consideration the liturgical focus on word and sacrament. Canon 1035, §2 suggests that the ministry of acolyte occurs after the ministry of lector and prior to ordination to the diaconate.

---

[6] See circular letter to US bishops by the general secretary of the NCCB, April 7, 1976. The clarification had been communicated to the apostolic delegate to the United States by the Congregation for the Sacraments and Divine Worship.

Transitional Diaconate

The code mandates a host of prescriptions, some on the part of the candidate, some on the part of the seminary personnel, some on the part of the major superior that must be fulfilled before ordination to the transitional diaconate.

- ◆ Qualifications affecting the candidate:

    profession of perpetual vows (or permanent commitment) in the institute or society;

    minimum age of twenty-three;

    completion of third year of theological studies;

    reception of baptism and confirmation;[7]

    institution in the ministries of lector and acolyte;[8]

    admission to candidacy (if applicable; see above, under Admission to Candidacy);

    an interval of at least six months from institution in the second ministry;

    a formal, handwritten letter by the candidate to his major superior in which he requests ordination, indicating both that he is seeking this freely and that he intends to dedicate himself permanently to ecclesiastical ministry as a celibate;

    a profession of faith by the candidate in the presence of the major superior or his delegate;

    proper training in the diaconal ministry and knowledge of the obligations inherent in it;

    a retreat of at least five days duration.

- ◆ From the rector of the seminary (or director of formation):

    submission of a report on the suitability of the candidate to the major superior;[9]

---

[7] A record of the reception of the sacraments is in the candidate's personal file since proof of reception is necessary for admission to religious life.

[8] A record of institution in the ministries is kept in the candidate's file.

[9] The report makes reference to "the sound doctrine of the candidate, his genuine piety, good morals, and aptitude to exercise the ministry, as well as, after a properly executed inquiry, about his state of physical and psychological health" (c. 1051, 1°). Frequently, a vote on the candidate taken by the formation personnel accompanies the report. The major superior can also use other means to ascertain the person's suitability, such as testimonial letters, the publication of ordination banns, etc.

- From the major superior:

    formal acceptance of the candidate's request, communicated to him in writing;

    some institutes or societies may require in their proper law that he consult with his council or obtain their consent before accepts the candidate's request for ordination;

    issuance of dimissorial letters (testifying to the fulfillment of all the requirements) to the ordaining bishop.[10]

- Records

    After the candidate is ordained to the diaconate, the ordaining prelate signs a formal document indicating both the date and place of the ordination. A copy of this document is presented to the individual and a copy is placed in his personal file. A copy likewise is retained in the archives of the diocese where the ordination was celebrated. Notification of diaconal ordination must be sent to the individual's place of baptism or place of reception into full communion.

- Canonical effects

    With ordination to the diaconate comes formal entrance into the clerical state and incardination into the religious institute or society.[11] The deacon may not validly marry.[12] Likewise, he now has the obligation of daily praying of the Liturgy of the Hours.

---

[10] The letters may be sent to any bishop of the rite to which the member belongs. The author of these dimissorial letters depends on the type of institute or society. The major superior is competent to issue dimissorial letters in clerical institutes of consecrated life of pontifical rite and in clerical societies of apostolic life of pontifical rite. In lay institutes whether pontifical or diocesan and in clerical institutes or societies of diocesan rite, the letters are not issued by the major superior of the institute or society but rather by the bishop of the diocese of domicile of the candidate at the request of the major superior. The diocesan bishop is technically the proper ordaining prelate as well. He issues dimissorial letters to the ordaining prelate only if he will not be the one conferring the sacrament. (See c. 1019 and also cc. 1016 and 1018.) See the appendix for a sample dimissorial letter.

[11] The revised rite for the ordination of bishops, presbyters, and deacons requires members of institutes of consecrated life who are to be ordained to the rank of deacon and presbyter to promise obedience to the diocesan bishop. See "De Ordinatione Episcopi, Presbyterorum et Diaconorum" in *Notitiae* 26 (1990), number 6.

[12] This impediment to marriage for members in perpetual vows already exists. However, the revised rite for the ordination of bishops, presbyters, and deacons requires those who have professed perpetual vows in a religious institute to make the profession of celibacy during the ordination rite. See "De Ordinatione Episcopi, Presbyterorum et Diaconorum," numbers 5 and 177. The decree promulgating the revised rite notes that this requirement is a derogation of canon 1037.

- Irregularities:

    Canonical legislation stipulates certain irregularities to ordination. The major superior must ensure and so state in his dimissorial letters that the candidate has not contracted any of these. Here is a listing of the current irregularities (see canon 1041):

    > one who suffers from insanity or from any other psychological disorder which disorder is judged to render him incapable of properly exercising the ministry after consulting with experts;[13]

    > one who in the past was guilty of formal heresy, schism, or apostasy;

    > one who has attempted marriage even civilly either while he himself was prohibited from doing so by an existing marriage bond, by ordination, or by the public and perpetual vow of chastity, or who attempted marriage with a woman validly married or bound by the same vow;

    > one who has committed deliberate homicide, or who has actually procured an abortion, or who has positively cooperated in either of these;

    > one who has gravely and maliciously mutilated himself or another person, or who has attempted suicide;

    > one who has exercised an act of the sacrament of order reserved to those in the episcopal or presbyteral rank while lacking that rank himself or while prohibited from the exercise of the sacrament of order by some canonical penalty either formally declared or imposed.

- Impediments

    While it may seem that the impediments to ordination listed below (see canon 1042) may hardly seem to apply to someone living the consecrated life, it is possible that they may exist. The impediments are:

    > a married man, unless he is seeking the permanent diaconate;

    > one who exercises an office or administration prohibited to clerics in accordance with canons 285 and 286 for which he must render an account;

    > a neophyte,[14] unless in the judgment of the major superior the man has been sufficiently tested (i.e., lived a suitable amount of time as a Catholic).

---

[13] The consultation with an expert is very important. It implies that before the major superior makes such a determination he should use competent, professional advice.

[14] The term *neophyte* in this context applies both to those baptized as an adult as well as to those who entered into full communion with the Church as an adult.

- Dispensation from irregularities and impediments
    If the fact on which an irregularity is based has been brought to the judicial forum, ecclesiastical or civil, the dispensation from the irregularity is reserved to the Holy See. Likewise reserved to the Holy See, if public, are the following irregularities:

    apostasy, heresy, or schism;

    attempted marriage even civilly when already bound by an existing marriage bond, ordination, or by a public and perpetual vow of chastity; or attempted marriage to a woman bound by a marriage bond or by the public and perpetual vow of chastity;

    deliberate commision of homicide or procurement of an abortion or has cooperation in either such crime, whether public or occult (see canon 1047, §2, 2 °).

    All other irregularities or impediments can be dispensed by the major superior in clerical institutes or societies. The local ordinary can dispense for other institutes or societies.

- Irregularities and Impediments after ordination
    The existence of irregularities or impediments render the exercise of the sacrament of order illicit but not invalid. In most aspects the existence of irregularities or impediments mirrors the irregularities for ordination as presented above. Here are those who have irregularities to the exercise of an order already received:

    one who while affected by an irregularity for ordination illicitly was ordained;

    one who is guilty of public apostasy, heresy, or schism;

    one who attempted marriage either while himself prohibited from marriage by an existing marital bond, ordination, or a public and perpetual vow of chastity; or who attempted marriage with a woman already validly married or bound by the same vow;

    one who has committed deliberate homicide or procured an abortion or who has positively cooperated in the same;

    one who has gravely and maliciously mutilated himself or another, or who has attempted suicide;

    one who has exercised an act of the sacrament of order reserved to those in the ranks of the episcopate or presbyterate while himself either lacking that rank or while barred from its exercise by a canonical penalty, declared or imposed.

The two categories of men who have impediments to the exercise of orders already received are:

one who while hindered by an impediment to ordination was illicitly ordained;

a person who has become insane or suffers from some other serious psychological disorder which renders him incapable of fulfilling the order received.[15]

♦ Dispensation from the above irregularities or impediments to the exercise of an order already received

If the fact on which an irregularity is based has been brought to an ecclesiastical or civil judicial forum, the dispensation from that irregularity is reserved to the Holy See. Also reserved to the Holy See are the cases of:

one who has attempted marriage in public cases as described above;[16]

one guilty of deliberate homicide or procurement of abortion, or who has positively cooperated in the same, whether public or occult (see canon 1047, §2, 2°).

All other irregularities or impediments to the exercise of an order already received may be dispensed by the major superior in clerical institutes or societies. The local ordinary can dispense in other institutes or societies.

Permanent Diaconate

This order is open to lay members of clerical institutes of consecrated life as well as to lay members of clerical societies of apostolic life and to members of lay institutes and societies. A prerequisite for ordination to the permanent diaconate is the making of a permanent commitment in the institute or society by vows, promises, or other bond.

The fundamental requirements for the transitional diaconate hold as well for the permanent diaconate with the following differences:

♦ minimum age of twenty-five;

---

[15] This impediment involves consultation with experts. The impediment to exercising an order received continues until the major superior after consulting experts allows the order to be exercised.
[16] The irregularity is public whether it is actually known or there is a strong possibility it will become known.

- completion of a three year preparation program (c. 236);[17]
- dimissorial letters.[18]

All the other requirements (e.g., formal letter requesting ordination, the profession of faith, the report of formation personnel, certification of the completion of the training program, the five day retreat, the recording of ordination and the notification of the place of baptism) for the transitional diaconate hold also for ordination to the permanent diaconate.

Denying ordination to the presbyterate

Canon 1026 forbids coercing a person to be ordained and canon 1038 focuses on the freedom of a transitional deacon to refuse presbyteral ordination and permission to exercise the diaconal ministry with all things being equal. Canon 1030 addresses the issue of a major superior prohibiting presbyteral ordination to a transitional deacon. The superior's prohibition must be founded on a canonical cause or reason and not on his mere whim. Such a cause is found among the irregularities and impediments to receiving orders listed above or in a deficiency of the broad requisites enumerated in canon 1051, 1° noted above or as delineated in canon 1029: an "integral faith ...right intention, ...requisite knowledge, ...a good reputation, ...integral morals, and proven virtue, ...and the other physical and psychological qualities in keeping with the order to be received." While it is true that ordination to the transitional diaconate does not confer an automatic right to subsequent presbyteral ordination, it implies that ordination to the presbyterate will follow in due time.

The most commonly occurring basis for denying presbyteral ordination is found in canon 1041, 1° which lists among the irregularities to receiving the sacrament of order: some form of insanity or another psychic defect which renders one unsuitable for properly fulfilling the ministry. Experts must be consulted according to this canon. Ultimately, it is the major superior who makes the decision.

Even an occult reason (i.e., one incapable of proof in the external forum) suffices to prohibit ordination. The sacrament of order exists primarily for the good of the Church and not simply for the benefit of the person who is ordained. Therefore, when there is a serious doubt about the suitability of the individual, the benefit of the doubt must be given to the Church community and not the individual. Justice requires the major superior to share the reason for denying ordination with the individual.

---

[17] Also see canon 659, §3 on the formation of members preparing to receive holy orders.
[18] See footnote 10 above.

A deacon who is refused presbyteral ordination by his major superior retains the right of appeal to the superior general of the institute or society. He has recourse to the Congregation for Institutes of Consecrated Life and Societies of Apostolic Life if the general upholds the denial of ordination. If the denial of priestly ordination is based on evidence of a psychic disorder, it is possible that the disorder can be treated by psychological therapy or controlled by medication. When psychological therapy seems hopeful, the major superior can delay ordination until the therapy is completed. He can do the same if the deacon's behavior has improved or changed due to medication. Then, after consultation with the therapist or expert, the major superior renders a decision on presbyteral ordination. If uncertainties or doubts remain unresolved, the benefit of the doubt goes to the Church, not to the deacon.

The Presbyterate

Basically the same prerequisites for diaconate ordination hold as well for presbyteral ordination with the following differences:

- minimum age of twenty-five;[19]
- prior reception of the diaconate;
- completion of four years of theological studies and the exercise of diaconal ministry in a pastoral setting for a suitable time period;
- an interval of at least six months from the reception of diaconate; and
- the absence of any irregularity or impediment.[20]

All other stipulations for diaconate (i.e., written request of candidate, formal written acceptance by the major superior, testimony on the person's suitability, the issuance of dimissorial letters, a five days retreat, recording of the ordination, and notifying the place of baptism or reception into full communion) hold for presbyteral ordination.[21]

---

[19] The major superior in clerical institutes or societies may dispense for up to a year's lack of age.
[20] A profession of faith is not required.
[21] See footnote 14 above regarding a promise of obedience to the diocesan bishop.

Faculties

The term *faculties* refers to authorization by a competent superior to allow priests and deacons to perform certain acts of the sacrament of order. The acts for a deacon that require faculties are preaching and officially witnessing the celebration of marriage. In addition to these acts, presbyters also need faculties to grant sacramental absolution. The law itself (c. 764) gives presbyters and deacons the faculty to preach everywhere with some possible exceptions.

Clerical religious institutes or societies of pontifical right

Major superiors in these institutes can usually grant faculties for sacramental absolution to other members of the institute or society. The constitutions and statutes of the institute or society will govern this power and need to be consulted. The faculties do not extend outside of the institute or society. Superiors in these institutes or societies receive their faculties from the universal law.[22]

Outside the institute or society

Presbyters who are members of institutes or societies receive faculties for granting sacramental absolution from the local ordinary of the diocese in which they have a domicile. Members of religious institutes and societies of apostolic life receive their domicile from the house to which they are attached (c. 103). They do not necessarily need to be living in the house to have their domicile there.

Ordinarily the presbyter's major superior requests faculties from the local ordinary. The current practice in the United States is that the major superior gives a written statement to the local ordinary about the presbyter's good standing.

Faculties to witness marriage usually accompany assignment to a parish. If the presbyter is not assigned to a parish, he receives the faculty to witness the marriage from the pastor of the parish in which the marriage is to be celebrated. There may be ministries other than parochial, such as campus ministry, for which the local ordinary will grant a general faculty to witness marriages.

---

[22] Canon 968, §2. They can also grant the faculty for their subjects and other presbyters staying in the house to any (c. 969, §2). This term "day and night" can be broadly interpreted to include those who visit the house for one day.

Departure of an Ordained Member from the Institute or Society[23]

Deacon

Previous chapters treat dismissal and transfer of a member to another religious institute or society of apostolic life. This chapter presents two other means for a deacon to depart from the institute or society. The individual may wish to leave the consecrated life but continue as a diocesan cleric; i.e., to be incardinated into a diocese (c. 693). The procedure is the same for a deacon as it is for a priest and the canonical process will be treated below. When a permanent deacon seeks incardination into a diocese, the issue of economic support must be addressed beforehand. He can sustain himself by secular employment or he might find full-time employment in an ecclesiastical setting.

Another possibility is that the deacon may wish to both leave the institute or society and be relieved of the obligations of the diaconate, including that of celibacy. The following are required for the canonical procedure:

- a formal letter of petition offering grave reasons (c. 290, 3°);
- results of the evaluation by the seminary or formation faculty of the person prior to his ordination along with any written observations or comments entered in the evaluation process;
- the evaluation of the person's suitability in summary form for life in the institute or society and the diaconate given by his formation directors during his period of training for institute or society and the diaconate;
- a curriculum vitae which includes his place and date of birth, place and date of his permanent commitment to the institute or society, the place and date of his diaconal ordination, and his appointments since ordination; and
- a *votum* of the major superior including his judgment of the reasons offered by the person, attempts he made to dissuade the man from seeking the dispensation, and his own opinion about the request.

The documents are transmitted to the general curia of the institute or society. The actual dispensation is granted by the Congregation for Divine Worship and the Discipline of the Sacraments.

---

[23] See Randolph R. Calvo and Nevin J. Klinger, eds., *Clergy Procedural Handbook*, (Washington, DC: The Canon Law Society of America, 1992), 67-89 and 238-275.

When the dispensation has been received, a copy is sent to the individual along with a statement of notification to be signed by him. The dispensation takes effect when the individual is notified. He does not need to accept the dispensation for it to be effective. The signed document of notification is kept in the individual's personal file and a copy is sent to the general curia. The rescript itself (or a copy) is also retained there. Notification of the dispensation is also sent to his place of baptism or place of reception into full communion.

Departure of a Presbyter from the Institute or Society

Besides dismissal or transfer to another institute or society, three additional possibilities exist:

- incardination into a diocese as a secular cleric (c. 691-693). When incardination is granted, it in effect dispenses the person from all the obligations of the vows (or promises) and renders him a cleric attached to a local Church. (The obligation of celibacy remains in effect). The following are required for this procedure:

    a formal letter of petition by the individual to the Holy Father providing serious reasons for the request;

    a formal statement from a local ordinary expressing a willingness to accept the person either immediately or on an experimental basis;[24]

    the *votum* or recommendation of the major superior.

Either the major superior or the receiving diocesan bishop can present the petition. If the major superior presents the request, all the documents are then transmitted to the general curia of the institute or society. The actual indult is granted by the Congregation for Institutes of Consecrated Life and Societies of Apostolic Life.

When the indult is received, it is retained in the person's file. A copy is given to the individual along with a formal statement of notification. The priest forwards the signed notification to his major superior to place in his file. A copy is sent to the general curia and likewise, a copy of the indult is sent by the major superior to the bishop who is receiving the man into his diocese. Until the priest is officially incardinated in the diocese, he remains technically a member

---

[24] If the permission is on an experimental basis, the member is automatically incardinated after five years unless the bishop at some earlier point formally incardinates him. The priest is bound to return to his institute or society if the diocesan bishop discontinues the permission before the five year period has expired or at its expiration. Similarly, if the person wishes to return to his institute or society at any point during the five year probationary period, he may do so.

of the institute or society. Therefore he may return to the institute or society any time prior to the incardination and does not need any approval to return.

- ♦ Possibility of departure from the institute or society with a dispensation from vows or promises and from all the obligations of the clerical state with the obligation of celibacy remaining[25]

    Essentially the documentation of this process must clearly manifest that the petitioner will remain firm in his intention of maintaining celibacy as a lay person and will not change his mind at some future point in this regard. The latter requirement ordinarily prohibits any priest younger than forty years old ineligible for the dispensation in the mind of the Congregation for Divine Worship and the Discipline of the Sacraments except for cases of most serious sexual misconduct. The required documents for the procedure are:

    a formal petition in which the person explains in detail his reasons for requesting the dispensation and his assurance of a firm purpose of observing celibacy;

    a curriculum vitae of the petitioner providing his full name, place and date of birth, place and date of permanent commitment in the institute or society, place and date of both his diaconal and presbyteral ordination, and his assignments;

    the evaluation of the man's suitability for membership and clerical life given by the formation personnel at the time of his preparation for vows or promises and ordination;

    the results of the evaluation of the individual prior to his making permanent commitment in the institute or society and prior to his diaconal and presbyteral ordinations along with any observations or notations entered in the evaluation report;

    formal *votum* of the major superior referring to attempts he made to dissuade the person from seeking the indult, his assessment of the reasons offered by the petitioner, references to how the man conducted himself in the priestly ministry, his character, and his conduct in general, mention of abandoning the institute or society illegally, if such is the case, and his own opinion about the request.

---

[25] Admittedly, this request rarely comes from a cleric. The Congregation of Institutes of Consecrated Life and Societies of Apostolic Life issues such indults and sometimes maintains the obligation of celibacy when it confirms the dismissal of an ordained member from an institute or society.

The documents are forwarded to the general curia of the institute or society. The actual indult is granted by the Congregation for Divine Worship and the Discipline of the Sacraments.

When the indult is received, a copy is sent to the person along with a statement of notification. The individual returns the signed document to the major superior to be kept in the person's file and a copy is sent to the general curia. The original indult, or at least a copy, is also placed in the person's file.

- Departure from the institute or society with both a dispensation from the obligations of the religious vows or promises and the obligations of the clerical state, including that of celibacy[26]

The investigation of the request for laicization is to be done either by the major superior or by the local ordinary of the person's actual residence. If the local ordinary conducts the investigation, the *votum* of the person's major superior must be included in the documentation. Three copies of the documentation are sent to the Congregation for Divine Worship and the Discipline of the Sacraments. Permission must be obtained from the Congregation for Divine Worship and the Discipline of the Sacraments for an ordinary other than the man's major superior or bishop of his residence to investigate the case.

The documents that must be obtained in the course of the investigation are:

a table of contents;

a formal letter to the Holy Father in which the person clearly indicates his wish to be dispensed;[27]

a curriculum vitae of the petitioner;

a mandate for a qualified priest to serve as instructor of the case and another priest to be the notary;

testimony of the petitioning priest covering his early family life, his formation, his presbyteral ministry, and the reason for his departure from active ministry;

---

[26] This procedure is commonly called *laicization*.

[27] Upon receiving this letter, the superior is to suspend the priest formally from the exercise of orders. However, this action is not ordinarily taken because it can cause more harm than good. If the person has already attempted marriage, such a suspension on the part of the superior is unnecessary because the person was automatically suspended when he attempted marriage (c. 1394, §1).

- the testimony of several witnesses who know him well;
- the testimony of experts who may have treated him;
- evaluation reports from his formation;
- a summary by the priest-instructor of the case;
- a *votum* by the major superior;
- a *votum* from the petitioner's local ordinary regarding possible scandal;
- a certificate of authenticity by the notary.

The documentation is then sent to the general curia of the institute. The Congregation for Divine Worship and the Discipline of the Sacraments is responsible for issuing the indult. A copy of the indult and a statement of notification is sent to the priest. The dispensation becomes effective when the priest receives it. He returns the signed statement to the major superior who will forward the statement to the general curia. The parish of baptism or reception into full communion is informed of the indult.

Dismissal

Although this topic is presented earlier in the handbook, it is presented again in this section because of the civil liability that an institute may face with an ordained member who refuses to seek a dispensation from obligations arising from his ordination or transfer to another institute or to a diocese. The institute's leadership can follow the procedure for dismissal of a member. It may want to inform the member prior to initiating the procedure what it intends to do and the rationale for the using this particular procedure.

Appendix: Sample Documents[28]

PETITION FOR ADMISSION TO CANDIDACY FOR THE DIACONATE AND FOR THE PRIESTHOOD

Current date
The Reverend N.
Provincial Superior (Superior General)
Street address
City, State, Zip Code

Dear Father N.
In accordance and compliance with canon 1034, §1 of the *Code of Canon Law*, I hereby formally petition for admission to candidacy for the orders of the diaconate and the priesthood. In making this request, I declare that I wish to dedicate my life to the service of the Church for the glory of God and the good of souls.

I realize that admission to candidacy for the sacrament of order does not carry with it any of the duties, rights, or privileges of clerics. However, I realize that in virtue of your acceptance of me as a candidate for the orders of diaconate and priesthood, I must care for my vocation in a special way and foster it. I also realize that I acquire the right to the necessary spiritual assistance by which I can develop my vocation and submit unconditionally to the will of God.

In presenting this petition, I solemnly declare that I am not by motivated by fear, either physical or moral. In no way am I coerced by parents, relatives, or any other agency whatsoever. Finally, I declare that I am making this request for admission to candidacy for the sacrament of order of my own free will.

Sincerely,
Signature

1. The petition must be handwritten on 8.5 x 11 stationery. If it is necessary to go to a second page, write on the back of the paper.
2. The petition is to be addressed to the petitioner's own major superior.
3. The petition is submitted to the formation director to be forwarded to the major superior.

---

[28] Samples One, Two, and Three are excerpts from *Handbook for Vocation and Seminary Personnel* (Washington, DC: United States Catholic Conference, n.d.) Reprinted with permission. All rights reserved.

SAMPLE PETITION FOR INSTALLATION INTO THE MINISTRY OF LECTOR

Current date
The Reverend N.
Provincial (Superior General)
Street Address
City, State, Zip Code

Dear Father N.:

In accordance and compliance with canon 1035, §1 of the *Code of Canon Law*, I am petitioning to be installed in the ministry of Lector.

I realize that as lector I am appointed for my own proper function, that of reading the Word of God in the liturgical assembly. In order that I may more fittingly and perfectly fulfill this function, I realize that I should meditate on the Sacred Scripture.

I am aware of the ministry I am undertaking and I shall make every effort and employ suitable means to acquire that love and knowledge of the Scripture that will make me more a disciple of the Lord. I also realize that the conferral of this ministry does not imply the right to sustenance or salary from the Church.

In presenting this petition, I solemnly declare that I am not motivated by fear, either physical or moral. I am not coerced in any way by parent, relative, or any other agency whatsoever. Finally, I declare that I am making this request for installation in the ministry of lector of my own free will.

Sincerely,
Signature

1. The petition must be handwritten on 8.5 x 11 stationery. If it is necessary to go to a second page, write on the back of the paper.
2. The petition is to be addressed to the petitioner's own major superior.
3. The petition is submitted to the formation director to be forwarded to the major superior.

SAMPLE PETITION FOR INSTALLATION INTO THE MINISTRY OF ACOLYTE

Current date
The Reverend N.
Provincial (Superior General)
Street Address
City, State, Zip Code

Dear Father N.:

In accordance and compliance with canon 1035, §1 of the *Code of Canon Law*, I am petitioning to be installed in the ministry of Acolyte.

I realize that as an acolyte I am appointed to aid the deacon and to minister to the priest. I understand the corresponding ordinary and extraordinary duties. In order that I may more worthily perform these functions, I realize that I should participate in the Holy Eucharist with increasingly fervent piety, that I should receive nourishment from it, and that I should deepen my knowledge of it.

Destined in a special way for the service of the altar, I realize that I should learn all matters concerning public divine worship and strive to grasp their inner spiritual meaning. In that way I shall be able to offer myself daily entirely to God, be an example to all by my seriousness and reverence in the sacred building, and have a sincere love for the Mystical Body of Christ, the people of God, especially the weak and the sick.

I realize that the conferral of this ministry does not imply the right to sustenance or salary from the Church.

In presenting this petition to you, I declare that I am not motivated by any fear, either physical or moral. In no way am I coerced by parents, relatives, or any other agency whatsoever. Finally, I declare that I am making this request for installation into the ministry of acolyte of my own free will.

Sincerely,
Signature

1. The petition must be handwritten on 8.5 x 11 stationery. If it is necessary to go to a second page, write on the back of the paper.
2. The petition is to be addressed to the petitioner's own major superior.
3. The petition is submitted to the formation director to be forwarded to the major superior.

STATEMENT TO LOCAL ORDINARY IN REQUESTING FACULTIES

STATEMENT OF THE RELIGIOUS SUPERIOR
concerning a Member of the (name of institute or society)
being presented for ministry in the
(Arch)diocese of (name)

Under guidelines proposed by the National Conference of Catholic Bishops (and approved by the Conference on November 18, 1993), the Conference of Major Superiors of Men, the Leadership Conference of Women Religious, and the Council of Major Superiors of Women Religious, and the policies of (name of the institute), I certify that (member's name) is a religious in good standing in the (name of) Province. To the best of my knowledge in the external forum, I am of the opinion that (name) is of good character and reputation.

I believe that he is qualified to perform his ministerial duties in an effective and suitable manner. More specifically, I am unaware of anything in his background which would render him unsuitable to work with minor children. Further, I have no knowledge that (name) has a current, untreated alcohol or substance abuse problem. Therefore, I present Reverend (member's name) for faculties in the (Arch)diocese of (name).

Signature
Provincial

Date

DIMISSORIAL LETTER

DIMISSORIAL LETTER

By virtue of this letter, I grant permission to (Name of the one to be ordained) to receive the Order of (Deacon or Presbyter) from the Most Reverend (Name of Diocesan Bishop where ordination is to take place), or, according to the norm of canon 1021 of the Code of Canon Law, by any other Bishop who is in Communion with the Apostolic See.

By this letter, I affirm that the above-named candidate has complied with the following requirements:

1. he became a permanently professed member of (Name of Institute) on (Date of Permanent Profession);
2. he has manifested his free intention to receive the Order of (Deacon or Presbyter);
3. he has the required age;
4. he has received approbation from the rector and faculty of the seminary and has completed the required studies;
5. he has been instituted into the required ministries for the Order he is requesting and has observed the prescribed intervals;
6. he has made the Profession of Faith, Declaration of Freedom, and fulfilled his spiritual obligation;
7. he is free of any impediments, irregularities, or censures and his moral character corresponds to the requirement of the Order he is about to receive.

Given at (Place)
on this (day) day of (Month), Year

Provincial

Provincial Notary

CHAPTER TWELVE

Procedures for Secular Institutes

SHARON HOLLAND, I.H.M.

Introduction

Although secular institutes have existed in some form in the Church for over two hundred years, their official recognition as a true form of consecrated life dates only from 1947.[1] Vatican Council II clearly recognized them as distinct from religious institutes in *Perfectae caritatis* 11 and the code now provides for them, for the first time, in the Church's universal law. Canons 573-606 apply to them as institutes of consecrated life; canons 710-730 address their specificity as secular institutes.

Certain canons of the latter section help to indicate what is characteristic of secular institutes. The member's consecration in a life of the evangelical counsels is lived out in the midst of secular realities. It is within that context that members seek their own growth in charity, and work to effect the sanctification of the world from within (c. 710). Consequently, the biblical image of leaven is often used to convey the notion of an individual presence, seeking to bring about the transformation of temporal realities through the power of the Gospel (c. 712).

Members of each institute are urged to a strong sense of communion in a common vocation (c. 602) without, however, the obligation of common life. Of its nature, consecrated secularity calls for the flexibility in living situations provided by canon 714.

While some institutes do have one or more corporate apostolates, it is clear from the canons that such works are not the expectation. Rather the more individual leaven-like presence in one's place of work and the diversity of living situations are characteristic.

---

[1] Pius XII, apostolic constitution *Provida Mater Ecclesia* (February 2, 1947) *AAS* 39 (1947) 114-124; CLD 3, 135-146.

Like other institutes of consecrated life, secular institutes can be either clerical or lay (c. 588). The sphere of their apostolic endeavors follows accordingly (cc. 711, 713).

In a 1976 address, Pope Paul VI offered a new image for the role of secular institutes. He saw them as the potential "experimental laboratory" in which the Church could test concrete ways of relating to the world.[2]

The post-synodal apostolic constitution *Vita Consecrata* speaks of secular institute members as "a leaven of wisdom and a witness of grace within cultural, economic, and political life.[3]

ERECTION AND RECOGNITION

Secular institutes, in accordance with the norms common to all institutes of consecrated life (cc. 573-606) are erected and recognized as diocesan or pontifical institutes in accordance with the procedures outlined in chapter two above. Likewise, their constitutions are approved by the same ecclesiastical authority in accord with canon 587.

STATUS OF MEMBERS

Members of secular institutes are consecrated and remain in the state of life they have as lay persons or clerics (c. 711). Consequently other parts of canon law apply to them in those respective states while religious law, unless expressly invoked, does not.

In keeping with this fact, a member's way of involvement in service to the ecclesial community will be as an individual lay man or woman or as a diocesan cleric (c. 713). Only if an institute actually has or accepts an institutional apostolate would there be consultations or written agreements between the institutes as such and the bishop.

Beyond their secular occupation, lay members are subject to the diocesan norms for lay participation in the life of the Church. Likewise the diocesan norms for clerical personnel would be followed for clerics, with the exception of cases mention in canon 715, §2 regarding clerics incardinated in an institute.

---

[2] Paul VI, "A Living Presence in the Service of the World and of the Church," in *Secular Institutes, Documents* (Rome: CMIS, 1998) 97.
[3] *VC* 10. *AAS* 88 (1996) 377-486; *Origins* 25 (April 4, 1996) 681; 683-720.

Similarly, the living arrangements of members follow from their status as laity or as secular clerics. Canon 714 provides for living alone, with family or in groups, according to the "ordinary conditions of the world" and to the institute's constitutions.

INCARDINATION

The norm for clerical secular institutes is incardination in the diocese (cc. 715, 266, §3). Studies, admission to orders, apostolic obedience, and the observance of particular law are essentially those of the secular clergy. (See chapter 11 above.)

As is clear from canon 266, §3, it is reserved to the Apostolic See to permit incardination in a secular institute. If this is granted, it would most probably be at the time of pontifical recognition of the institute. However, it must be noted that major superiors of clerical secular institutes of pontifical right are not ordinaries in the sense of canon 134, §1 and thus do not have the authority to grant dimissorial letters for their members. Rather, the member's ordination will be governed by the law for seculars (c. 1019, §2).

The major superior in such cases would need to provide the necessary information and guarantees of preparation to the member's proper bishop who, according to canon 1018, §1, 1° may issue the dimissorials if he himself will not be the ordaining bishop.

An ordained member who is incardinated in the institute will, according to canon 715, §2, relate to the diocesan bishop more in the manner of a religious when assigned to proper works of the institute or when exercising governance in the institute.

Should it happen that an institute with diocesan incardination also has some proper work, an agreement would have to be reached with the bishop when initiating its presence in diocese, including the way in which members would be appointed to that work. Likewise, if a member incardinated in the diocese is elected to a position of internal governance which would significantly affect his commitments in the diocese, an agreement would need to be reached with the bishop. Canon 718 addresses the institute's financial responsibility for such members.

Participation in Life and Governance

Chapters and Assemblies

Although there is no direct reference to a collegial governing body in the canons on secular institutes, canon 596 from the common norms, recognizes for both superiors and chapters, the authority given them in universal law and constitutions. Further, secular institutes enjoy that just autonomy of life, especially of governance, described in canon 586. In fact, a general chapter or assembly does exist in each institute and must be provided for in the constitutions.[4]

Moderators

Although it is not stated in canon 717, it is common practice that the supreme moderator be elected by the collegial governing body referred to above, following the norms for canonical elections, as presented in the constitutions.

The supreme moderator must be definitively incorporated. The length of a moderator's term of office and the manner of choosing them is to be defined in the constitutions.

In addition to the moderator's role stated in canon 717, §3 of seeking to preserve unity of spirit and to promote the active participation of members (c. 716), other responsibilities of moderators may be gleaned from the canons. These illustrate not only their role but also the necessity of their having a council.

Moderators have a role in the administration of any temporal goods belonging to the institute (c. 718); they are expected to be available to members for spiritual direction and advice (c. 719, §4); major moderators with their councils decide on the admission of candidates to probation and to the assumption of sacred bonds (c. 720) and they handle questions of separation from the institute (cc. 726-727; 729-730).

When canon law, or the constitutions, requires the advice or consent of the major moderator's council, the process is regulated by canon 127, §§1 and 3. For consent it is required that there be a meeting of the council and that the consent of an absolute majority of those present be obtained. In the case of needing the advice (counsel) of the council, there is to be a meeting unless proper law determines otherwise, and the counsel of all who are present must be sought. These elements are necessary for a valid act on the part of the mod-

---

[4] When approving secular institutes, *Provida Mater Ecclesia* (IX) provided for them to adopt offices and organs of governance based on those religious societies but with adaptation.

erator (c. 127, §1). In all cases the members of the council are to give their opinions sincerely and when the matter requires it, they must observe secrecy (c. 127, §3).

The guidelines for the general moderator's periodic report to the Apostolic See are provided in chapter two.

Administration of Goods

As public juridic persons, secular institutes have a right to acquire, retain, administer, and alienate temporal goods (c. 1255). As institutes which do not, as a rule, have common life or corporate apostolates, their transactions of this kind will be fewer than those of religious institutes or societies of apostolic life.

The norms of Book V of the Code (c. 718) apply and the basic procedures described in chapter nine above would be followed. Proper law must determine when a major moderator with the consent of his or her council may act and when transactions are reserved to the supreme moderator.

Proper law must also establish how it will handle its financial responsibilities toward members who, because of work for the institute, are not earning a living elsewhere. It is common practice that institutes have a system by which members contribute from their earnings to provide funds to cover the expenses of formation and governance. Moderators and formation personnel are not necessarily engaged full-time in internal work; however, where these roles or engagement in some corporate work involves a member more fully, provision must be made for their living expenses, insurance, and retirement.

ADMISSION

Canon 720 requires that the constitutions of each institute provide for which major moderator may act, with what role of the council, in admitting candidates to probation (cc. 721-722), to temporary incorporation, (c. 723, §§1-2), and to perpetual or definitive incorporation (c. 723, §§3-4).

Canon 721 lists three invalidating impediments to admission to probation in a secular institute. Here the minimum age is majority, age 18 (c. 97, §1). The impediments of marriage bond, sacred bonds, or incorporation in a society of apostolic life may be supplemented by others in the constitutions. In addition, canon 597 from the common norms must be observed, requiring that a candidate must be Catholic, of right intention, possess the necessary qualities, and be free of impediments.

Although the canons on secular institutes do not detail all of the same documents and requirements for admission as are given for religious institutes, the procedures discussed in chapter four above can be helpful. It must be kept in mind, however, that the absence of a common life as a norm and the life of secular consecration in the ordinary working world can significantly affect the criteria used by an institute in admitting candidates.

If the evaluation of experts is used to judge the maturity of the individual (c. 721, §3) then canon 220 must be observed, protecting the individual's right to his or her good reputation and to privacy. This involves the usual release of information forms and the strictly confidential use of information on the part of those whose authority to admit candidates gives them access to it.

FORMATION

The canons regulating formation in secular institutes (cc. 722 and 724) leave a great deal to proper law. In keeping with their secular nature, the institutes do not require a common residence in which formation takes place. Rather, it is often carried out through correspondence, individually used courses of study followed in regular contact with a formator, tapes, occasional visits, participation in local gatherings of members, and annual retreats. In some areas, seminary or university courses in spirituality, theology, scripture, liturgy, etc. may be available. In this way, formation goes forward without professional work being interrupted.

Constitutions must establish the length and method of formation before the first assumption of sacred bonds. However, it cannot be shorter than two years (c. 722, §3). The fact that formation is a life-long project is clear from canon 724 which calls for uninterrupted formation after first incorporation in matters both human and divine. Likewise, moderators must concern themselves with the continuous spiritual formation of members.

From various canons the broad areas of the content of formation can be gleaned:

- ♦ candidates must understand the vocation to secular consecration and be formed in the particular spirit and way of life of the institute;
- ♦ they must learn to fully translate their life into apostolate which, like leaven, strives to imbue all things with the spirit of the Gospel;
- ♦ lay members will be formed to share in the Church's evangelizing tasks using the means which most clearly respond to the purpose, spirit, and character of the institute;
- ♦ candidates for ordination will be formed for sacred ministry;

- all, according to their state, will study how to order and inform the temporal order according to the values of the Gospel;
- candidates must be formed as ecclesial men and women who think with the Church;
- All will receive formation for a life of prayer, both personal and liturgical, enabling them to fulfill fruitfully those obligations mentioned in canon 719.

Incorporation

As mentioned above, constitutions must establish which major moderator is to judge the suitability of the candidate for incorporation at the end of initial probation and with what role of the council. Consequently, each institute must also give thought to how they can provide for contact between candidates and major moderators or councillors and for appropriate evaluation from those responsible for formation. Where candidates have the possibility of participating in local groupings of members on a regular basis, those members also might have a role in evaluating the suitability of the potential new member.

The code leaves to the constitutions of each institute the determination of the sacred bonds by which the evangelical counsels will be assumed (c. 712). The bonds, whether vows (cc. 1191-1192), oaths (cc. 1199-1200), acts of consecration binding in conscience, or promises, are recognized as sacred, that is, effecting the consecration of the members to God. The constitutions must also provide detail on the obligations which further specify the content of canons 599-601 of the common norms preserving "the proper secularity of the institute" (c. 712). It is also customary for the constitutions to contain the formula used at the time of incorporation.

It is clear from the canons (c. 723, §2) that first incorporation is "temporary," that is, taken for a specified amount of time. While it may not be less than five years, constitutions are to specify whether the original commitment is renewed annually, is made immediately for five years or is made in some other combination of renewal periods.

Since the code expresses only the minimum and not the maximum time in temporary incorporation, the constitutions should provide (a) after how many years one may be admitted to perpetual incorporation or definitive incorporation, (b) whether all members are incorporated in the same way or if there is an option between perpetual and definitive incorporation.

The law is silent on the point of a moderator receiving the sacred bonds because that is a characteristic of the public vows of religious which are received in the name of the Church (c. 1192, §1). Proper law, however, should indicate in what setting the sacred bonds are assumed, whether they are witnessed in silence or if they are received on behalf of the institute. Likewise, there should be provision for how they are recorded in the archives of the institute.

Associates

Since their formal recognition by the Church as a form of consecrated life, many secular institutes have also had other persons associated with them. It is clear from the preceding canons that members, in what *Provida Mater* (III, 2) called the "strict sense," are those who assume the evangelical counsels through sacred bonds, either perpetually or definitively. The fundamental difference between celibate chastity and conjugal chastity most clearly highlights the difference between the two states.

The constitutions of each secular institute with associates must clarify what bond is used to associate a person with the institute (c. 725). Furthermore, proper law or policies should identify (a) the requirements for becoming associated, (b) the rights and obligations which flow from association both on the part of the individual and of the institute, (c) how those associated are formed and assisted in striving for evangelical perfection according to the spirit of the institute, (d) the way in which those associated may participate in its mission. Only members in the strict sense have the right and duty to participate in the life and governance of the institute in the sense of canons 716 and 717, §3.

SEPARATION OF MEMBERS

Departure during Temporary Incorporation

Canon 726 envisions three ways in which those in temporary incorporation may leave the institute. The fact that the similar canons of religious law are neither invoked nor fully repeated indicates that they should not be applied in these cases.

- ♦ When the time of temporary incorporation elapses, the individual, not having requested renewal or definitive incorporation is free. The matter should be discussed in advance with the competent moderator and the fact noted in the records of the institute.

- ♦ The competent major superior may exclude a member from the renewal of sacred bonds. He or she is required to hear the council first. The just cause which is required must be evaluated in terms of the requirements of universal law and the proper law of the institute and knowledge of the member during the previous period of temporary incorporation.

- One who feels urged by a grave cause to leave the institute before the time of temporary incorporation has lapsed presents a written request for an indult of departure to the supreme moderator expressing the reasons for the request. Proper law may ask that the petition be channeled through a more immediate major moderator but granting the indult is reserved to the supreme moderator with consent of the council.

The canon makes no distinction between pontifical and diocesan institutes. The effects of the indult are in canon 728.

Departure of the Perpetually Incorporated

For the departure of a perpetually incorporated member, there must be recourse to ecclesiastical authority (c. 727).

- In pontifical institutes, the petition, written after serious prayer, is forwarded to the supreme moderator who sends it to the Apostolic See. While not stated in the canon, it would be appropriate for the supreme moderator to add his or her opinion in the forwarding letter.
- In diocesan institutes the constitutions should provide further precision. The indult could be sought from the Apostolic See or also from the diocesan bishop of (a) the principal seat of the institute or (b) the diocese where the member lives and works. It is always channeled through the supreme moderator.
- In the case of a cleric incardinated in the institute the provisions of canon 693 are invoked requiring that a benevolent bishop be found before the indult is granted.

In institutes where some or all of the members are definitively, rather than perpetually, incorporated constitutions must indicate whether the above or a purely internal procedure is followed in cases of departure.

Effect of the Indult

In any case, the indult of departure takes effect when granted legitimately. The sacred bonds cease to bind and all rights and obligations arising from incorporation cease (c. 728). The normal procedure is that the indult is communicated back to the petitioner using the same channels through which it was submitted to the competent ecclesiastical authority.

For a secular institute cleric incardinated in the diocese, the indult terminates incorporation in the institute leaving him incardinated in the diocese and fully subject to the diocesan bishop.

Dismissal

For cases of dismissal, canon 729 applies a number of canons from religious law to parallel situations in secular institutes. The reader may refer to chapter seven for those procedures.

- *Ipso facto* dismissal is handled according to canon 694.
- Mandatory dismissal is handled according to canon 695.
- For discretionary dismissal, causes must be established in the constitutions of each secular institute. While they must be proportionately grave, external, imputable, and juridically proven; the causes listed in canon 696 are not repeated here for secular institutes.
- The procedure for discretionary dismissal is that of the religious canons 697-700 with the effects expressed in canon 701.
- Canon 702 is not invoked since it is presumed that secular institute members are self-supporting through their work. However, when proper law does call for some form of community of goods, attention must be given to the equity and evangelical charity due to members separating from the institute (c. 702, §2).

Transfers

In the case of transfers between two secular institutes, the religious canons are again employed omitting only canon 684, §3 on monasteries (c. 730). The basic principles explained in chapter seven would apply.

If, however, the transfer involves a secular institute and either a religious institute or a society of apostolic life, the written petition and the letters of consent from the supreme moderators given with the consent of their respective councils must be forwarded to the Apostolic See. In granting the permission, certain particular mandates may be added to accommodate differences such as the presence or absence of vows or the mode of incorporation which are not provided for in the canons on transfer between two institutes of the same kind.

CHAPTER THIRTEEN

SOCIETIES OF APOSTOLIC LIFE

MICHAEL P. JOYCE, C.M.

Societies of apostolic life have their origins in the sixteenth and seventeenth centuries with the Oratories of Saint Philip Neri in Rome and Pierre Berulle in Paris, along with the Congregation of the Mission and the Daughters of Charity of Saint Vincent Depaul, the Society of Saint Sulpice founded by Jean Jacques Olier, and others. The founders did not intend the members to live the religious life for a variety of reasons. However, the lifestyle of these societies approached that of religious institutes in many ways. The 1917 *Code of Canon Law* called these groups societies of common life without vows. The law for the societies in that code treated them as religious congregations. The commission for revision of the law for institutes of consecrated life gradually accepted the position that societies of apostolic life should not be considered institutes of consecrated life. This position is reflected in the schema of 1980. Since societies of apostolic life are not institutes of consecrated life, they have their own section of law although they share in some ways a law in common with institutes.[1]

Inasmuch as this handbook treats procedures for societies of apostolic life, it is not appropriate to present a history of the societies here. The above paragraph shows briefly the treatment they have received in canon law. The remainder of the chapter will examine the codal law for societies canon by canon. The reader is referred to previous chapters when appropriate because certain canons require societies to follow the law for institutes of consecrated life. This chapter gives specific procedures for societies when the law requires.

---

[1] Cecil L. Parres, C.M., "Societies of Apostolic Life" in *A Handbook on Canon 573-746*, Jordan Hite, T.O.R., Sharon Holland, I.H.M., Daniel Ward, O.S.B., eds. (Collegeville, Minnesota: The Liturgical Press, 1985), 289.

Those implementing procedures for societies of apostolic life always need to attend to the proper law of the society (the constitutions, statutes, directories, etc.) because the general law gives precedence to the proper law of the society as the canons indicate. While this principle is effective as well for institutes of consecrated life, it is particularly pertinent for societies because each society has a unique character which the *Code of Canon Law* recognizes.

The Bond with the Society

While there are several notable distinctions between societies of apostolic life and institutes of consecrated life, the most remarkable is that members of societies are not consecrated by religious vows (c. 731, §1). Societies in some respects resemble religious institutes; however, the members do not have public vows as defined by canon 1192, §1.

Some societies do establish the bond between the members and the society through vows. These vows, however, are private as defined in canon 1192, §1. As section 2 of canon 731 notes, there are other ways that societies can establish the bond. The method is described in the constitutions of each society. Likewise, if the society does use vows as a method for creating the bond, the effects of the vows are also determined in the constitutions. Canons 598 to 602 also apply to these societies.

The society needs to determine clearly how the bond is created. Competent superiors and members should sign some form of a document indicating how, when, and where the bond became effective. A copy of the document is placed in the individual's personnel file and notification is sent to the general headquarters of the society. See the appendix to this chapter for a sample form of attestation.

The general law does not legislate the manner in which the common life is experienced. As section 1 of canon 731 states, this matter is treated in the constitutions of the society. Usually, the constitutions will give a general prescription for the observance of the common life. Major superiors and local levels of leadership then make more concrete criteria for how it is exercised.

When there is a need for a society or its members to communicate with the Holy See, the proper congregation to contact is the Congregation for Institutes of Consecrated Life and for Societies of Apostolic Life. The title of the congregation indicates its competency.

General Norms

Rather than repeat principles already enunciated in the code, canon 732 refers members of societies of apostolic life back to canons introducing institutes of consecrated life. The topics those canons cover are the intent of the founder or foundress, establishment of societies by diocesan bishops, aggregation, divisions, and mergers of societies. Subsequent canons address changes subject to the Holy See, suppression, autonomy, and proper law. The introductory canons also describe the various types of institutes, exemption, communication with the Holy See, and relationship to ecclesiastical authority. This section of the law on institutes of consecrated life also explains the authority of superiors and chapters, and general norms for admission. Canon 606 invokes the principle of equal application of the law to societies of men and women.

While societies of apostolic life are to use the canons, the particular character of each society is still respected. The great difference between societies highlights the critical importance of their proper law.[2]

The reader can see chapter two of this handbook for procedures used in establishing new societies (c. 579). The same chapter explains the aggregation of a society to another society or to an institute of consecrated life (c. 580). The chapter also gives the procedures for mergers and union of institutes and societies (c. 582) as well as procedures for suppression of a society (c. 584).

A society of apostolic life needs to look to its proper law for the procedures for dividing into parts, establishing new divisions, joining previously erected ones, or defining the parts in another way. One should consult with the supreme authority of the society for these procedures (c. 581). Suppression of various parts of the society (c. 585) belongs to the competent authority of the society. The supreme authority of the society should be consulted for the proper procedures.

Changes in matters which have been approved by the Apostolic See cannot be made without its permission (c. 583). As mentioned above, the Congregation for Institutes of Consecrated Life and Societies of Apostolic Life handles these matters.

While institutes have a rightful autonomy of life and local ordinaries are to safeguard and protect that autonomy (c. 586), there are many instances in which societies and local ordinaries need to cooperate, especially in the apostolate. Chapter eight of this handbook presents procedures for working with local ordinaries regarding the apostolate.

---

[2] Sharon Holland, I.H.M., "Societies of Apostolic Life," *The Code of Canon Law: Text and Commentary* 535, ed. James A. Coriden et al. (New York/Mahwah, NJ: Paulist Press, 1985) 535.

Canon 587 addresses constitutions, statutes, and directories of societies. Chapter one concerning governance explains these documents.

Societies of apostolic life can enjoy the privilege of exemption (c. 591) as spelled out in their constitutions. At the same time, supreme moderators of societies of apostolic life must give regular reports to the Apostolic See on the status and life of the society. Chapter two explains this report. For societies of apostolic life of diocesan right, the diocesan bishop of the principal seat of the institute approves the constitutions and confirms any changes in them (c. 595). He also deals with matters of greater importance which affect the whole institute and are beyond the power of its internal authority. He can also grant dispensations from the constitutions in particular cases. An example of matters of greater importance is alienation of temporal goods. See chapter nine for procedures in this area.

The law for societies of apostolic life and their members applies equally to either sex (c. 606) unless the context of the wording or the nature of the matter indicates otherwise. The nature of clerical societies of apostolic life requires some differences in applying canon law to the members of the society. Chapter eleven explains procedures that are needed for the sacrament of order.

If members of a particular society undertake living the evangelical counsels, they are also bound by canons 598 to 602. Again, the proper law of the society describes in more detail how the counsels are lived by the members. Each of the mentioned canons refers to the proper law of institutes of consecrated life.

Houses and Local Communities

Unlike institutes of consecrated life, societies of apostolic life can establish local communities in addition to erecting houses (c. 733). The erection of houses and the establishment of local communities is done by the competent authority of the society after receiving the written consent of the diocesan bishop. When a house or local community is suppressed, the competent authority must consult the diocesan bishop before the suppression.

The proper law of the society determines the governance, the manner of life in common of the members, and the relationship to other parts of the society for local communities. The general law is silent on these matters. Houses have the right to have at least an oratory in which to celebrate and reserve the Holy Eucharist.

Governance

Governance in societies of apostolic life is determined by the constitutions of the society (c. 734). However the constitutions must take into consideration canons 617 to 633. Canons 617 to 630 address superiors and their councils. See chapter one of this handbook for further information. Canon 620 establishes who in societies of apostolic life are major superiors; namely, the general superior of a society, those who govern a province or its equivalent, and their vicars. Canon 621 describes what the universal law considers a province. There are four requirements for a province. It must be (1) a union of several houses, (2) under the same superior, (3) constituting an immediate part of the society, and (4) established by the legitimate authority of the society. One needs to consult the proper law of a society regarding further requirements for establishing a province. Canon 623 requires the proper law to indicate what are the qualifications for valid appointment or election to the office of superior in terms of the length of membership in the society. Furthermore, proper law must determine terms of office and methods for removal or transfer from the office (c. 624).

General superiors of societies of apostolic life are chosen by canonical elections as indicated in their proper constitutions. Diocesan bishops preside at the election of a supreme moderator of societies of diocesan right (c. 635). Superiors, apart from supreme moderators, are instituted according to the constitutions of the society. They have councils to assist them in carrying out their office. The council members must give their consent or counsel for various matters according to universal or proper law (c. 627). The reader can consult chapter one for a more complete explanation of relationships between major superiors and their councils, and the requirements for consent or counsel.

Superiors in societies who are charged with the responsibility of visitation are to fulfill the duty according to the norms of the proper law of the society (c. 628). All superiors of a society have the obligation to reside in their respective houses or local community (c. 629). However, proper law may provide for the use of a regional superior for several houses or local communities within a given area. Superiors are not to hear the confessions of their subjects unless a subject takes the initiative and requests it (c. 630, §4). This norm provides protection for both superiors and subjects in regard to the internal forum. Canon 630 requires ordinary confessors for lay societies in houses of formation and in large communities.

Societies of apostolic life must have an institute akin to the general chapter of religious institutes (c. 631). These bodies may have other names in societies to distinguish the society from religious institutes; however, their functions are the same for the society as a general chapter is for a religious institute. The reader may refer to chapter one on governance for further explanation of chapters. Societies may have other organs as well for consultation and participation of members (c. 633). These bodies must be carefully established and regulated.

Admission, Incorporation, and Initial Formation

Each society is allowed to determine in its proper law its own norms for admission, probation, incorporation, and formation of its members (c. 735). However, the society must follow the requirements of canons 642 to 645 for admission. Canon 642 demands that those seeking admission must have the required age, health, character, and maturity that the society requires. The reader can consult chapter four for more explanation of these requirements. Canon 643 lists factors that render admission invalid. One also needs to consult the proper law of the society because it can establish further impediments. If the person seeking admission is a diocesan presbyter or deacon, the superior must consult his local ordinary before admitting the cleric (c. 644). Likewise, the superior is not to admit someone so burdened by debt that the person cannot retire it. Canon 645 indicates what documentation is required for admission. Chapter four provides explanations of these documents as well as sample forms for them.

Although the canons referred to are in the context of a novitiate, societies are not required to have a novitiate. The canons need to be read in the context of the first probationary period of membership in the society.

Incardination

Members of clerical societies of apostolic life are incardinated into the society unless the constitutions provide otherwise (c. 736). One exception is the Society of St. Sulpice in which members are incardinated into their diocese of origin. Initial formation programs for ordination are to follow those for diocesan clergy which can be found in the national *Program for Priestly Formation*.[3]

Societies that have clerical members incardinated into dioceses must clearly define in the constitutions or in a contract the relationship of the member with the diocesan bishop. A diocesan cleric entering into a society maintains incardination in the diocese until he is definitively incorporated into the society unless the constitutions of the society maintain incardination in a diocese (see cc. 268, §2 and 266,§2).

---

[3] The latest edition for the United States is National Conference of Catholic Bishops, *Program of Priestly Formation*, fourth edition (Washington, DC: United States Catholic Conference, 1993).

Rights and Obligations of Members

The rights and obligations of members of societies of apostolic life are found in the constitutions of the society (c. 737). Canons 662 to 672 concerning the rights and obligations of members of institutes of consecrated life do not apply to members of societies of apostolic life. Constitutions must attend to the distinction between temporary and definitive incorporation. The rights and obligations of members in temporary incorporation will differ from those belonging to members who are definitively incorporated

Although members of societies of apostolic life are not bound to the rights and obligations of religious, they are bound to the rights and obligations of clerics (c. 739).[4] These obligations include reverence and obedience to the pope and to their proper ordinary (c. 273), union and cooperation with one another in a mutual and prayerful bond (c. 275), the pursuit of holiness (c. 276), the observance of perfect and perpetual continence (c. 277, §§1-2), and avoidance of activities alien to their state and way of life (c. 285, §§1-2). There are some rights and obligations that do not belong to lay members of societies. The context determines those that require the sacrament of order to exercise them. The reader may refer to chapter six for a fuller presentation on the applicability of the obligations and rights of clerics to members of societies of apostolic life.

Relationship with the Diocesan Bishop

Members of societies of apostolic life are subject to the diocesan bishop in the spheres of public worship, the care of souls, and other works of the apostolate (c. 738). Please refer to chapter eight for more information. When members of a society are incardinated in a diocese, their relationship with the diocesan bishop is governed by the constitutions of the society or particular agreements. The diocesan bishop has the right of pastoral visitation for churches, oratories, and other works of a society with the exception of schools for its own members (c. 683).

A diocesan bishop can prohibit a member of a society for a very serious reason from living in the diocese (c. 679). He is first to inform the major superior of the intended prohibition. If the major superior does not remove the member, the diocesan bishop refers the matter to the Holy See. The member can appeal the bishop's decision through the supreme moderator of the society.

Works entrusted to a society by a diocesan bishop are subject to the bishop (c. 681). This situation is different than a work of the society. The reader can refer to chapter eight on the apostolate for more information on how to proceed with works entrusted by the diocesan bishop.

A diocesan bishop may confer an ecclesiastical office upon a member of a society of apostolic life with at least the assent of the competent superior. The member can be removed from the office either at the discretion of the diocesan bishop or the superior, having notified the bishop. The law is applicable to pastors and parochial vicars according to canons 523; 538, §2; 547; and 552. Neither ordinary needs to consent to the removal by the other (c. 682).

Common Life

Members of societies of apostolic life are obliged to live the common life in a legitimately constituted house or local community (c. 740). The constitutions determine what forms common life for the society. The proper law of the society determines lawful absences from the common life.

Temporal Goods

Societies, their parts, and their houses are made juridic persons by the law itself (c. 741). Therefore each of these units are capable of acquiring, administering, and alienating temporal goods. Provinces and houses are not subsidiaries of the society or of one another. See chapter nine on temporal goods for further explanation about acquisition, administration, and alienation. Each society and each province is to have a finance officer distinct from the major superior (c. 636). Every house of the society is also to have a distinct finance officer to the extent possible. The finance officers and other administrators are to give accounts of their administration according to the norms of the proper law.

The proper law of the society determines acts of extraordinary administration that need approval of another agency and the procedures necessary for obtaining the permission (c. 638). Persons other than superiors may be designated for validly incurring expenses and performing juridic acts of ordinary administration. The designation should be in writing and include the powers and limits of the designee.

Members of societies of apostolic life are capable according to the constitutions of the society of acquiring, administering, and alienating temporal goods because they are not bound by a public vow of poverty. However, whatever comes to them on account of their membership in the society belongs to the society.

---

[4] Commentators disagree on the meaning of canon 739. Since this book addresses procedures rather than commentary, it is beyond the scope of this work to discuss the disagreements here.

Departure and Dismissal of Members in Temporary Incorporation

Voluntary departures and dismissals of members not definitively incorporated are governed by the constitutions of the society (c. 742). The following section addresses members who are definitively incorporated.

Departure of Members Definitively Incorporated

Members definitively incorporated who wish to depart may obtain an indult of departure from the society from the supreme moderator with the consent of the council unless the constitutions reserve the indult to the Holy See (c. 743). When the indult has been obtained, the member no longer has the rights and obligations that incorporation entail. However if the member is a presbyter or deacon, the indult is not granted until he has found a bishop who will incardinate him or at least receive him for five years with a view to incardination. In the latter case, he is incardinated after the five years have passed unless the bishop refused to incardinate him.

Societies that require an indult from the Holy See for departure should consult chapter seven for proper procedures to follow. The reader may also refer to chapter eleven for the departure of members who are presbyters or deacons.

Transfer

Supreme moderators of societies of apostolic life can give a member permission with the consent of the council to transfer to another society of apostolic life (c. 744). Before the member is definitively transferred into the receiving society, the rights and obligations from membership in the society of origin are suspended for the member. The member has a right during this time to return to the original society. See chapter seven for proper procedures to follow.

If a member desires to enter an institute of consecrated life, he or she must receive permission from the Holy See. Likewise, if a member of an institute of consecrated life wishes to enter a society of apostolic life, the member must also receive permission from the Holy See. The reader again can refer to chapter seven for these procedures.

Living Outside the Society

Supreme moderators of societies of apostolic life can grant permission with the consent of the council for a member to live outside the society for a period up to three years and suspend the rights and obligations of the member not suitable to the new situation (c. 745). If the member is a presbyter or deacon, the local ordinary of the diocese in which he will live must also grant permission. Chapter seven has procedures for these actions.

Dismissal of Members Definitively Incorporated

Superiors seeking the dismissal of a definitively incorporated member follow the same procedures as for the dismissal of a member of an institute of consecrated life (c. 746). The reader may consult chapter seven of this work for those procedures.

SAMPLE FORM

Attestation of Definitive Bond

I, *Name of Member*, a member of *Name of Society* born in *Name of City or Town*, diocese of *Name of Diocese*, on the *Date* day of the month of *Month* in the year *Year*, son/daughter of *Name of Father* and of *Name of Mother with Maiden Name*; received into the *Name of Society and Province, if applicable* at *Name of Place* on the *Date* day of the month of *Month* in the year *Year*, made definitive bond with the same Society according to its Constitutions, which I understand well, at *Name of Place* on the *Date* day of the month of *Month* in the year *Year*, in the presence of *Name of Superior or Witness to Bond*, who is a member of the same Society.

Signature of Member making definitive bond

Signature of Witness to Definitive Bond

INDEX

A

abortion, irregularities and impediments to ordination involving, 225–227
acolyte, ministry of, 221–222, 238
active voice
  exclaustrated members, 28
  general chapters, 28
acts, 14, 16
  cession, act of, *See* cession, act of
administration of temporal goods, 198–206
admission of candidates, 63–94
  applications
    information about (sample form), 71–72
    records and recordkeeping, 66
    sample application form, 76–82
  autobiographical essay, 87–88
  committee or admissions board, 70, 75
  common procedures, 65–68
  directories, value of, 70
  education of candidate in institutional traditions and practices, 65
  financial obligations of candidates, 64, 66, 90
  forms and figures
    admissions board information, 75
    application, 76–82
    autobiography of candidates, 87–88
    dental examination, 91
    eye examination, 92
    HIV/AIDS testing, 93–94
    information about application for admission, 71–72
    information-gathering form, 73–74
    letters of recommendation/references, 83–84
    psychological testing release form, 85–86
  HIV/AIDS testing, 66, 93–94
  implementation of codes, 65–68
  information-gathering process, 65–68, 73–74
  invalid admissions, 64
  letters of recommendation, 67, 83–84
  major superiors' right to admit candidates, 63–94
  medical examinations, 66–68, 91–94
  medical records, 91–94
  ordination, 219–220, 236
  postulancy or pre-novitiate, *See* postulancy or pre-novitiate
  psychological testing, 64, 67, 85–86
  records and recordkeeping
    applications, 66
    canonical requirements, 64
    criteria fulfillment, 65
    ordination, 220
    sample forms, *See* subhead 'forms and figures,' this heading
  references, 67, 83–84
  requirements for admission, 63–64, 65
  secular clerics, diocesan bishop's notification required for, 64
  secular institutes, 245–248
  societies of apostolic life, 256
  specific code requirements, 63–64
age requirements
  ministry of lector or acolyte, institution into, 221
  novitiate, admission to, 64
  ordination, admission to candidacy for, 220
  permanent diaconate, 227
  perpetual profession, 102

presbyterate, ordination to, 229
secular institutes, admission to candidacy in, 245
temporary profession, 99
transitional diaconate, 223
agency status of exclaustrated religious, 145
agreements
  apostolates, regarding
    diocesan bishop, agreement between religious institute and, 193
    entrusted by diocesan bishop to religious institute, 171
    individual religious, new apostolates initiated by, 178
    inter-institute agreement to jointly sponsor a work, 194
    partnership agreements with sponsored works, 185–186
  exclaustrated members, 147
  living apart from community, 123
  mergers and unions, 44, 46
  sponsored works, partnership agreements, 185–186
AIDS/HIV testing prior to admission of candidates, 66, 93–94
alcohol or drug abuse
  policies, 58–59
  privacy and confidentiality regarding, right to, 127
alien activities, requirement to abstain from, 130–133
alienation, business transactions, and indebtednesses, 201–207
  amounts triggering approval requirements, 201–203, 204–205
  Apostolic See, requiring approval of, 202–203, 204–205
  approval of, 201–202, 205–206
  charitable trusts, temporal goods held in, 206–207
  civil structures used to avoid, 199
  Congregation for Institutes of Consecrated Life and Societies of Apostolic Life, approval required of, 201, 203–204
  definition of alienation, 207
  experts as to valuation of goods, 205
  juridic person, affecting, 201
  leases, 206
  major superior requiring consent of council for, 5, 206
  procedures for, 202–203
  proper law, 201
  reorganization of corporation as alienation, 206
  time to seek approval, 205–206
  valuation of goods, 204–205
apostasy, irregularities and impediments to ordination involving, 225–227
apostolates, 167–194
  abuses, correction of, 179, 181
  agreements regarding, *See* agreements
  bans
    individual religious forbidden to reside in diocese, 179
    religious institute forbidden conduct apostolic work in diocese, 179–180
  catechetics, 169
  changes in, 170, 172–175
  Church's apostolate, institutional apostolate as part of, 168
  civil law requirements, 182–184
  coordination
    collaboration and cooperation with other institutes, societies, and secular clerics, 172, 194
    diocesan bishop's responsibility of, 178
    superiors, responsibilities of, 180

defined, 167
diocesan bishops, relationship with, 169–179, 192, 193
ecclesiastical offices
  conferred by diocesan bishop on institute, 171
  individual religious taking up, 175–177
  societies of apostolic life, entrusted to members of, 257
education, 169–170
entrusted by diocesan bishop to institute or society, 171, 257
exemptions from jurisdiction of diocesan bishop to fulfill, 169
formation, 169
forms and figures
  agreement between religious institute and diocesan bishop, 193
  assignment from congregation, letter of, 191
  testimonial letter of permission to diocesan bishop, 192
fostering, diocesan bishop's duty of, 178
governance of apostolic works
  diocesan bishops, by, 178–180
  major superiors, 179–181
  sponsored works, 185
individual religious, 175–178
  assignment from congregation, letter of, 191
  civil law requirements, 182–183, 184
  diocese, forbidden to reside in, 179
  ecclesiastic office held by, 175–177
  new works initiated by, 177–178
  remuneration, 182–183
  rights and obligations, 181
  testimonial letter of permission to diocesan bishop, 192
joint works, 172, 194
liabilities related to, 183
major superiors, 179–181
  abuses, correction of, 181
  coordination of apostolate by, 180
  individual religious, oversight of, 181
  participation in mission, 180
  rights and obligations, 181
media, 170
modifying, 170, 174
new apostolic works, 170, 172–173, 177–178
parochial duties, 171
preaching, 170
publishing and writing, 170
radio, 170
religious authorized to live apart from community for purposes of, 122–123
remuneration for, 182–183
rights and obligations regarding, 181
societies of apostolic life, entrusted to members of, 257
specific religious houses, rights of, 170–171
sponsored works, *See* sponsored works
television, 170
terminating, 170, 174–175
traditions of institute, remaining true to, 170, 172–175
visitations as form of oversight of, 178
withdrawing from, 170, 174–175
writing and publishing, 170
apostolic life, societies of, *See* societies of apostolic life
Apostolic See
  diocesan institutes, forming, 38
  exclaustration, approval of
  durante necessitate exclaustration only grantable by Holy See, 139

involuntary exclaustration, 144
voluntary exclaustration, 142
living apart from community, disapproval of, 118–119
mergers and unions, 42
new institutes and societies, forming
  diocesan institutes, 38
  mergers and unions, 42
  pontifical recognition, 41
reports to, *See* reports to Apostolic See
secular institutes, pontifical recognition of, 242
secularization, approval of, 149, 151
societies of apostolic life, 253
suppression reserved to, 46
transfers between religious institutes and secular institutes or societies of apostolic life, approval of, 135, 250, 259
women's contemplative communities, rules of cloister for, 125–126
appeals
  denial of ordination to presbyterate, 229
  dismissals, 155
  right of, 214
arbitration, 211–213
archives, 15–19, *See* also records and recordkeeping
assets, *See* temporal goods
associates of secular institutes, 248
association with persons, prudence enjoined as to, 129
associations of the faithful (Pious Unions), 36–38
automatic or *ipso facto* dismissal, 154, 155, 156, 158, 216
automobiles used by exclaustrated religious, 145–146

B

Berulle, Pierre, 251
bishops, *See* diocesan bishops
boards of reconciliation, 209–210
business or trade, engagement in, 130, 131–132
business transactions adversely affecting patrimonial condition of juridic person, *See* alienation, business transactions, and indebtednesses

C

candidates, admission of, *See* admission of candidates
canon law
  fidelity to traditions and openness to world, balancing, v–vii
  freedom allowed institutes and societies to determine specific modalities or procedures, 2–3
catechetics, apostolate of, 169
"Catholic" as title, use of, 196–197
cession, act of, 102–106
  changes to, 106
  purpose of, 102–103
  sample forms, 103–105
  transfers between institutes, 136
chapters and other gatherings
  directories and handbooks as to, 11
  general chapters, *See* general chapters
  secular institutes, 244
  societies of apostolic life, 255–256
  universal law concerning, 8
charitable trusts, 206–207
charts, *See* forms and figures
chastity, vow of, *See* evangelical counsels
civil and criminal law, 19–24
  alienation, avoiding, 199
  apostolates and, 182–184
  exclaustration, 145–147

medical care, advance directives regarding, 110
records and recordkeeping, 19–24
sexual misconduct of members, 58
temporal goods, administration of, 199–200
civil offices and duties, *See* duties and offices outside institute
clerical status
  acolyte, ministry of, 221–222, 238
  admission into candidacy for ordination, 219–220
  diaconate, *See* diaconate
  dismissal or departure, effect on clerical status of, 231–235
  laicization, clerics leaving institutes without seeking, 152, 231–235
  lector, ministry of, 221–222, 237
  ministries of lector and acolyte, institution into, 221–222, 237–238
  ordination, *See* ordination
  presbyterate
    denial of ordination to, 228–229
    ordination to, 229
  secular, *See* secular clerics
  secular clerics, *See* secular clerics
  secular institutes, clerical members of, 241, 242–243
cloister, 125–126
Code of Canon Law
  fidelity to traditions and openness to world, balancing, v–vii
  freedom allowed institutes and societies to determine specific modalities or procedures, 2–3
common good, rights and obligations regarding, 4
common life, 117–121
  cloistered communities, 125–126
  living apart from community, *See* living apart from community

religious institutes, 117–119
secular institutes, 119–120, 241
societies of apostolic life, 120–121, 251, 252, 258
variants on, 118–119
communion with church
  obligation of members to maintain, 4
  sponsored works, 186–188
compensation
  civil law requirements, 182–183
  claims of former members regarding work performed during membership, 148
complementary book, 9
compulsory or mandatory dismissal, 154, 156, 216
conciliation process, 210–211
confidentiality, *See* privacy and confidentiality
constitutions, 8–9, 39
contemplative communities
  cloister, 125–126
  women religious, 125–126
coordination of apostolates
  collaboration and cooperation with other institutes, societies, and secular clerics, 172, 194
  diocesan bishop's responsibility of, 178
  superiors, responsibilities of, 180
councils of major superiors, 5–7
  consent *versus* counsel required from, 5
  minutes of council meetings, 13–14, 23
credit cards used by exclaustrated religious, 145
criminal law of secular state, *See* civil and criminal law

D

debt
  admission of candidates with, 64, 66, 90, 256
  institutes and societies undertaking, *See* alienation, business transactions, and indebtednesses
definitions and terminology
  apostolate, 167
  dismissal, 154
  exclaustration, 138
  faculties, 230
  governance, 1–3
  interventions, 59
  law, types of, 8
  plurality of terms, 3
  policies, language used in
    clarity and unambiguousness, striving for, 55
    sexual misconduct policies, 56
  sponsored works, 184
  temporal goods, 195, 207–208
  transfers between institutes, 135
definitive departure, *See* secularization
departure from institute or society, *See* dismissal or departure from institute or society
Depaul, Vincent (Saint), 251
diaconate
  canonical effects of admission to, 224
  dismissal or departure from institute or society, 231–232
  permanent, 227–228
  transitional, 223–224
dignity of position and requirement to abstain from unbecoming activities, 129–130
diocesan bishops
  abuses, correction of, 179
  admission of secular clerics as candidates, 64
  apostolate and institutional relationship with, 169–179, 192, 193
  cloister, right of entry to, 126
  collaboration and cooperation with, 172
  ecclesiastical offices conferred by, 171
  exclaustrated religious and, 140, 142, 144
  exemption from jurisdiction of, 169
  faculties, granting, 230
  new institutes and societies, responsibilities regarding formation of, *See* new institutes and societies, forming
  secular institutes
    incardination of clerical members of, 243
    recognition of, 242
  secularization, 149, 151, 152
  societies of apostolic life, 253, 254, 257
  sponsored works, recognition as Catholic, 188
  temporal goods, acquisition of, 197, 200
diocesan institutes
  founding and approval, 38–41
  secularization, approval of, 149, 151, 152
  suppression, 46–47
  temporal goods, administration of, 200
directories, 10–13
  admission of candidates, 70
  diocesan institutes, forming, 39
dismissal or departure from institute or society
  admission into candidacy for ordination, no canonical effects of, 220
  appealing dismissal, 155

266

automatic or *ipso facto* dismissal, 154, 155, 156, 158, 216
clerics, status of, 231–235
compulsory or mandatory dismissal, 154, 156, 216
decree of dismissal, 155, 162–163, 217
definitive departure, *See* secularization
diaconate, persons admitted to, 231–232
discretionary dismissal, 156
dismissal specifically, 154–169
   defined, 154
   ordained members, 235
   penal process, 215–218
   procedures, 155
   rights and obligations, 154
   sample forms pertaining to, 157–163
   secular institutes, 250
   societies of apostolic life, 260
   time periods, 154–155
   types of, 155–156
exclaustration, *See* exclaustration
fact sheet regarding, 166
facultative dismissal, 216
forms and figures, *See* forms and figures
indults
   exclaustration, 142–143, 150–151
   secular institutes, departure from, 249
   secularization, 149, 151, 152, 232–235
ipso facto or automatic dismissal, 154, 155, 156, 158, 216
major superior's council, decisions requiring consent of or consultation with, 6–7, 217
mandatory or compulsory dismissal, 154, 156, 216

medical reasons for, 151, 165
medical records, release of, 165
mental illness, due to, 151
ministries of lector and acolyte, no canonical effects of institution into, 222
notice of dismissal, 155
novitiate, dismissal or departure from
   involuntary dismissal, 97
   voluntary departure, 97
ordained members, 231–235
penal process for dismissal, 215–218
procedures
   dismissal specifically, 154–155
   involuntary exclaustration, 143–144
   secularization, 148–149
   voluntary, ordinary, or simple exclaustration, 141–143
procedures for, 157
psychological problems, 151
readmission, *See* readmission
records and recordkeeping
   forms and figures, *See* forms and figures
   ordained members, 231–235
refusal of renewal of temporary profession or admittance to perpetual profession, 100
remuneration for work performed during membership, 148
rights and obligations
   dismissal specifically, 154
   exclaustration, 139–140
   transfers between institutes, 135–136
sample forms relating to, *See* forms and figures
secular institutes, 248–250
secularization, *See* secularization
societies of apostolic life, 259, 260

temporary profession, expiration of, 100
time periods
  dismissal specifically, 154–155
  exclaustration, 140–141
  transitional diaconate, canonical effects of admission to, 224
  votum or recommendation, 232, 235
  warnings leading up to dismissal, 160–162
dispute resolution, 209–214, *See also* judicial processes
documentation, *See* records and recordkeeping
dress or habit, religious; use by exclaustrated members, 139
drug or alcohol abuse
  policies, 58–59
  privacy and confidentiality regarding, right to, 127
due process, right to, 213–214
duties and rights, *See* rights and obligations
duties or offices outside institute
  acceptance by religious of, 128
  alien activities, requirement to avoid, 130, 132
  financial responsibilities, 130–131
  jury duty, 132
  military service, 130, 132
  political activities or public office, 130, 132

E

ecclesiastical goods, *See* temporal goods
ecclesiastical offices
  conferral by diocesan bishop on institute, 171
  individual religious taking up, 175–177

societies of apostolic life, entrusted to members of, 257
education
  admission of candidates, education of candidate in institutional traditions and practices prior to, 65
  apostolate of, 169–170
  catechetics, apostolate of, 169
  policies addressing
  sexual misconduct, 56
  substance abuse, 58–59
  religious authorized to live apart from community for purposes of, 122–123
elections and voting
  general chapters, 25, 27–30
  secular institutes, supreme moderators of, 244–245
erections
  new institutes and societies, *See* new institutes and societies, forming
  novitiates, 5, 95
  secular institutes, 242
evangelical counsels
  cession, act of, *See* cession, act of
  exclaustration, 139–140
  renunciation of temporal goods, 106–108
  rights and obligations of faithful, affecting, 4
  secular clerics, religious held to same requirements as, 128–129
  societies of apostolic life, 254
  temporal goods, *See* temporal goods
exclaustration, 121, 138–147
  ad experimentum, 139
  agreements regarding, 147
  Apostolic See, approval of
    durante necessitate exclaustration only grantable by Holy See, 139
    involuntary exclaustration, 144

268

voluntary exclaustration, 142
civil law and, 145–147
defined, 138
diocesan bishops and, 140, 142, 144
durante necessitate, 139, 141
effects of, 139–140
evangelical counsels, 139–140
finances, 139–140, 145–147
granting authority
   durante necessitate exclaustration, 139
   involuntary or imposed exclaustration, 144
   voluntary, ordinary, or simple exclaustration, 142
imposed, 138, 141, 143–144
indefinite duration, of, 139
indults, 142–143, 150–151
involuntary, 138, 141, 143–144
local ordinaries and, 140
major superior's council, decisions requiring consent of, 6
ordinary, 138, 140, 141–143
petitions
   involuntary or imposed exclaustration, 144
   voluntary, ordinary, or simple exclaustration, 141–142
procedures
   involuntary exclaustration, 143–144
   voluntary, ordinary, or simple exclaustration, 141–143
qualified, 138, 141
readmission following, 144
rights and obligations, 139–140
simple, 138, 140, 141–143
societies of apostolic life, 124
time period for, 140–141
voluntary, 138, 140, 141–143
exemptions
apostolates, to fulfill, 169

societies of apostolic life, 254
extensions of time
novitiate, time in, 98
temporary profession, 99–101

F

facultative dismissal, 216
faculties
defined, 230
outside institute or society, 230
requesting, 230, 239
suspension of, 153
within institute or society, 230
faith dimension of Catholic identity of sponsored works, 187
family of members, care of
policy regarding, 113–114
religious authorized to live apart from community for purposes of, 122
federation prior to merger or union, 45
fidelity to traditions and openness to world, balancing, v–vii
figures, *See* forms and figures
files, ordering of, 14–15
finances
admission of candidates, 64, 66, 90, 256
alien activities, requirement to abstain from, 130–131
constitutions providing norms for, 9
directories and handbooks as to, 12–13
exclaustration, 139–140, 145–147
mergers and unions, 44, 46
remuneration
   civil law requirements, 182–183
   claims of former members regarding work performed during membership, 148

responsibilities or liabilities on behalf of another, taking up, 130–131
societies of apostolic life
  admission to, 256
  officer in charge of finances, 258
  temporal goods, administration of, 198–206
  transfers between institutes, 136
formation
  admission of candidates, *See* admission of candidates
  apostolate, 169
  constitutions providing norms for, 9
  directories and handbooks as to, 12
  novitiate, *See* novitiate
  ongoing, 114–116
  secular institutes, 246–247
  societies of apostolic life, 256
formation of new institutes and societies, *See* new institutes and societies, forming
former members
  rights and obligations regarding, 164
  sexual misconduct, accusations of, 57–58
forms and figures
  acts, form for recording, 16
  admission of candidates, *See* admission of candidates
  apostolates
    agreement between religious institute and diocesan bishop, 193
    assignment from congregation, letter of, 191
    testimonial letter of permission to diocesan bishop, 192
  cession, act of, 103–105
  civil law, recordkeeping requirements of, 20–24
  decree of dismissal, 162–163
  dismissal or departure from institute or society
    decree of dismissal, 162–163
    dismissal specifically, 157–163
    exclaustration, indult of, 150–151
    fact sheet regarding, 166
    ipso facto dismissal, declaration of, 158
    laicization, letter of clerics leaving institutes without seeking, 152
    medical leave agreement, 165
    suspension of faculties, letter ordering, 153
    transfers between institutes, petition for and approval of, 137
    warnings leading up to dismissal, 159–161
  exclaustration, indult of, 150–151
  faculties
    requesting, 239
    suspension of, 153
  files for office of local superior, 15
  indult of exclaustration, 150–151
  ipso facto dismissal, declaration of, 158
  laicization, letter of clerics leaving institutes without seeking, 152
  novitiate, decree of erection, transfer, or suppression of, 96
  ordination
    acolyte, petition for installation as, 238
    dismissorial letter, 240
    faculties, requesting, 239
    lectorate, petition for installation into, 237
    petition for admission to candidacy, 236
  reports to Apostolic See, circular letter from Congregation for Religious and Secular Institutes regarding, 49–52

societies of apostolic life, form for attestation of definitive bond with, 260
suspension of faculties, letter ordering, 153
transfers between institutes, petition for and approval of, 137
warnings leading up to dismissal, 159–161
wills, 108–109

G

general chapters, 24–30
  convoking, 25
  distinction from other types of chapter, 24
  elections and voting, 25, 27–30
  membership, 26–27
  officials, 25–26
  participation in, 25–26
  rights and obligations, 25, 27
  societies of apostolic life, 255–256
general norms
  religious institutes, 112–115
  secular institutes, 116
  societies of apostolic life, 115–116, 253–254
goods, temporal, *See* temporal goods
governance, 1–30
  acts, 14, 16
  apostolates
    diocesan bishops, by, 178–180
    major superiors, 179–181
    sponsored works, 185
  archives, 15–19, *See also* records and recordkeeping
  constitutions, 8–9, 39
  defined, 1–3
  directories, 10–13
    admission of candidates, 70
  diocesan institutes, forming, 39
  handbooks, 10–13
  law, types of, 8–13
  major superior and council, 5–7
  provincial statutes and policies, 13
  purpose of, 1–2
  records and recordkeeping, *See* records and recordkeeping
  regional statutes and policies, 13
  rights and obligations, *See* rights and obligations
  secular institutes, 244–245
  societies of apostolic life, 255–256
  sponsored works, 185
  temporal goods, administration of, 198–206

H

habit or dress, religious; use by exclaustrated members, 139
handbooks, 10–13
health, *See* entries at medical
heresy, irregularities and impediments to ordination involving, 225–227
HIV/AIDS testing prior to admission of candidates, 66, 93–94
Holy See, *See* Apostolic See
homicide, irregularities and impediments to ordination involving, 225–227

I

impediments with respect to ordination, 225–227
incardination
  secular institutes, clerical members of, 243
  secularization of incardinated clerics, 152, 231–235
  societies of apostolic life, 256
  transitional diaconate, admission to, 224

income tax
    exclaustrated religious, 146
    remuneration of individual religious, 182

incorporation
    baptismal consecration, relationship to, 33–34
    fully incorporated members, 111–133
    perpetual profession, *See* perpetual profession
    secular institutes, into, 245, 247–248
    societies of apostolic life, into, 256, 259
    temporary profession, *See* temporary profession

indebtedness
    admission of candidates with, 64, 66, 90, 256
    institutes and societies undertaking, *See* alienation, business transactions, and indebtednesses

indults
    exclaustration, 142–143, 150–151
    secular institutes, departure from, 249
    secularization, 149, 151, 152, 232–235

insurance
    exclaustrated religious, 144, 145, 147

interventions, 58, 59–61

investigations, 214

ipso facto or automatic dismissal, 154, 155, 156, 158

irregularities with respect to ordination, 225–227

J

joint apostolates, 172, 194

judicial processes, 209–218
    appeals
        denial of ordination to presbyterate, 229
        dismissals, 155
        right of, 214
    arbitration, 211–213
    boards of reconciliation, 209–210
    conciliation, 210–211
    dispute resolution procedures, extra-judicial, 209–214
    due process, right to, 213–214
    mediation, 211
    penal procedures, 214, 215–218
    reconciliation boards, 209–210
    rights and obligations, 213–215
        penal processes, 218
        reconciliations, penalties imposed in course of, 214
    secular state, civil and criminal law of, *See* civil and criminal law

juridic personality
    business transactions adversely affecting patrimonial condition of, *See* alienation, business transactions, and indebtednesses
    sponsored works, 187–188, 189
    temporal goods, acquisition of, 197

jury duty, 132

justice, duty to foster peace and harmony based on, 132

L

labor unions, involvement in, 132

laicization, clerics leaving institutes without seeking, 152, 231–235

last will and testament of religious, 108–109

law
    canon law
        fidelity to traditions and openness to world, balancing, v–vii
        freedom allowed institutes and societies to determine specific modalities or procedures, 2–3

civil and criminal law, *See* civil and criminal law
mergers and unions, juridic preparation for, 45–46
particular law, 8
proper law, *See* proper law
special law, 8
suppression of institutes and societies, juridic steps in, 46–47
types of, 8–13
universal law, 8
    chapters, concerning, 8
    living apart from community, 121
lawsuits involving exclaustrated religious, 145–147
leases as alienation, 206
lector, ministry of, 221–222, 237
letters of recommendation for admission of candidates, 67, 83–84
liabilities
    apostolic works, 183
    exclaustrated religious, 145–147
    others, taking up responsibilities or liabilities on behalf of, 130–131
living apart from community, 118–119, 121–124
    agreements regarding, 123
    Apostolic See's disapproval of, 118–119
    exclaustration, *See* exclaustration
    open-endedness, avoiding, 123
    proper law, 124
    religious institutes, 122–123
    societies of apostolic life, 124, 260
    time restraints on, 122, 123
    trend towards, 118–119
    universal law providing criteria for, 121
    variants of common life involving, 118–119
local communities

common life, variants on, 118–119
societies of apostolic life, 254
local ordinaries
    defined, 200
    diocesan bishops, *See* diocesan bishops
    exclaustrated religious and, 140
    faculties, granting, 230
    societies of apostolic life, 253, 254, 257
    temporal goods, authority regarding administration of, 200

M

major superiors
    admission of candidates, right of, 63–94
    apostolates, role in carrying out, *See* apostolates
    councils of, 5–7
    faculties, granting, 230
    novitiate, decisions regarding, 5, 95
    secular institutes, supreme moderators of, 244–245
    societies of apostolic life, 253, 255
    transitional diaconate, admission to, 224
    votum or recommendation regarding dismissal or departure from institute or society, 232, 235
mandatory or compulsory dismissal, 154, 156, 216
marriage
    diaconate, canonical effects of admission to, 224
    faculties to witness, 230
    irregularities and impediments to ordination, 225–227
media apostolate, 170
mediation, 211
medical care
    advance directives, 110

cloister, right of entry to, 126
dismissal or departure from institute or society, medical reasons for, 151, 165
exclaustrated religious, 146
provision by institute or society, 110, 113
religious authorized to live apart from community for purposes of, 122–123
medical examinations for admission of candidates, 66–68, 91–94
medical records
    admission of candidates, 91–94
    privacy and confidentiality, 127
    release on separation from institute, 165
members, 111–133
    cloister, 125–126
    common life, *See* common life
    former members
        rights and obligations regarding, 164
        sexual misconduct, accusations of, 57–58
    fully incorporated, 111–133
    general norms for
        religious institutes, 112–115
        secular institutes, 116
        societies of apostolic life, 115–116
    living apart from community, *See* living apart from community
    mergers and unions, status following, 43, 46
    novices, *See* novitiate
    perpetual profession, admittance to, *See* perpetual profession
    policies, involvement in formulating, 54
    privacy and confidentiality, *See* privacy and confidentiality
    restrictions on, 128–133
    rights and obligations, *See* rights and obligations
    secular institutes, status of members of, 242–243
    temporarily professed, *See* temporary profession
mental disorders
    denial of ordination to presbyterate, 228–229
    dismissal or departure from institute or society, 151
    irregularities and impediments to ordination, 225–227
mergers and unions, 41–46
    agreement, 44, 46
    Apostolic See, role of, 42
    discernment regarding, 42
    distinction between, 41, 44
    federation, formation of, 45
    individuals opposed to, options for, 43, 45–46
    juridic preparation for, 45–46
    member status, 43, 46
    psychological preparation for, 45
    purpose of, 41–42, 44
    records and recordkeeping
        financial agreement, 44, 46
        institute requesting merger, 43
        procedural account, 44
        receiving institute, 44
        unions, 45–46
    smaller institutes, considerations regarding, 42
    specific requirements
        mergers, 42–44
        unions, 44–46
    spiritual preparation for, 45
    suppression, preferred to, 46
military service, volunteering for, 130, 132

ministries of lector and acolyte, institution into, 221–222, 237–238

N

neophyte status as irregularity to ordination, 225

Neri, Philip (Saint), 251

new institutes and societies, forming, 31–52
- Apostolic See
  - diocesan institutes, 38
  - mergers and unions, 42
  - pontifical recognition, 41
- associations of the faithful (Pious Unions), 36–38
- authentic charisms, identifying, 35–36
- baptismal consecration, relationship to, 33–34
- criteria for discernment regarding, 32–33
- diocesan bishops, responsibilities of
  - associations, 36–37
  - criteria for discernment, 31, 32, 35
  - diocesan institutes, 38–41
  - spirit and purpose, determining, 36–37
  - unions, letters regarding, 46
- diocesan institutes, 38–41
- experimental forms, 34–35
- federation prior to merger or union, 45
- inspiration of founder, 31–36
- mergers and unions, *See* mergers and unions
- Pious Unions (associations of the faithful), 36–38
- pontifical recognition, 41
- purpose and spirit, determining, 37–38
- renewals of existing institutes, 34

spirit and purpose, determining, 37–38

nihil obstat required to form diocesan institute, 38, 39

norms, general
- religious institutes, 112–115
- secular institutes, 116
- societies of apostolic life, 115–116, 253–254

notice
- admission of secular clerics as candidates, diocesan bishop's notification required for, 64
- dismissal, 155
- penal processes, 218

novitiate
- admission of candidates to, *See* admission of candidates
- dismissal or departure from
  - involuntary dismissal, 97
  - voluntary departure, 97
- erecting, 5, 95
- extension of time in, 98
- major superior's council, decisions requiring consent of, 5, 95, 97, 98
- postulancy or pre-novitiate, *See* postulancy or pre-novitiate
- request of admittance to temporary profession by novice, 99
- societies of apostolic life, 256
- suppressing, 5, 95
- transferring, 5, 95

O

obedience, vow of, *See* evangelical counsels

obligations, *See* rights and obligations

offices, ecclesiastical
- conferral by diocesan bishop on institute, 171

individual religious taking up, 175–177
societies of apostolic life, entrusted to members of, 257
offices or duties outside institute, *See* duties or offices outside institute
Olier, Jean Jaques, 251
ordination
acolyte, ministry of, 221–222, 238
admission into candidacy for, 219–220, 236
denial of ordination to presbyterate, 228–229
diaconate, to, *See* diaconate
dismissal or departure of ordained members, 231–235
dismissorial letter, 224, 228, 229, 240
forms and figures, *See* forms and figures
illicit ordination of one hindered by impediment, 227
impediments, 225–227
irregularities, 225–227
lector, ministry of, 221–222, 237
ministries, institution into, 221–222, 237–238
petitions
admission to candidacy for, 220
diaconate, 223
ministries of acolyte or lector, 221, 237–238
presbyterate, to
admission to, 229
denial of, 228–229
records and recordkeeping
acolyte, institution as, 222
diaconate, transitional, 224
lectorate, institution into, 222
ministries, institution into, 222
ordained members' dismissal or departure from institute or society, 231–232
sample documents, *See* forms and figures

P

papacy, *See* Apostolic See
papal cloister, 126
parishes
faculties, 230
religious institutes, responsibilities of, 171
particular law, 8
partnerships to undertake sponsored works, 185–186
passive voice
exclaustrated members, 28
general chapters, 28
penal procedures
criminal law of secular state, *See* civil and criminal law
ecclesiastical, 214, 215–218
penalties imposed in process of reconciliation, 214
permanent diaconate, 227–228
perpetual profession
admission to, 100
refusal of, 100
renunciation of temporal goods prior to, 106–108
requesting, 100
requirements for validity of, 102
secular institutes, perpetual or definitive incorporation into, 245, 249
will made prior to, 108–109
petitions
exclaustration
involuntary or imposed, 144

voluntary, ordinary, or simple, 141–142
ordination
  admission to candidacy for, 220
  diaconate, 223
  ministries of acolyte or lector, 221, 237–238
  secularization, 149, 151, 152
  transfers between institutes, 137
physical necessities of life, member entitlement to, 113
Pious Unions (associations of the faithful), 36–38
policies, 53–61
  alcohol abuse, 58–59
  application of, even-handed, 54–55
  changing or revising, 54
  communication of, 54
  development of, 54, 55
  drug abuse, 58–59
  educational elements
    sexual misconduct policies, 56
    substance abuse, 58–59
  family of members, care of, 113–114
  HIV/AIDS testing for admission of candidates, 66, 93
  institution-wide policies, 53
  internal administrative policies, 53
  interventions, 58, 59–61
  language used in
    clarity and unambiguousness, striving for, 55
    sexual misconduct policies, 56
  member involvement in formulating, 54
  purpose of, 53, 54
  records and recordkeeping, 54, 55
  sexual misconduct, addressing, 56–58
  substance abuse, 58–59
  types of, 53

political activities, requirement to abstain from, 130, 132
pontifical right, institutions of; approval of secularization for members, 149, 151
Pope, *See* Apostolic See
postulancy or pre-novitiate
  Benedictine Sisters, postulancy materials of, 68–69
  canonical requirements regarding, lack of, 63, 68
  secular institutes, probationary period for, 245
  societies of apostolic life, probationary period for, 256
  Trappist monastery, postulancy materials of, 69
poverty, vow of, *See* evangelical counsels; temporal goods
pre-novitiate, *See* postulancy or pre-novitiate
presbyterate
  denial of ordination to, 228–229
  ordination to, 229
  secular, *See* secular clerics
  status regarding, *See* clerical status
privacy and confidentiality
  medical care, 127
  records and recordkeeping, 127
  rights and obligations regarding, 4, 126–127
  substance abuse, 127
probationary period
  postulancy or pre-novitiate, *See* postulancy or pre-novitiate
  secular institutes, 245
  societies of apostolic life, 256
  transfers between institutes, 136
profession
  baptismal consecration, relationship to, 33–34

perpetual, *See* perpetual profession
temporary, *See* temporary profession
professional counseling of exclaustrated religious, 147
proper law, 8, 208
   alienation, 201
   living apart from community, 124
   rights and obligations of members according to, 112–113, 116
   societies of apostolic life, 252, 253
   temporal goods, acquisition of, 196
property law, *See* temporal goods
provincial statutes and policies, 13
psychological disorders
   denial of ordination to presbyterate, 228–229
   dismissal or departure from institute or society, 151
   irregularities and impediments to ordination, 225–227
psychological testing prior to admission of candidates, 64, 67, 85–86
publishing and writing as apostolate, 170

R

radio, media apostolate involving, 170
readmission
   exclaustration, following, 144
   legitimate departure, following, 164
   major superior's council, decisions requiring consent of, 6
reassignment of duties
   sexual misconduct, following, 57
   substance abuse, due to, 58
recognition
   new institutes and societies, pontifical recognition of, 41
   secular institutes, 242
   sponsored works, recognition as Catholic, 188

reconciliation boards, 209–210
reconciliation process, 209–214
records and recordkeeping, 13–24
   acolyte, institution as, 222
   acts, 14, 16
   admission of candidates, *See* admission of candidates
   archival materials, 15–19
   civil law, requirements of, 19–24
   diaconate, transitional, 224
   diocesan institutes, forming, 38–41
   dismissal or departure from institute or society
      forms and figures, *See* forms and figures
      ordained members, 231–235
   files, ordering of, 14–15
   lectorate, institution into, 222
   medical records, *See* medical records
   mergers and unions, *See* mergers and unions
   ministries, institution into, 222
   minutes of council meetings, 13–14, 23
   novitiate, decree of erection, transfer, or suppression of, 95–96
   official documents, 17, 20
   ordination, *See* ordination
   policies, 54, 55
   privacy and confidentiality, 127
   reports to Apostolic See, *See* reports to Apostolic See
   secret archives, 18–19
   societies of apostolic life
      admission to society, 256
      designation of financial responsibilities, 258
      form for attestation of definitive bond with, 260
   transfers between institutes, 137

references required for admission of candidates, 67, 83–84
regional statutes and policies, 13
relations with other institutes or societies
  apostolate, collaboration and cooperation regarding, 172, 194
  sexual misconduct, accusations of, 57–58
religious habit or dress used by exclaustrated members, 139
religious institutes
  alien activities, requirement to abstain from, 130
  association with persons, prudence as to, 129
  common life, 117–119
  duties or offices outside institute, acceptance of, 128
  general norms, rights, and obligations, 112–115
  living apart from community, 122–123
  restrictions on members, 128–132
  secular clerics, religious held to same requirements as, 128–132
  societies of apostolic life distinguished from, 251, 252
  transfers between religious institutes and secular institutes or societies of apostolic life, approval of, 135, 250, 259
  unbecoming activities, requirement to abstain from, 129–130
remuneration
  civil law requirements, 182–183
  claims of former members regarding work performed during membership, 148
renewal of profession, 100
renunciation of temporal goods, 106–108

reorganization of corporation as form of alienation, 206
reports to Apostolic See, 47–52
  circular letter from Congregation for Religious and Secular Institutes regarding, 49–52
  contents, 47–48
  purpose of, 47
  religious institutes and societies of consecrated life, letter to, 49–50
  secular institutes, letter to, 51–52
reputation
  prudence as to company kept, 129
  rights and obligations regarding, 127
  unbecoming activities, requirement to abstain from, 129–130
retirement of exclaustrated religious, 146
rights and obligations, 3–5, 111–112
  apostolate of specific religious houses, rights of, 170–171
  apostolates, 181
  appeal, right of, 214
  applicability to members, 3, 111
  cloister, 125–126
  common good, 4
  communion with church, obligation to maintain, 4
  dismissal or departure from institute or society
    dismissal specifically, 154
    exclaustration, 139–140
    transfers between institutes, 135–136
  due process, right to, 213–214
  equality, 4
  evangelical counsels, 4
  exclaustration, 139–140
  formation, ongoing, 114–116
  former members, 164
  fully incorporated members, 111–112

general chapters, 25, 27
judicial processes, 213–215
　penal processes, 218
　reconciliations, penalties imposed in course of, 214
justice, fostering peace and harmony based on, 132
penal processes, 218
physical necessities of life, member entitlement to, 113
privacy and confidentiality, 4, 126–127
proper law, according to, 112–113, 116
religious institutes, members of, 112–115
reputation, right to, 127
secular institutes, members of, 116
sexual misconduct, accusations of, 57
societies of apostolic life, members of, 115–116, 257, 258
spiritual necessities, member entitlement to, 112–113
transfers between institutes, 135–136
vocational necessities, member entitlement to, 3–4, 112–113, 115

S

sacraments
　baptismal consecration and profession, relationship between, 33–34
　faculties, 153, 230
　improper exercise of, 226–227
　marriage
　　diaconate, canonical effects of admission to, 224
　　faculties to witness, 230
　　irregularities and impediments to ordination, 225–227
　orders, See ordination
salaries
　civil law requirements, 182–183
　claims of former members regarding work performed during membership, 148
sample forms, See forms and figures
schism, irregularities and impediments to ordination involving, 225–227
schools, See education
secret archives, 18–19
secular clerics
　admission as candidates, diocesan bishop's notification required for, 64
　collaboration and cooperation with, 172
　dismissal or departure from institute without laicization, 152, 231–235
　religious held to same requirements as, 128–132
secular institutes, 241–250
　admission of candidates, 245–246
　alien activities, not bound by restrictions on, 133
　Apostolic See, recognition by, 242
　associates of, 248
　chapters and other gatherings, 244
　clerical members, 241, 242–243
　common life, 119–120, 241
　diocesan bishops
　　incardination of clerical members, 243
　　recognition by, 242
　diocesan norms, subject to, 242
　dismissal or departure from institute or society, 248–250
　erection of, 242
　formation, 246–247
　governance, 244–245
　history of, 241–242
　incardination of clerical members, 243
　incorporation into, 245, 247–248
　lay members, 241, 242–243

280

members, status of, 242–243
perpetual or definitive incorporation
   admission to, 245
   departure from, 249
probationary period, 245
recognition of, 242
requirements for admission into, 245–246
separation of members, 248–250
supreme moderators, 244–245
temporal goods, administration of, 245
temporary incorporation
   admission to, 245, 247
   departure from, 248–249
transfers, 135, 250
secularization, 148–152
Apostolic See, approval of, 149, 151
approval of, 149, 151, 152
diocesan bishops, 149, 151, 152
incardinated clerics, 152
indults, 149, 151, 152
laicization, clerics leaving institutes without seeking, 152, 231–235
perpetually professed members, 149–152
petitions, 149, 151, 152
procedures, 148–149
suspension of faculties, 153
temporarily professed members, 148–149
self-mutilation, irregularities and impediments to ordination involving, 225–227
separation of members, 135–169
   departure or dismissal, *See* dismissal or departure from institute or society
   exclaustration, *See* exclaustration
   fact sheet regarding, 166
   secular institutes, 248–250
   secularization, *See* secularization
   transfers, *See* transfers between institutes
sexual misconduct, policies addressing, 56–58
Social Security for exclaustrated religious, 146
societies of apostolic life, 251–260
   admission of candidates, 256
   alien activities, restrictions on, 133
   Apostolic See, 253
   apostolic works entrusted by bishop to, 257
   autonomy of, 253
   bond with society, creation of, 252, 260
   canonical treatment of, 251–252
   changes to, 253
   chapters and other gatherings, 255–256
   cloister, 125
   common life, 251, 252, 258
   diocesan bishops, 253, 254, 257
   dismissal or departure of members, 259, 260
   ecclesiastical offices entrusted by bishop to individual member, 257
   evangelical counsels, 254
   exclaustration, 124
   exemptions available to, 254
   finances
      admission to society and, 256
      officer in charge of, 258
   form for attestation of definitive bond, 260
   formation, 256
   general chapters, 255–256
   general norms, 253–254
   governance, 255–256
   historical background, 251

houses of, 254
incardination, 256
incorporation into, 256, 259
living apart from community, 124, 260
local communities, 254
local ordinaries, 253, 254, 257
major superiors, 253, 254
novitiates, 256
probationary period, 256
proper law, 252, 253
records and recordkeeping
   admission to society, 256
   designation of financial responsibilities, 258
   form for attestation of definitive bond with, 260
religious institutes, distinguished from, 251, 252
rights and obligations, 115–116, 257, 258
suppression, 253
supreme authority of, 253
temporal goods, 258
transfers involving, 135, 250, 259
vows, private nature of, 251, 252
women and men, rules the same for, 254
special law, 8
spiritual requirements
   mergers and unions, preparation for, 45
   new institutes and societies, forming, 37–38
   rights and obligations of members regarding, 112–113
   sponsored works, faith dimension of Catholic identity of, 187
vocation
   member entitlement to necessities related to, 3–4, 112–113, 115

religious authorized to live apart from community for purposes of discerning, 122
sponsored works, 184–190
   advocacy role of religious institute, 186
   Catholic identity of, 186–188
   communion with church, 186–188
   definitions and terminology, 184
   faith dimension of Catholic identity, 187
   governance, 185
   influence over, 185–186
   institutions operating within Catholic tradition but without juridic bonds, 189–190
   juridic personality, 187–188, 189
   partnerships, 185–186
   recognition as Catholic, 188
   relationship to institute or society, 185–186
   secular frameworks, Catholic entities within, 189
   secular institutions operating under management of ecclesiastical entity, 190
   structural relationship to Church, 187, 188–190
substance abuse
   policies, 58–59
   privacy and confidentiality regarding, right to, 127
suicide, irregularities and impediments to ordination involving, 225–227
superiors, supreme moderators, and supreme authorities, *See* major superiors
suppression
   institutes and societies, 46–47, 253
   novitiate, 5, 95

T

taxation
  alienation, approval of, 201–202
  exclaustrated religious, 146
  remuneration of individual religious, 182
television, media apostolate involving, 170
temporal goods, 195–213
  acquisition of, 196–197, 207
    "Catholic" as title, use of, 196–197
    defined, 207
    diocesan bishop, authority of, 197, 200
    juridic personality, 197
    proper law, 196
  administration of, 198–206, 207, 208, 245
  alienation of, *See* alienation, business transactions, and indebtednesses
  business transactions adversely affecting patrimonial condition of juridic person, *See* alienation, business transactions, and indebtednesses
  cash, 195
  charitable trusts, held in, 206
  civil law requirements, 199–200
  definitions and terminology, 195, 207–208
  extraordinary administration, 198, 207
  finances, 198–206
  fixtures, 195
  immovable property, 195, 208
  leases, 206
  ordinary administration, 198, 208
  patrimonial condition and, 201, 208
  renunciation of, 106–108
  secular institutes, 245
  societies of apostolic life, 258
  stable patrimony and, 201, 208
  types of, 195
temporary profession, 99–101
  act of cession prior to, *See* cession, act of
  expiration without renewal or advancement to perpetual profession, 100
  extension of, 99–101
  major superior's council, decisions requiring consultation of, 7, 99
  receipt of, 100
  renewal of, 100
  request for, 99
  requirements for, 99
  secular institutes, temporary incorporation into, 245, 247, 248–249
  secularization of temporarily professed members, 148–149
time periods
  alienation, business transactions, and indebtednesses, approval of, 205–206
  dismissal or departure from institute or society
    dismissal specifically, 154–155
    exclaustration, 140–141
  extensions of
    novitiate, time in, 98
    temporary profession, 99–101
  living apart from community, time restraints on, 122, 123
  secular institutes, temporary incorporation into, 247
trade or business, engagement in, 130, 131–132
tradition
  apostolates, 170
  balancing fidelity to traditions and openness to world, v–vii

common life, variants on, 118–119
experimental forms of institutes and societies varying from, 34–35
sponsored works operating within Catholic tradition but without juridic bonds, 189–190
transfers between institutes, 135–137
    approval form, 137
    cession, act of, 136
    definition of, 135
    effect of, 136
    finances, 136
    major superior's council, decisions requiring consent of, 6
    permission for, 6, 135–136
    petition for transfer, 137
    probationary period, 136
    procedures for, 136
    reasons given for, 135–136
    records and recordkeeping, 137
    religious institutes and secular institutes or societies of apostolic life, transfers between, 135, 250, 259
    rights and obligations, 135–136
    secular institutes, involving, 135, 250
    societies of apostolic life, involving, 135, 250, 259
transfers of novitiate houses, 5, 95

U

unbecoming activities, requirement to abstain from, 129–130
unions, labor; involvement in, 132
unions of institutes and societies, *See* mergers and unions
universal law, 8
    chapters, concerning, 8
    living apart from community, 121

V

visitations as form of oversight of apostolates, 178
vocation
    member entitlement to necessities related to, 3–4, 112–113, 115
    religious authorized to live apart from community for purposes of discerning, 122
voting and elections
    general chapters, 25, 27–30
    secular institutes, supreme moderators of, 244–245
votum or recommendation regarding dismissal or departure from institute or society, 232, 235

W

wages
    civil law requirements, 182–183
    claims of former members regarding work performed during membership, 148
warnings leading up to dismissal, 159–161
wills, 108–109
women religious
    contemplative communities, rules of cloister for, 125–126
    societies of apostolic life, 254
writing and publishing as apostolate, 170

AUTHORS

BEVERLY K. DUNN, S.P. is in tribunal ministry in Stockton, Calif. She received a doctorate in canon law from the University of St. Paul in Ottawa, Canada.

EMMETT J. GAVIN, O.CARM. is a Carmelite priest of the Province of the Most Pure Heart of Mary. He is prior and director of formation at Whitefriars Hall, the Carmelite house of studies in Washington, D.C. He received his licentiate in canon law from the Catholic University of America in Washington, D.C.

SHARON L. HOLLAND, I.H.M. is a member of the Sisters Servants of the Immaculate Heart of Mary. She is an office head at the Congregation for Institutes of Consecrated Life and Societies of Apostolic Life. She received a doctorate in canon law from from the Gregorian University in Rome.

DAVID M. HYNOUS, O.P. is a Dominican priest of the Saint Albert Province. He is currently serving as a judge on the Metropolitan Tribunal of the Archdiocese of Chicago. He received a doctorate in canon law from the Angelicum in Rome.

MICHAEL P. JOYCE, C.M. is a Vincentian priest of the Midwest Province. He is pastor of St. Francis de Sales Parish in St. Louis, Moderator of Hispanic Ministry for the Archdiocese of St. Louis, and a judge on the Provincial Court of Appeals of Chicago. He received a doctorate in canon law from the Catholic University of America in Washington, D.C.

ROBERT J. KASYLN, S.J. is a Jesuit priest of the New York Province. He received a doctorate in canon law from St. Paul University in Ottawa.

ROSE MCDERMOTT, S.S.J. is a member of the Sisters of St. Joseph. She is assistant professor of canon law at the Catholic University of America. She received a doctorate in canon law from the Catholic University of America in Washington, D.C.

Rosemary Smith, S.C. is a member of the Sisters of Charity of St. Elizabeth. She is director of Women's Advocacy for the Sisters of Charity of the Incarnate Word. She received a doctorate in canon law from the Catholic University of America in Washington, D.C.

Therese Guerin Sullivan, S.P. is a member of the Sisters of Providence. She is vicar for religious and a judge in the tribunal of the Diocese of Gary. She received a licentiate in canon law from the University of St. Paul in Ottawa, Canada.

Victoria Vondenberger, R.S.M. is a member of the Sisters of Mercy of the Americas. She is the Tribunal Director, Promoter of Justice, and Defender of the Bond for the Archdiocese of Cincinnati as well as a member of the Archdiocesan Board of Mediation. She received a licentiate in canon law from the University of St. Paul in Ottawa, Canada.

Daniel Ward, O.S.B. is a Benedictine priest. He is Executive Director of Legal Resource Center for Religious, Silver Springs, Md. He received a licentiate in canon law from the Catholic University of America in Washington, D.C.

Contributors

The Committee also wishes to thank those individuals who served as contributors to the various authors of the text:

Kathleen Ann Bierne, P.B.V.M.
Rita-Mae Bissonnette, R.S.R.
M. Dominica Brennan, O.P.
Marianne Burkhard, O.S.B.
James J. Conn, S.J.
Jonathan P. DeFelice, O.S.B.
Vincent B. Grogan, O.F.M.
Joyce Hoben, S.N.D.N.
David M. Hynous, O.P.
Paulissa Jirik, S.S.N.D.
Bernard M. Johnson, O.S.C.O.
Gary M. Luiz, C.PP.S.
Margaret M. Modde, O.S.F.
Francis G. Morrisey, O.M.I.
David M. O'Connell, C.M.
Kevin D. O'Rourke, O.P.
Esther Redmann, O.S.U.
Nancy Reynolds, S.P.
Elissa A. Rinere, C.P.
Kevin R. Seasoltz, O.S.B.
Patrick T. Shea, O.F.M.
Margaret A. Stallmeyer, C.D.P.
Sally J. Tolles, D.H.S.;
Marlene C. Weisenbeck, F.S.P.A.
M. Madeline Welch, O.S.U.
Richard B. Williams, O.P.